The Free Market Reader

The Ludwig von Mises Institute gratefully acknowledges the Patrons whose generosity made the publication of this book possible:

O. P. Alford, III
J. C. Arthur, MD
Lemuel R. Boulware
E. O. Buck
Jerry D. Busch
Mr. and Mrs. Edgar Capen
Philip L. Carret
Edward E. Culver
Charles G. Dannelly
Roland S. DeMott
John L. Doyle
Dr. William A. Dunn
Mrs. Card G. Elliott, Jr.
Jason H. Fane
Arthur C. Fennekohl
Willard Fischer
Mr. and Mrs. James R. Focht
Don L. Foote
Heritage Mark Foundation
William A. Galbraith, Jr.
Mrs. St. John Garwood
Bernard G. Geuting
Captain Maino des Granges
W. Grover
Freeway Fasteners
Thomas R. Haig, Jr.
David J. Hosbein, MD
John F. Kieser
D. Covington Logan
David Manley
Dorothea Marica
James T. Morton
Victor Niederhoffer
James Panyard
Pennsylvania Manufacturers Association
Francis M. Powers, MD
Lewis E. Randall
Donald Mosby Rembert
James M. Rodney
Sheldon Rose
Jean C. Sanford
Adolph Schoepe
Fluidmaster, Inc.
Ed Schoppe
E. D. Shaw, Jr.
Shaw Oxygen Company
Donald R. Stewart
Twin Oil Company
C. S. Trosper

THE FREE MARKET READER

ESSAYS IN THE ECONOMICS OF LIBERTY

EDITED BY
LLEWELLYN H. ROCKWELL, JR.

The Ludwig von Mises Institute

To O. P. Alford, III,

entrepreneur and activist
for liberty

CONTENTS

Introduction: Tax Payers and Tax Eaters
Llewellyn H. Rockwell, Jr. 13

1. FUNDAMENTALS

Ten Great Economic Myths
Murray N. Rothbard 19

Creative Economic Semantics
Murray N. Rothbard 32

Competition at Work: Xerox at 25
Murray N. Rothbard 35

Looking Beneath the Surface
Llewellyn H. Rockwell, Jr. 37

The Fraud of GNP
Llewellyn H. Rockwell, Jr. 39

Racial Discrimination and the Free Market
Mark D. Hughes 40

Mises Contra Marx
David Gordon 45

Keynesian Myths
Murray N. Rothbard 50

Liberty and Property
Ludwig von Mises 56

The Interest Rate Question
Murray N. Rothbard 62

How the Market Creates Jobs and
How the Government Destroys Them
Walter Block 65

The National Bureau and Business Cycles
Murray N. Rothbard 70

2. FIAT MONEY AND THE GOLD STANDARD

Confidence and Money
Llewellyn H. Rockwell, Jr. 75

Bank Runs and Water Shortages
Murray N. Rothbard 77

The World Currency Crisis
Murray N. Rothbard 83

Understanding the Business Cycle
Mark D. Skousen 88

Money Inflation and Price Inflation
Murray N. Rothbard 93

First Step Back to Gold
Murray N. Rothbard 97

Sound Money: Gold or Denationalized?
Llewellyn H. Rockwell, Jr. 100

Alan Greenspan: A Minority Report
Murray N. Rothbard 103

Fiat Paper Money: Tyranny's Credit Card
Tucker Alford 105

Back to Fixed Exchange Rates
Murray N. Rothbard 109

Monetary Crises
Llewellyn H. Rockwell, Jr. 114

The Real Secrets of the Temple
Llewellyn H. Rockwell, Jr. 116

3. FREE TRADE AND PROTECTIONISM

The Case for Free Trade
Ron Paul 123

Turgot and Iacocca
Llewellyn H. Rockwell, Jr. 128

The Crusade Against South Africa
Murray N. Rothbard 131

We the People vs. the Loot Seekers
Mark D. Hughes 134

The Myth of the Trade Deficit
Sam Wells 138

Another Federal Crime Against Consumers
Llewellyn H. Rockwell, Jr. 144

Economic Warfare Hurts Us More Than Them
Robert Higgs and Charlotte Twight 146

Protectionism and the Destruction of Prosperity
Murray N. Rothbard 148

4. GREAT ECONOMISTS

A Call to Activism
Margit von Mises 163

Ludwig von Mises: Hero
Llewellyn H. Rockwell, Jr. 170

Memories of Ludwig von Mises
William H. Peterson 177

Mises vs. the Green-Eyed Monster
Bradley Miller 180

Hazlitt, Hutt, and Rothbard:
Three Economists Who Are National Treasures
Llewellyn H. Rockwell, Jr. 184

Murray N. Rothbard: Giant of Liberty
Walter Block and Llewellyn H. Rockwell, Jr. 195

Henry Hazlitt: Giant of Liberty
Various Authors 200

The Life and Work of a Dissident Scholar
Jeffrey Tucker 216

5. SOCIALISM

The Politics of Famine
Murray N. Rothbard 223

Mises and Gorbachev: Why Socialism Still Doesn't Work
Tom Bethell 226

A Trip to Poland
Murray N. Rothbard 231

The Misesian Revolution in Poland
Lawrence W. Reed 233

Mises and the Soviet Free Market
Lawrence W. Reed 235

Freedom vs. Planning
Richard Ebeling 239

Why Socialism Must Fail
Hans-Hermann Hoppe 244

Massachusetts and the Mussolinization of America
Llewellyn H. Rockwell, Jr. 250

The Collapse of Socialism
Murray N. Rothbard 254

6. PRIVATIZATION VS. GOVERNMENT OWNERSHIP

Airport Congestion: A Case of Market Failure?
Murray N. Rothbard 257

Privatization
Murray N. Rothbard 260

Government vs. Natural Resources
Murray N. Rothbard 263

Privatize the Roads!
Walter Block 266

The Case for a Free Market in Body Parts
Walter Block 270

Abolish the SEC
Graeme B. Littler 273

Cancel the Postal Monopoly
Llewellyn H. Rockwell, Jr. 276

Lies, Damned Lies, and Social Security
Patrick W. Watson 280

The Conservative Sanctification of Big Government
Llewellyn H. Rockwell, Jr. 284

The Case Against Government Child Care
Kathleen M. Spotts 286

7. BUDGETS, TAXES, BUREAUCRACY, AND INTERVENTIONISM

Love in the Bureaucracy
Bradley Miller 291

Rotation in Office
Llewellyn H. Rockwell, Jr. 295

The Balanced Budget Amendment Hoax
Murray N. Rothbard 296

How Government Intervention Plagued Our 19th-Century Economy
Lawrence W. Reed 299

Send Out the Clowns
Llewellyn H. Rockwell, Jr. 304

How Our Economic Constitution Has Deteriorated
Robert Higgs 306

Nine Myths About the Crash
Murray N. Rothbard 308

The Crash Commission Report
Ron Paul 314

The Regulatory-Industrial Complex
Sam Wells 316

Who Really Benefits From Foreign Aid?
Sam Wells 320

A Plague From Both Their Houses: The Economic Advisors to Bush and Dukakis
Llewellyn H. Rockwell, Jr. 323

The Coming World Central Bank
Ron Paul 335

8. REAGANOMICS

A Walk on the Supply-Side
Murray N. Rothbard 339

The Case Against the Flat Tax
Murray N. Rothbard 342

Is There Life After Reaganomics?
Murray N. Rothbard 362

Ronald Reagan: Protectionist
Sheldon L. Richman 381

The Sad Legacy of Ronald Reagan
Sheldon L. Richman 385

Index 391

Introduction: Tax Payers and Tax Eaters

In countries with openly tyrannical governments, we expect lies. From government newspapers, government officials, and every other aspect of the state propaganda apparatus, we assume deception.

What we do not expect is that the U.S. government does not operate much differently, even if the means are subtler.

Ludwig von Mises always distinguished between the two methods of acquiring wealth: the voluntary way of the free market and the coercive means of the state.

With an interventionist state like ours, dedicated to extracting our money for itself and favored interest groups, whose officials revel in dominating others, no one will admit openly what he is about. The talk will be of the public interest, the common good, the national security. But the real issues will always be cash and control.

Even in the early 19th century, John C. Calhoun described the United States as divided between the "tax payers and tax eaters." And today, we can use that same analysis. Ludwig von Mises called the battle between these two artificially created groups a "caste conflict," in contradistinction to Karl Marx's class conflict.

There can be no natural class conflict in society, since the free market harmonizes all economic interests. But in an interventionist system, there must be a struggle between the caste that lives off the government and the rest of us.

To keep us from struggling too much, the government—from our earliest days—trains us to be good little citizens: to salute and say "Yes, sir!" when ordered to pay redistributionist taxes, instructed how to run our businesses, told how to lead our personal lives, or drafted for foreign wars.

And part of the training is the painstakingly inculcated acceptance of the government as "we."

"Are we spending too much on the space shuttle?" someone asked me recently. But "we" are not spending anything. The U.S. government is.

The government is separate from us, and almost always opposed to our interests. We do not have a government of the people, by the people, and for the people. We have a government *to* the people. And one important tool in keeping it going is the lie.

For example, almost every economic statement from the Reagan administration has been a lie. We—and I *do* mean we—got the most protectionist eight years since Herbert Hoover, and they called it free trade. We got five tax increases, including the single largest in human history, and they called it lower taxes. We got the biggest deficits ever, and they called it fiscal conservatism. We got a doubled federal budget, and they called it cutting back. We got a vast increase in the power and scope of federal control and snooping, and they called it freedom.

In analyzing any government action, we should always ask: who's getting the money and the power?

During the Carter administration, conservatives told us how terrible the Occupational Safety and Health Administration (OSHA) was. It oppressed businesspeople, imposed crazy regulations, and violated civil liberties. And it was all true. But why is there silence on Reagan's OSHA? Because it is really a big-business agency, set up by the Nixon administration.

OSHA exists not to protect workers' health and safety, but to defend established corporations from competition. It's not an anti-business agency, it's an anti-*small*-business agency.

Exxon, with its thousands of lawyers, has no trouble dealing with OSHA. But the small company can be put out of business by OSHA's fines and harassment. And it is—not by coincidence—the small businesses that OSHA concentrates on.

Recently, OSHA imposed its largest fine ever for alleged safety violations on a small meat-packing house. The agency had acted at the behest of the largest meat-packing firm in the area. This is why unscrupulous big businesses love OSHA. It's anti-competitive.

We used to hear about the awful Environmental Protection Agency (EPA) during the Carter administration. It oppressed businesspeople, imposed crazy regulations, etc. But again, this is a big-business agency established under the Nixon administration to hobble competition and subsidize favored local politicians and special interests—especially construction firms. It does not exist to improve the environment.

Like OSHA, EPA regulations are much less of a relative burden on large firms than small ones. And most of the EPA budget is spent on gigantic building contracts for supposed pollution-control facilities. But since friends of the administration are getting the contracts now, all conservative criticism has disappeared.

The Consumer Product Safety Commission (CPSC) was another product of the Nixon administration specifically set up to hurt small business and to help big business, this time under cover of consumer safety.

During the Carter years, we heard about how appalling this agency was. But there's silence now. Yet CPSC is still intervening, and still setting guidelines at the behest of established businesses designed to foil competition.

The Federal Trade Commission—emblematic of the older Progressive and New Deal agencies—is no different. Denounced during the Carter years as a crazed regulator—which it was—it is now praised as a bastion of free enterprise. Yet special interest groups founded the agency specifically to restrict competition and therefore free enterprise. The FTC now brags, for example, about eight years of increased enforcement of the anti-trust laws, statutes designed to allow politically connected businessmen to suppress their non-politically connected rivals.

One of the glories of America, and of the American free market, has always been our entrepreneurs. But especially since the days of the big railroads, there have always been some established businesses scheming to use government to reward themselves and punish their competitors. These traitors to free enterprise have been a major force in the growth of government, which is the horror story of our century.

To be able to fight for the ideals of the Founding Fathers, to be able to work for free markets and individual freedom, we have to be able to see through the government-generated smoke.

If we do not understand, and help others understand, what the government and its associated special interests are trying to do to us, there's no way we can fight them.

One rule of thumb is to assume that the government is lying until proven truthful, and to look carefully to see who's benefiting from any government action. It's not enough to make economic arguments against government control, as important as that is.

To mobilize the tax-*eaten* to make necessary changes—as the Jeffersonians and Jacksonians knew—we have to tell people the truth. And that means showing them the injustice, as well as the inefficiency, of government intervention.

Only correct economics, combined with a clear-eyed caste-analysis of who's doing what to whom, can help us make the changes we need to make. And that has been one of the roles of the Ludwig von Mises Institute.

The first publication, indeed the first activity, of the new Institute, was the *Free Market*. More than six years later, this publication has become an influential advocate of the uncompromising laissez-faire, anti-tax eater position. It is widely reprinted and cited, and increasingly useful to members of the general public, the media, the academy, and the policy community.

But newsletters are necessarily ephemeral. And so much of lasting significance has been published in the *Free Market* that I thought a more permanent collection was justified. It also makes a good, if not comprehensive, primer on free-market theory and policy from an Austrian perspective.

On monetary and fiscal policy, trade, regulation, socialism, privatization, and a host of other areas, these articles offer a perspective—and a tone—that once permeated the American Right, but which almost disappeared.

The fact that it is now flourishing, even if as a minority voice, is due in part to the *Free Market* and the Mises Institute.

This has been due to many people, but I would especially like to thank Perry Alford, to whom this volume is gratefully dedicated. His commitment to the vision of the Founding Fathers, to individual liberty and the free market, and his fighting spirit, have been lasting inspirations to all of us associated with the Institute.

Special thanks are also due to the indispensable Jeffrey A. Tucker. Norma A. Marchman did essential work in preparing the manuscript for typesetting and the production process, and Lianne M. Araki and Judy Thommesen did their usual excellent work as well.

Llewellyn H. Rockwell, Jr.
The Ludwig von Mises Institute
October 1988

•

1

FUNDAMENTALS

Ten Great Economic Myths

Murray N. Rothbard

Our country is beset by a large number of economic myths that distort public thinking on important problems and lead us to accept unsound and dangerous government policies. Here are ten of the most dangerous of these myths and an analysis of what is wrong with them.

Myth #1: Deficits are the cause of inflation; deficits have nothing to do with inflation.

In recent decades we *always* have had federal deficits. The invariable response of the party *out* of power, whichever it may be, is to denounce those deficits as being the cause of our chronic inflation. And the invariable response of whatever party is *in* power has been to claim that deficits have nothing to do with inflation. *Both* opposing statements are myths.

Deficits mean that the federal government is spending more than it is taking in in taxes. Those deficits can be financed in two ways. If they are financed by selling Treasury bonds to the public, then the deficits are not inflationary. No new money is created; people and institutions simply draw down their bank deposits to pay for the bonds, and the Treasury spends that money. Money has simply been transferred from the public to the Treasury, and then the money is spent on other members of the public.

On the other hand, the deficit may be financed by selling bonds to the banking system. If that occurs, the banks create *new* money by creating new bank deposits and using them to buy the bonds. The new money, in the form of bank deposits, is then spent by the Treasury, and thereby enters permanently into the spending stream of the economy, raising prices and causing inflation. By a complex process, the Federal Reserve enables the banks to create the new money by generating bank reserves of one-tenth that amount. Thus, if banks are to buy 100 billion of new bonds to finance the deficit, the Fed buys approximately $10 billion on *old* Treasury bonds. This purchase increases bank reserves by $10 billion, allowing the banks to pyramid the creation of new bank deposits or money by ten times that amount. In short, the government and the banking system it controls in effect "print" new money to pay for the federal deficit.

Thus, deficits are inflationary to the extent that they are financed by the banking system; they are *not* inflationary to the extent they are underwritten by the public.

Some policymakers point to the 1982-83 period, when deficits were accelerating and inflation was abating, as a statistical "proof" that deficits and inflation have no relation to each other. This is no proof at all. General price changes are determined by two factors: the supply of, and the demand for, money. During 1982-83 the Fed created new money at a very high rate, approximately at 15% per annum. Much of this went to finance the expanding deficit. But on the other hand, the severe depression of those two years increased the demand for money (i.e. lowered the desire to spend money on goods), in response to the severe business losses. This temporarily compensating increase in the demand for money does not make deficits any the less inflationary. In fact, as recovery proceeds, spending will pick up and the demand for money will fall, and the spending of the new money will accelerate inflation.

Myth #2: Deficits do not have a crowding-out effect on private investment.

In recent years there has been an understandable worry over the low rate of saving and investment in the United States. One worry is that the enormous federal deficits will divert savings to unproductive government spending and thereby crowd out productive investment, generating ever-greater long-run problems in advancing or even maintaining the living standards of the public.

Some policymakers have once again attempted to rebut this charge by statistics. In 1982-83, they declare deficits were high and increasing while interest rates fell, thereby indicating that deficits have no crowding-out effect.

This argument once again shows the fallacy of trying to refute logic with statistics. Interest rates fell because of the drop of business borrowing in a recession. "Real" interest rates (interest rates minus the inflation rate) stayed unprecedentedly high, however—partly because most of us expect renewed heavy inflation, partly because of the crowding-out effect. In any case, statistics cannot refute logic; and logic tells us that if savings go into government bonds, there will necessarily be less savings available for productive investment *than there would have been*, and interest rates will be higher than they would have been without the deficits. If deficits are financed by the public, then this diversion of savings into government projects is direct and palpable. If the deficits are financed by bank inflation, then the diversion is indirect, the crowding-out now taking place by the new money "printed" by the government competing for resources with old money saved by the public.

Milton Friedman tries to rebut the crowding-out effect of deficits by claiming that *all* government spending, not just deficits, equally crowds out private savings and investment. It is true that money siphoned off by taxes could also have gone into private savings and investment. But deficits have a far greater crowding-out effect than overall spending, since deficits financed by the public obviously tap savings and savings alone, whereas taxes reduce the public's consumption as well as savings.

Thus, deficits, whichever way you look at them, cause grave economic problems. If they are financed by the banking system, they are inflationary. But even if they are financed by the public, they will still cause severe crowding-out effects, diverting much-needed savings from productive private investment to wasteful government projects. And, furthermore, the greater the deficits the greater the permanent income tax burden on the American people to pay for the mounting interest payments, a problem aggravated by the high interest rates brought about by inflationary deficits.

Myth #3: Tax increases are a cure for deficits.

Those people who are properly worried about the deficit unfortunately offer an unacceptable solution: increasing taxes. Curing deficits by raising taxes is equivalent to curing someone's bronchitis by shooting him. The "cure" is far worse than the disease.

For one reason, as many critics have pointed out, raising taxes simply gives the government more money, and so the politicians and bureaucrats are likely to react by raising expenditures still further. Parkinson said it all in his famous "Law": "Expenditures rise to meet income." If the government is willing to have, say, a 20% deficit, it will handle high revenues by raising spending still more to maintain the same proportion of deficit.

But even apart from this shrewd judgment in political psychology, why should anyone believe that a *tax* is better than a higher price? It is true that inflation is a form of taxation, in which the government and other early receivers of new money are able to expropriate the members of the public whose income rises later in the process of inflation. But, at least with inflation, people are still reaping some of the benefits of exchange. If bread rises to $10 a loaf, this is unfortunate, but *at least* you can still eat the bread. But if taxes go up, your money is expropriated for the benefit of politicians and bureaucrats, and you are left with no service or benefit. The only result is that the producers' money is confiscated for the benefit of a bureaucracy that adds insult to injury by using part of that confiscated money to push the public around.

No, the only sound cure for deficits is a simple but virtually unmentioned one: cut the federal budget. How and where? Anywhere and everywhere.

Myth #4: Every time the fed tightens the money supply, interest rates rise (or fall); every time the fed expands the money supply, interest rates rise (or fall).

The financial press now knows enough economics to watch weekly money supply figures like hawks; but they inevitably interpret these figures in a chaotic fashion. If the money supply rises, this is interpreted as lowering interest rates and inflationary; it is *also* interpreted, often in the very same article, as raising interest rates. And vice versa. If the Fed tightens the growth of money, it is interpreted as both raising interest rates and lowering them. Sometimes it seems that *all* Fed actions, no matter how contradictory, must result in raising interest rates. Clearly something is very wrong here.

The problem here is that, as in the case of price levels, there are several causal factors operating on interest rates and in different directions. If the Fed expands the money supply, it does so by generating more bank reserves and thereby expanding the supply of bank credit and bank deposits. The expansion of credit necessarily means an increased supply in the credit market and hence a lowering of the price of credit, or the rate of interest. On the other hand, if the Fed restricts the supply of credit and the growth of the money supply, this means that the supply in the credit market declines, and this should mean a rise in interest rates.

And this is precisely what happens in the first decade or two of chronic inflation. Fed expansion lowers interest rates; Fed tightening raises them. But after this period, the public and the market begin to catch on to what is happening. They begin to realize that inflation is chronic because of the systemic expansion of the money supply. When they realize this fact of life, they will also realize that inflation wipes out the creditor for the benefit of the debtor. Thus, if someone grants a loan at five percent for one year, and there is seven percent inflation for that year, the creditor loses, not gains. He loses two percent, since he gets paid back in dollars that are now worth seven percent less in purchasing power. Correspondingly, the debtor gains by inflation. As creditors begin to catch on, they place an inflation premium on the interest rate, and debtors will be willing to pay. Hence, in the long-run anything which fuels the expectations of inflation will raise inflation premiums on interest rates; and anything which dampens those expectations will lower those premiums. Therefore, a Fed tightening will now tend to dampen inflationary expectations and *lower* interest rates; a Fed expansion will whip up those expectations again and *raise* them. There are two, opposite causal chains at work. And so

Fed expansion or contraction can either raise or lower interest rates, depending on which causal chain is stronger.

Which will be stronger? There is no way to know for sure. In the early decades of inflation, there is no inflation premium; in the later decades, such as we are now in, there is. The relative strength and reaction times depend on the subjective expectations of the public, and these cannot be forecast with certainty. And this is one reason why economic forecasts can never be made with certainty.

Myth #5: Economists, using charts or high speed computer models, can accurately forecast the future.

The problem of forecasting interest rates illustrates the pitfalls of forecasting in general. People are contrary cusses whose behavior, thank goodness, cannot be forecast precisely in advance. Their values, ideas, expectations, and knowledge change all the time, and change in an unpredictable manner. What economist, for example, could have forecast (or *did* forecast) the Cabbage Patch Kid craze of the Christmas season of 1983? Every economic quantity, every price, purchase, or income figure is the embodiment of thousands, even millions, of unpredictable choices by individuals.

Many studies, formal and informal, have been made of the record of forecasting by economists, and it has been consistently abysmal. Forecasters often complain that they can do well enough as long as current trends continue; what they have difficulty in doing is catching *changes* in trend. But of course there is no trick in extrapolating current trends into the near future. You don't need sophisticated computer models for *that*; you can do it better and far more cheaply by using a ruler. The real trick is precisely to forecast when and how trends will change, and forecasters have been notoriously bad at that. No economist forecast the depth of the 1981-82 depression, and none predicted the strength of the 1983 boom.

The next time you are swayed by the jargon or seeming expertise of the economic forecaster, ask yourself this question: If he can really predict the future so well, *why* is he wasting his time putting out newsletters or doing consulting when he himself could be making trillions of dollars in the stock and commodity markets?

Myth #6: There is a tradeoff between unemployment and inflation.

Every time someone calls for the government to abandon its inflationary policies, Establishment economists and politicians warn that the result can only be severe unemployment. We are trapped, therefore, into playing off inflation against high unemployment, and become persuaded that we must therefore accept some of both.

This doctrine is the fallback position for Keynesians. Originally, the Keynesians promised us that by manipulating and fine-tuning deficits and government spending, they could and would bring us permanent prosperity and full employment without inflation. Then, when inflation became chronic and ever-greater, they changed their tune to warn of the alleged tradeoff, so as to weaken any possible pressure upon the government to stop its inflationary creation of new money.

The tradeoff doctrine is based on the alleged "Phillips curve," a curve invented many years ago by the British economist A. W. Phillips. Phillips correlated wage rate increases with unemployment, and claimed that the two move inversely: the higher the increases in wage rates, the lower the unemployment. On its face, this is a peculiar doctrine, since it flies in the face of logical, commonsense theory. Theory tells us that the higher the wage rates, the *greater* the unemployment, and *vice versa*. If everyone went to their employer tomorrow and insisted on double or triple the wage rate, many of us would be promptly out of a job. Yet this bizarre finding was accepted as gospel by the Keynesian economic establishment.

By now, it should be clear that this statistical finding violates the facts as well as logical theory. For during the 1950s, inflation was only about one to two percent per year, and unemployment hovered around three or four percent, whereas nowadays unemployment ranges between eight and 11%, and inflation between five and 13%. In the last two or three decades, in short, *both* inflation *and* unemployment have increased sharply and severely. If anything, we have had a *reverse* Phillips curve. There has been anything but an inflation-unemployment tradeoff.

But ideologues seldom give way to the facts, even as they continually claim to "test" their theories by acts. To save the concept, they have simply concluded that the Phillips curve still remains as an inflation-unemployment tradeoff, except that the curve has unaccountably "shifted" to a new set of alleged tradeoffs. On this sort of mind-set, of course, no one could ever refute any theory.

In fact, inflation now, even if it reduces unemployment in the short-run by inducing prices to spurt ahead of wage rates (thereby reducing *real* wage rates), will only create more unemployment in the long run. Eventually, wage rates catch up with inflation, and inflation brings recession and unemployment inevitably in its wake. After more than two decades of inflation, we are all now living in that "long run."

Myth #7: Deflation—falling prices—is unthinkable, and would cause a catastrophic depression.

The public memory is short. We forget that, from the beginning of the Industrial Revolution in the mid-18th century until the beginning of World War II, prices generally went down, year after year. That's because continually increasing productivity and output of goods generated by free markets caused prices to fall. There was no depression, however, because costs fell along with selling prices. Usually, wage rates remained constant while the cost of living fell, so that "real" wages, or everyone's standard of living, rose steadily.

Virtually the only time when prices rose over those two centuries were periods of war (War of 1812, Civil War, World War I), when the warring governments inflated the money supply so heavily to pay for the war as to more than offset continuing gains in productivity.

We can see how free-market capitalism, unburdened by governmental or central bank inflation, works if we look at what has happened in the last few years to the prices of computers. A computer used to have to be enormous, costing millions of dollars. Now, in a remarkable surge of productivity brought about by the microchip revolution, computers are falling in price even as Iwrite. Computer firms are successful despite the falling prices because their costs have been falling, and productivity rising. In fact, these falling costs and prices have enabled them to tap a mass market characteristic of the dynamic growth of free-market capitalism. "Deflation" has brought no disaster to this industry.

The same is true of other high-growth industries, such a electronic calculators, plastics, TV sets, and VCRs. Deflation, far from bringing catastrophe, is the hallmark of sound and dynamic economic growth.

Myth #8: The best tax is a "flat" income tax, proportionate to income across the board, with no exemptions or deductions.

It is usually added by flat-tax proponents, that eliminating such exemptions would enable the federal government to cut the current tax rate substantially.

But this view assumes, for one thing, that present deductions from the income tax are immoral subsidies or "loopholes" that should be closed for the benefit of all. A deduction of exemption is only a "loophole" if you assume that the government owns 100% of everyone's income and that allowing some of that income to remain untaxed constitutes an irritating "loophole." Allowing someone to keep some of his own income is neither a loophole nor a subsidy. Lowering the overall tax by abolishing deductions for medical care, for interest payments, or for uninsured losses, is simply lowering the taxes of one set of people (those that have little interest to pay, or medical expenses, or uninsured losses) at the expense of raising them for those who have incurred such expenses.

There is furthermore neither any guarantee nor even likelihood that, once the exemptions and deductions are safely out of the way, the government would keep its tax rate at the lower level. Looking at the record of governments, past and present, there is every reason to assume that more of our money would be taken by the government as it raised the tax rate back up (at least) to the old level, with a consequently greater overall drain from the producers to the bureaucracy.

It is supposed that the tax system should be roughly that of pricing or incomes on the market. But market pricing is *not* proportional to incomes. It would be a peculiar world, for example, if Rockefeller were forced to pay $1,000 for a loaf of bread—that is, a payment proportionate to his income relative to the average man. That would mean a world in which equality of incomes was enforced in a particularly bizarre and inefficientmanner. If a tax were levied like a market price, it would be *equal* to every "customer," not proportionate to each customer's income.

Myth #9: An income tax cut helps everyone because not only the taxpayer but also the government will benefit, since tax revenues will rise when the rate is cut.

This is the so-called "Laffer curve," set forth by California economist Arthur Laffer. It was advanced as a means of allowing politicians to square the circle; to come out for tax cuts, keeping spending at the current level, *and* balance the budget all at the same time. In that way, the public would enjoy their tax cuts, be happy at the balanced budget, and still receive the same level of subsidies from the government.

It is true that if tax rates are 99%, and they are cut to 95%, tax revenue will go up. But there is no reason to assume such simple connections at any other time. In fact, this relationship works much better for a local excise tax than for a national income tax. A few years ago, the government of the District of Columbia decided to procure some revenue by sharply raising the District's gasoline tax. But, then, drivers could simply nip over the border to Virginia or Maryland and fill up at a much cheaper price. D.C. gasoline tax revenues fell, and much to their chagrin and confusion, they had to repeal the tax.

But this is not likely to happen with the income tax. People are not gong to stop working or leave the country because of a relatively small tax hike, or do the reverse because of a tax cut.

There are some problems with the Laffer curve. The amount of time it is supposed to take for the Laffer effect to work is never specified. But still more important: Laffer assumes that what all of us want is to maximize tax revenue to the government. If—a big if—we are really at the upper half of the Laffer Curve, we should then all want to set tax rates at that "optimum" point. But why? *Why* should it be the objective of every one of us to maximize government revenue? To push to the maximum, in short, the share of private product that gets siphoned off to the activities of government? I should think we would be more interested in *minimizing* government revenue by pushing tax rates far, far below whatever the Laffer Optimum might happen to be.

Myth #10: Imports from countries where labor is cheap cause unemployment in the United States.

One of the many problems with this doctrine is that it ignores the question: *why* are wages low in a foreign country and high in the United States? It starts with these wage rates as ultimate givens, and doesn't pursue the question why they are what they are. Basically, they are high in the United States because labor productivity is high—because workers here are aided by large amounts of technologically advanced capital equipment. Wage rates are low in many foreign countries because capital equipment is small and technologically primitive. Unaided by much capital, worker productivity is far lower than in the United States. Wage rates in every country are determined by the productivity of the workers in that country. Hence, high wages in the United States are not a standing threat to American prosperity; they are the *result* of that prosperity.

But what of certain industries in the U.S. that complain loudly and chronically about the "unfair" competition of products from low-wage countries? Here, we must realize that wages in each country are interconnected from one industry and occupation and region to another. All workers compete with each other, and if wages in industry A are far lower than in other industries, workers—spearheaded by young workers starting their careers— would leave or refuse to enter industry A and move to other firms or industries where the wage rate is higher.

Wages in the complaining industries, then, are high because they have been bid high by *all* industries in the United States. If the steel or textile industries in the United States find it difficult to compete with their counterparts abroad, it is not because foreign firms are playing low wages, but because other *American* industries have bid up American wage rates to such a high level that steel and textile cannot afford to pay. In short, what's really happening is that steel, textile, and other such firms are using labor inefficiently as compared to other American industries. Tariffs or import quotas to keep inefficient firms or industries in operation hurt everyone, in every country, who is not in that industry. They injure all American consumers by keeping up prices, keeping down quality and competition, and distorting production. Tariff or an import quota is equivalent to chopping up a railroad or destroying an airline—for its point is to make international transportation artificially expensive.

Tariffs and import quotas also injure other, efficient American industries by tying up resources that would otherwise move to more efficient uses. And, in the long run, the tariffs and quotas, like any sort of monopoly privilege conferred by government, are no bonanza even for the firms being protected and subsidized. For, as we have seen in the cases of railroads and airlines, industries enjoying government monopoly (whether through tariffs or regulation) eventually become so inefficient that they lose money anyway, and can only call for more and more bailouts, for ever more of a privileged shelter from free competition.

Creative Economic Semantics

Murray N. Rothbard

If the federal government's economists have been good for nothing else in recent years, they have made great strides in what might be called "creative economic semantics." First they redefined the seemingly simple term "budget cut." In the old days, a "budget cut" was a reduction of next year's budget below this year's. In that old-fashioned sense, Dwight Eisenhower's first two years in office actually cut the budget substantially, though not dramatically, below the previous year. Now we have "budget cuts" which are not cuts, but rather substantial increases over the previous year's expenditures. "Cut" became subtly but crucially redefined as reducing something else. *What* the something else might be didn't seem to matter, so long as the focus was taken off actual dollar expenditures. Sometimes it was a cut "in the rate of increase," other times it was a cut in "real" spending, at still others it was a percentage of GNP, and at yet other times it was a cut in the sense of being below past *projections* for that year. The result of a series of such "cuts" has been to raise spending sharply and dramatically not only in old-fashioned terms, but even in all other categories. Government spending has gone up considerably any way you slice it. As a result, even the idea of a creatively semantic budget cut has now gone the way of the nickel fare and the Constitution of the United States.

Another example of creative semantics was the "tax cut" of 1981-1982, a tax cut so allegedly fearsome that it had to be offset by outright tax increases late in 1982, in 1983, in 1984, and undoubtedly on and on into the future. Again in the old days, a cut in income taxes meant that the average person would find less of a slice taken out of his paycheck. But while the 1981-82 tax changes did that for some people, the average person found that the piddling cuts were more than offset by the continuing rise in the Social Security tax, and by "bracket creep"—a colorful term for the process by which inflation (generated by the federal government's expansion of the money supply) wafts everyone into higher money income (even though a price rise might leave them no better off) and therefore into a higher tax bracket. So that even though the official schedule of tax rates might remain the same, the average man is paying a higher chunk of his income.

The much-vaulted and much-denounced "tax cut" turns out, on old-fashioned semantics, to be no cut at all but rather a substantial increase. In return for the dubious pleasure of this non-cut, the American public will have to suffer by paying through the nose for years to come in the form of "offsetting," though unfortunately all-too-genuine, tax increases. Of course, government economists have been doing their part as well to try to sugar-coat the pill of tax increases. They never refer to these changes as "increases." They have not been increases at all; they were "revenue enhancement" and "closing loopholes." The best comment on the concept of "loopholes" was that of Ludwig von Mises. Mises remarked that the very concept of "loopholes" implies that the government rightly owns all of the money you earn, and that it becomes necessary to correct the slipup of the government's not having gotten its hands on that money long since.

Despite promises of a balanced budget by 1984, we find that several years of semantically massaged "budget cuts" and "tax cuts" as well as "enhancements" have resulted in an enormous, seemingly permanent, and unprecedented deficit somewhere around $200 billion. Once again, creative semantics have come to the rescue. One route is to use time-honored methods to redefine the deficit out of existence. The Keynesians used to redefine it by claiming that in something called a "full employment budget" there was no deficit, that is, that if one subtracts the spending necessary to achieve full employment, there would be no deficit, perhaps even a surplus. But while such a sleight-of-hand might work with a deficit of $20 billion, it is a puny way to wish away a gap of $200 billion. Still, the government's economists are trying. They have already redefined the "deficits" as a "real increase" in debt, that is, a deficit discounted by inflation. The more inflation generated by the government, then, the more it *looks* as if the deficit is washed away. On the very same semantic magic, the apologists for the disastrous runaway German inflation of 1923 claimed that there was no inflation at all, since in terms of gold, German prices were actually falling! And similarly, they claimed, that since in real terms the supply of German marks was falling, that the *real* trouble in Germany was that there was too *little* money being printed rather than too much.

There is no general acceptance for the idea that, based on some legerdemain, the deficit doesn't really exist. But there is acceptance of the view that a tax increase constitutes a "down payment" on the deficit. Again, in the old days, a "down payment" on a debt meant that part of the debt was being paid off. Washington's creative economists have managed to redefine the term to mean a hoped-for reduction of next year's *increase* in the debt—a very different story indeed.

Competition at Work: Xerox at 25

Murray N. Rothbard

A little over 25 years ago a revolutionary event occurred in the world of business and in American society generally. It was a revolution accomplished without bloodshed and without anyone being executed. The Xerox 914, the world's first fully-automated plain-paper copier, was exhibited to the press in New York City.

Before then copiers existed, but they were clumsy and complex, they took a long time, and the final product was a fuzzy mess imprinted on special, unattractive pink paper. The advent of Xerox ushered in the photocopying age, and was successful to such an extent that within a decade the word "xerox" was in danger of slipping out of trademark and becoming a generic term in the public domain.

Many people, and even some economists, believe that large, highly capitalized firms can always outcompete small ones. Nothing could be further from the truth. In the pre-Xerox age, the photography industry was dominated, at least in the United States, by one giant, Eastman Kodak. And yet it was not Kodak or any other giant business or massive research facility that invented or even developed the Xerox process. It was invented, instead, by one man, Chester Carlson, a New York City patent attorney, who did the initial experiments in the kitchen of his apartment home in 1938. Carlson then looked around for a firm that would develop a commercial product from his invention. He first thought of Eastman Kodak, but Kodak told him it would never work, that it was too complex, would be too costly to develop, and, most remarkably of all, would have only a small potential market! The same answer was given to Carlson by 21 other large firms such as IBM. They were the "experts"; how could they all be wrong?

Finally, one small firm in Rochester took a gamble on the Xerox project. Haloid Co., a photographic paper manufacturer with annual sales of less than $7 million, bought the rights to the process from Carlson in 1947, and spent $20 million and 12 years before the mighty Xerox 914 came on the market in the fateful fall of 1959. Horace Becker, who was chief engineer on the Xerox 914, explains that "technically, it did not look like a winner. . . . That which we did, a big company could not have afforded to do. We really shot the dice, because it didn't make any difference." Small business can outcompete, and outinnovate, the giants.

Haloid Co., then Haloid Xerox Co., and finally Xerox, became one of the great business and stock-market success stories of the 1960s. By the early 1970s, it had captured almost all of the new, huge photocopier market, and its 1983 revenues totaled $8.5 billion. But by the mid 1970s, Xerox, too, was getting big, bureaucratic, and sluggish, and Japan invaded the photocopy market with the successful Savin copier. As competition by new originally small firms accelerated, Xerox's share of the market fell to 75% in 1975, 47% in 1980, and less than 40 percent in 1982. As one investment analyst commented, "They had an aging product line. They were caught off guard."

In the world of business, no firm, even the giants, can stand still for long. In trouble, Xerox fought back with its new and improved 10 Series of "Marathon" copiers, and in 1983 the company increased its share of the photocopy market for the first time since 1970; and its record considerably improved in 1984.

So, Happy Birthday Xerox! The Xerox success story is a monument to what a brilliant and determined lone inventor can accomplish. It is a living testimony of how a small firm can innovate and outcompete giant firms, and of how a small firm, become a giant, can rethink and retool in order to keep up with a host of new competitors. But above all, the Xerox story is a tribute to what free competition and free enterprise can accomplish, in short, what people can do if they are allowed to think and work and invest and employ their energies in freedom. Human progress and human freedom go hand in hand.

Looking Beneath the Surface

Llewellyn H. Rockwell, Jr.

I learned two lessons from my years on Capitol Hill as Congressman Ron Paul's chief aide: 1) Every act of government deliberately benefits an interest group coalition at the expense of the rest of us; and 2) The government and the interests always lie about it.

During the gasoline crisis, for example, Congress passed the "windfall profits" tax on oil. The politicians and their lapdogs in the media trumpeted this as a deserved comeuppance to Big Oil.

Seen from the inside, it was just the opposite. The large, multi-national oil companies, in cahoots with Jimmy Carter's Department of Energy, designed the tax and actively lobbied Congress for it. Why? Because it was to their comparative advantage. More money for energy programs flowed to the Establishment companies through such corporate welfare as the synfuels program, and the tax harmed only small domestic producers. The windfall profits tax is collected in Texas, not in Saudi Arabia.

So the imposition of this vicious tax served two interest groups: the government and the multinational oil companies, against U.S. oil producers and consumers.

Virtually every single act of government can be analyzed in this way. Since the Federal Reserve Act of 1913 cartelized the banking industry and allowed the banks to inflate together with the government, at the expense of the rest of us, we can assume—using interest-group analysis—that the industry promoted the bill. And in fact, Rockefeller and Morgan-connected commercial and investment banking interests wrote the act, lobbied for it, and staffed the resulting agency. Even today, Paul Volcker is a former vice president of Chase Manhattan Bank.

Teddy Kennedy is pushing for an increase in the minimum wage "to help the poor." In fact, the very existence of a minimum wage harms the poor, since it means that anyone whose production is worth less than that figure, plus Social Security and other business taxes, will remain unemployed. And in fact that is its purpose. It makes it harder for new, small businesses to start up, and—by outlawing low-wage competition—enables labor unions to continue to get higher-than-market wages through federal coercion. That is why labor unions love the minimum wage, and why their bought-and-paid-for Congressmen and Senators work to raise it.

The Reagan administration has spent more on foreign aid than all previous administrations from Eisenhower to Carter combined. But not to help the poor in foreign lands. Foreign aid is a massive subsidy to U.S. bankers with loans to foreign governments, and to U.S. exporters whose products are purchased with the funds. And—no surprise—it is big banks and exporters that push for foreign aid. As to the poor in foreign lands, they are made worse off as corrupt, dictatorial governments are cemented in power; the American taxpayer is impoverished by unconstitutional spending.

When looking or listening to the government, assume the reverse of what it claims, and look to see who is getting the cash. Only this way of looking beneath the surface, which Mises called "caste-conflict" analysis, helps explain government actions so clearly, or—when exposed—helps rally the people against further injustices.

The Fraud of GNP

Llewellyn H. Rockwell, Jr.

"The Gross National Product grew at an annual rate of 4.4% for the first quarter of 1987," the Commerce Department recently said. But corporate profits and people's earning dropped. We're all supposed to be better off when the GNP grows. Why aren't we? The reason, as shown by Professor Murray N. Rothbard, is that the GNP is a phony statistic.

The GNP records the dollar amount of goods and services produced in the economy during a period. But it equates government spending with private spending. And it ignores the wealth and potential growth destroyed by taxation.

Imagine that the economy consisted of two small, productive towns. The government decides to destroy one of them—a hotbed of tax resistance—by aerial bombardment, and to tax the other to pay for the clean-up. After a year, the destroyed town is restored. Calculating the net effect of this process, the Commerce Department would say that the GNP of the two-town economy grew by 50%.

GNP records the money spent on goods and services, not the wealth destroyed by bombs, taxation, regulation, or other government activities. So GNP would act as if a third town had been added to the economy, when in fact one had been deducted.

As Professor Rothbard has pointed out, *subtracting* government spending from GNP, and then adjusting for taxation, gives us a much better idea of the real economy. His "Private Product Remaining (to Producers)" or PPR does exactly that.

Working from Professor Rothbard's thesis, Professor Robert Batemarco of Manhattan College computed the PPR from 1960 to 1985 for an article in the first issue of the Institute's *Review of Austrian Economics*.

The gap shown on the chart between GNP and PPR represents the horrendous growth of government. And the gap is huge and growing, despite promises to get Washington off our backs.

The growth in GNP is almost all attributable to increased government spending, which represents capital consumption, not progress. As shown by the PPR the economy has barely moved, thanks to the government's incredible taxation, deficits, welfare, borrowing, subsidies, and controls.

Real growth in the U.S. registered a mere 1.3% last year. On the average, the GNP figure is about 52% higher than real growth. And the more government grows, the higher that percentage.

Always be wary of government statistics. They are usually designed to mislead, and GNP is part of that game.

Racial Discrimination vs. the Free Market

Mark D. Hughes

Not long ago I saw a poster at George Mason University advertising a talk on "The Development of Racism Under Capitalism." Sponsored by SCAR (the Student Coalition Against Racism), the implied position was wrong; it is capitalism that hinders racism.

"The term 'discrimination' has acquired an unambiguously negative meaning," writes Dr. Walter Block. "It conjures up the image of racial and sexual prejudice. Strictly speaking, however, the term is neutral."

As human beings, we face an unavoidable scarcity of time and resources: that is, we cannot have everything we want or need whenever we want or need it. To cope with this scarcity, we ration our time, skill, knowledge, and wealth.

This process must involve discrimination. For example, if I choose to read Mises's *Human Action* rather than the collected poetry of Keats, I am discriminating against Keats. And my choosing to read at all means I am discriminating against every other use of my time.

Different ways of rationing resources have emerged over the centuries. The barbarism of ancient times involved grabbing what you could, when you could, and however you could. In the barbarism of modern times, these same activities are carried out by governments.

But the best and only peaceful method for rationing scarce resources is the price system. Respecting private property and individual rights, the price system puts the power of choice into the hands of the person whose scarce resources are to be rationed.

If the owner of a resource wishes to exchange it with others, and he sets the price at zero, then people who discriminate in favor of it, by choosing to consume it, will want more of it than the owner wishes to exchange. The owner will therefore ration his resource by giving it a positive price. As the price of the resource rises, more and more people will choose to discriminate against it in favor of a less costly resource.

Their desire for the resource has not changed, but the cost of discriminating in favor of it has increased. For example, I will have the same desire for a European sports car regardless of its price, but its price makes discriminating in its favor too costly for me.

The more scarce and desirable a resource, the higher its price. But at some point, the owner will arrive at a price where the total discrimination in favor of it is just equal to the quantity he is willing to exchange.

Prices and the right of ownership give individuals the ability to increase or decrease the level of discrimination against their resources. This is the mechanism that makes free market competition work. And only this competition gives individuals control over their own scarce resources.

A consumer who refuses to purchase resources from a person (i.e. discriminates against that person) solely because of the color of that person's skin is discriminating. The act of discrimination itself is neither good nor bad, but the underlying values can be considered unethical.

Does the person who suffers because of racism have any recourse? He could try to use government power to force an exchange by coercion. But there is a better way: he can use the price system.

If I feel someone is discriminating against me for unethical reasons, then I can make his choice costly by lowering the price I charge. His discrimination then becomes more costly. A person discriminating against me can only continue to do so if he is willing to pay a higher relative price for his choice. I can't change his values, but I can make them more costly to hold.

This very process occurs every day. When a member of a minority group opens a new grocery store in an unfriendly neighborhood, say a Korean in a black area of Washington, D.C., he is likely to be discriminated against. Instead of demanding that the government force shoppers to buy from his store, he chooses the peaceful method: he reduces his prices. This increases the cost to consumers of discriminating against him, because they are now paying a premium to shop somewhere else. As a result, they begin to patronize his store. Racists may still be racists, but they no longer discriminate unethically.

But if the government had set the grocer's prices at the same level as other stores not owned by minorities, there would be no cost to consumers for racially discriminating against him. They would simply continue shopping at Safeway.

Henry Hazlitt wrote in his unforgettable book *Economics in One Lesson*:

> A wage is, in fact, a price. It is unfortunate for clarity of economic thinking that the price of labor's services (labor's scarce resource) should have received an entirely different name from other prices. This has prevented most people from recognizing that the same principles govern both.

Like the consumer of any resource, an employer will pay a wage no higher than the production the worker can generate. If the worker accepts a job paying less than his production, other employers will recognize they can profit by offering a higher wage. Eventually the worker receives a wage equal to the value he contributes.

If the government imposes a minimum wage, anyone who cannot add more than the minimum to the employer's business will not be hired. No employer can pay out more than his business produces for very long. The government's minimum wage law discriminates against the less productive members of society.

According to Professor Walter E. Williams of George Mason University, author of *The State Against Blacks*:

> As late as 1948, black youth labor market participation was higher than that of white youths and their unemployment rate was less. But with each and every increase in the level and coverage of the minimum wage law, that picture was changed. Now the very opposite is the case.

When the state imposes minimum wage laws, it reduces the cost for employers to discriminate racially. It also takes away a minority person's best weapon: the right to lower prices and make racially based discrimination costly.

Suppose there are two young women, one white and one black, both equally qualified. They are the only two people who have applied for a hostess's job in a restaurant owned by a white racist. The employer is willing to pay up to $5.00 per hour. The white woman has been offered a job she likes better at another business at $4.50 an hour, and will accept the restaurant job only if she can get $5.00 per hour.

The black woman knows the boss is a racist. She realizes that her only hope of getting the job is to ask for less than $5.00 per hour. And the less she asks for, the greater her chances of getting the job. If she lowers her price to $4.50, the employer must now pay 50 cents per hour to discriminate racially against her. And at some wage it will be too costly for him to continue his racial discrimination, and he will hire the black woman.

The story is different when the state imposes a minimum wage of $5.00 per hour. Far from aiding the black woman, it forbids her from competing with her white rival. The government has in effect made it illegal for the black woman to work at that restaurant.

This brings us back to "The Development of Racism Under Capitalism." SCAR and groups like it demand that the government intervene in the free market to eliminate racial discrimination. But the free market tends to reduce unethical discrimination; it is the state through its fettering of free enterprise that promotes racism.

Mises Contra Marx

David Gordon

If asked to name the foremost critic of Marxism, most economists sympathetic to the free market would name Eugen von Böhm-Bawerk, who in his treatise *Capital and Interest* and his separate brochure *Karl Marx and the Close of his System* demolished the labor theory of value, the linchpin of Marxist economics.

But the labor theory is but one part of Marxism: what about the remainder of the system? Here one must turn to the work of Böhm-Bawerk's greatest student, Ludwig von Mises, whose devastating analysis of Marxism is of surpassing excellence. His contribution to the critique of Marxism is principally to be found in two of his books: *Socialism* and *Theory and History*. (Both are available from the Mises Institute.)

The *Communist Manifesto* (1848) famously states: "The history of all hitherto existing society is the history of class struggles." Each social system, in the Marxist view, is characterized by a different variety of class conflict. In the capitalist system, of course, the protracted conflict finds capitalists opposed to proletarians. In the course of the social struggle between the classes, members or friends of each class elaborate theories of various sorts to advance the interests of that class. These theories, whatever they may claim, do not stem from the search for objective truth. Like all "ideological" thought, economic, social, and political theories reflect class interest.

Mises, more forcefully than any other critic of Marx, at once penetrates to the essence of this fallacious view. If all thought about social and economic matters is determined by class position, what about the Marxist system itself? If, as Marx proudly proclaimed, he aimed at providing a science for the working class, why should any of his views be accepted as true? Mises rightly notes that Marx's view is self-refuting: if all social thought is ideological, then *this* proposition is itself ideological and the grounds for believing it have been undercut. In his *Theories of Surplus Value*, Marx cannot contain his sneering at the "apologetics" of various bourgeois economists. He did not realize that in his constant jibes at the class bias of his fellow economists, he was but digging the grave of his own giant work of propaganda on behalf of the proletariat.

Mises never tired of emphasizing a theme he expresses tersely in *Liberalism*: "Man has only one tool with which to fight error: reason." By "reason," he meant a logical procedure claiming universal validity. To deny the power of reason is in effect to refute oneself. If reason must be subordinated to some other faculty, whether class interest, hermeneutic understanding, or whatever nonrational intellectual fad one pleases, the result can be nothing other than stultifying. Without logic, what *reason* can be given for the acceptance of the postulated account?

Mises did not confine his assault on Marxism to the essential, yet arcane, area of epistemology. He also analyzed in detail the principal themes of Marx's interpretation of history. According to Marx, the key to history lies in the forces of production. (Very roughly, the forces of production of a society consist of the society's technology.) These forces, throughout history, have a constant tendency to develop. As they do so, they compel changes in the relations of production, i.e., the economic and social system existing in a particular society. At one time, e.g., feudalism was best adapted to develop the forces of production. When it ceased to be the most efficient system, capitalism replaced it, breaking what Marx called the "fetters" on production imposed by the manorial economy of feudalism. In turn, at the dictate of the forces of production, capitalism will be replaced by socialism, a system Marx anticipated would be enormously more productive than its predecessor.

Mises in *Theory and History* posed a simple query that proved lethal to the alleged "science of historical materialism." As just explained, growth of the forces of production is supposed to explain all else of importance. But what determines this very growth? As Mises often reminds us, only individuals act: classes, "forces of production," "relations of production," etc., are in themselves but abstractions. Apart from the action of human beings, they are void and powerless. Like Hegel's *Geist* (Spirit), Marx's forces of production are a self-developing phenomenon governing human will. Marx never bothers to explain how such forces, in themselves the *effects* of human action, can exclusively determine all important human action.

Once one has grasped the point that it is individuals, not the forces of production, who act, the entire Marxist scheme of historical evolution falls by the wayside. If human beings create by their acts the forces of production, rather than the forces determining these acts, then nothing is inevitable about the transition from one economic system to another. Such changes will take place as persons act to create them, no more and no less. If one objects that there are laws determining human action, perhaps the objector would be good enough to produce them for inspection. That the results of what persons create may not be to their liking is another matter.

Marxism, as the Stalinist "philosopher" M. B. Mitin liked to declare portentously, is "a guide to action." And the action the Marxists have in mind is of course the replacement of capitalism by socialism. In a famous passage in Volume III of *Capital*, Marx foresees a rosy day ahead under the blessings of socialism in which people will be able to devote most of their time to leisure. Work for mere survival will become a thing of past.

Such is the Marxist promise: the reality, Mises demonstrated, was quite another matter. In his argument, Mises did not principally rely on the results of attempting to turn socialism from idea to reality in Soviet Russia. Instead, as those acquainted with his praxeological method will have anticipated, Mises offered proof that socialism was of its nature impossible.

He presented his argument in a famous article appearing in 1920 that, with much elaboration, was incorporated into his great work *Socialism* (1922). Characteristic of Mises, his point is in essence a simple one: the great Austrian economist had an unerring instinct for the heart of any issue of theory he considered. Given a list of goods to produce, whether those desired by the members of society in their roles as consumers or those on an agenda concocted by a dictator, any developed economy must have a way to decide how to employ its resources in the best possible way to produce the desired goods.

Under capitalism, this challenge receives a response fully adequate to the difficulty it poses. Resources, whether land, labor, or capital, exist subject to ownership by individuals. These persons, in a fashion elaborated in minute detail in Mises's *Human Action* and Murray N. Rothbard's *Man, Economy, and State*, will trade in markets. Doing so will enable them to price production goods according to their most efficient use in securing the desired consumption goals.

The details of the process cannot be here elaborated, and in any event, no one seriously denies that the free market *can* perform the task of economic calculation I have briefly described. The gravamen of Mises's indictment of socialism, and the controversial aspect of his argument, is his contention that *only* capitalism can solve the calculation problem. Socialism in particular cannot.

Again without descending into detail, the main point of Mises's reasoning can be quickly comprehended. Socialism by definition consists of the centralized direction of the economy, its main means of production being under "public," i.e. government, ownership. How can a centralized system, in the absence of markets, decide whether a use of resources to produce a good is more efficient than a rival use? Any "prices" the director of the economy imposes will be arbitrary and of no value for genuine calculation. (One technicality ought to be mentioned, lest the argument be misunderstood: it is production goods, not first-order or consumption goods, that Mises maintains a socialist system lacks the means to calculate.)

We can at once see how Mises's argument administers the *coup de grace* to Marxism. That system claims that socialism will arrive because the development of the forces of production will demand its institution. Even if one were to neglect Mises's point, that the growth of the forces of production is *not* inevitable, one can see that Marx's view is laughably inept. It is capitalism that is not only the most efficient economic system, but the *only* economic system that is efficient. If the forces of production did, *per impossible* inevitably grow of their own accord, it is not socialism but capitalism that they would establish.

Continuing his assault on Marxism, Mises explored Marx's reasons for not considering the problem of efficiency. Here Mises's answer admits of no dispute. Marx said nothing about the calculation problem because he devoted virtually no attention whatever to the economic institutions of socialism. To do so, he thought, would be to establish "blueprints" for the future, in the style of the Utopian socialists he was quick to scorn. With complete intellectual irresponsibility, he preached the overthrow of the intricate economy of capitalism he himself acknowledged as the most productive in history in order to establish a scheme whose institutions he had not bothered to analyze.

When one considers the responses of Mises's socialist critics, however, perhaps Marx's policy of averting his eyes from the problems of socialism was wiser than he knew. Mises had little difficulty in refuting all the attempted socialist solutions of his calculation problem. Some looked to mathematics: a system of simultaneous equations would enable the necessary prices to be discovered. How, in a regime of constant change, these equations were to operate, the proponents of this approach left unsaid. The most popular response to Mises, though, lay elsewhere. The Polish economist Oskar Lange, long resident in the United States until, following the Second World War, the blandishments of Communist Poland proved too much for him to resist, claimed that a socialist economy need not abandon the market. Though to some "market socialism" has little more sense the a "square circle," Lange was of course not among them. But his proposal, though original, fared no better than the others. Mises subjected it to withering attack, the details of which I leave the interested reader to explore in Mises's work. In particular, his illuminating discussion of his critics in *Human Action* should be consulted.

Mises exposed several irremediable and crucial errors in Marxism. A reader of his criticism cannot help but apply to Marxism the well-known line from "Ozymandias": "Round the decay of that colossal wreck, . . . /The lone and level sands stretch far away."

Keynesian Myths

Murray N. Rothbard

Inflation and Idle Capacity

The Keynesians have been caught short again. In the early and the late 1970s, the wind was taken out of their sails by the arrival of inflationary recession, a phenomenon which they not only failed to predict, but whose very existence violates the fundamental tenets of the Keynesian system. Since then, the Keynesians have lost their old invincible arrogance, though they still constitute a large part of the economics profession.

In the last few years, the Keynesians have been assuring us with more than a touch of their old *hauteur*, that inflation would not and could not arrive soon, despite the fact that "tight-money" hero Paul Volcker had been consistently pouring in money at double-digit rates. Chiding hard-money advocates, the Keynesians declared that, despite the monetary inflation, American industry still suffered from "excess" or "idle" capacity, functioning at an overall rate of something like 80%. Thus, they pointed out, expanded monetary demand could not result in inflation.

As we all know, despite Keynesian assurances that inflation could not reignite, it *did* despite the idle capacity, leaving them with something else to puzzle over. Inflation has risen this year from approximately 1% in 1986 to 6% now, interest rates are rising again, the fall of the dollar has raised import prices, and gold prices are rising again. Once again, the hard-money economists and investment advisors have proved far sounder than the Establishment-blessed Keynesians.

The best way to explain where the Keynesians went wrong is to turn against them their own common reply to their critics: that anti-Keynesians, who worry about the waste of inflation or government programs, are "assuming full employment" of resources. Eliminate this assumption, they say, and Keynesianism becomes correct in the through-the-looking-glass world of unemployment and idle resources. But the charge should be turned around, and the Keynesians should be asked: why should there be unemployment (of labor or of machinery), at all? Unemployment is not a given that descends from heaven. Of course, it often exists, but what can account for it?

The Keynesians themselves create the problem by leaving out the price system. The hallmark of crackpot economics is an analysis that somehow leaves out prices, and talks only about such aggregates as income, spending, and employment.

We know from "microeconomic" analysis that if there is a "surplus" of something on the market, if something cannot be sold, then the only reason is that its price is somehow being kept too high. The way to cure surplus or unemployment of anything, is to lower the asking price, whether it be wage rates for labor, prices of machinery or plant, or of the inventory of a retailer

In short, as Professor William H. Hutt pointed out brilliantly in the 1930s, when his message was lost amid the fervor of the Keynesian Revolution: idleness or unemployment of a resource can only occur because the owner of that resource is deliberately withholding it from the market and refusing to sell it at the offered price. In a profound sense, therefore, all unemployment and idleness is voluntary.

Why should a resource owner deliberately withhold it from the market? Usually, because he is holding out for a higher price, or wage rate. In a free and unhampered market economy, the owners will find out their error soon enough, and when they get tired of making no returns from their labor or machinery or products, they will lower their asking price sufficiently to sell them. In the case of machinery and other capital goods, of course, the owners might have made a severe malinvestment, often due to artificial booms created by bank credit and central banks. In that case, the lower market-clearing price for the machinery or plant might be so low as to not be worth the laborer's giving up his leisure—but then the unemployment is purely voluntary and the worker holds out permanently for a higher wage.

A worse problem is that, since the 1930s, government and its privileged unions have intervened massively in the labor market to keep wage rates above the market-clearing wage, thereby insuring ever higher unemployment among workers with the lowest skills and productivity. Government interference, in the form of minimum wage laws and compulsory unionism, creates compulsory unemployment, while welfare payments and unemployment "insurance" subsidize unemployment and make sure that it will be permanently high. We can have as much unemployment as we pay for.

It follows from this analysis that monetary inflation and greater spending will not necessarily reduce unemployment or idle capacity. It will *only* do so if workers or machine owners are induced to think that they are getting a higher return and at least some of their holdout demands are being met. And this can only be accomplished if the price paid for the resource (the wage rate or the price of machinery) *goes up*. In other words, greater supply or use of capacity will only be called forth by wage and price increases, i.e. by *price inflation*.

As usual, the Keynesians have the entire causal process bollixed up. And so, as the facts now poignantly demonstrate, we can and do have inflation along with idle resources.

The New International Money Scheme

Ever since the Western world abandoned the gold coin standard in 1914, the international monetary system has been rocketing from one bad system to another, from the frying pan to the fire and back again, fleeing the problems of one alternative only to find itself deeply unhappy in the other. Basically, only two alternative systems have been considered: (1) fiat money standards, each national fiat currency being governed by its own central bank, with relative values fluctuating in accordance with supply and demand; and (2) some sort of fixed exchange rate system, governed by international coordination of economic policies.

Our current System 1 came about willy nilly in 1973, out of the collapse of Bretton Woods System 2 that had been imposed on the world by the United States and Britain in 1944. System 1, the monetarist or Friedmanite ideal, at best breaks up the world monetary system into national fiat enclaves, adds great uncertainties and distortions to the monetary system, and removes the check of external discipline from the inflationary propensities of every central bank. At worst, System 1 offers irresistible temptations to every government to intervene heavily in exchange rates, precipitating the world into currency blocs, protectionist blocs, and "beggar-thy-neighbor" policies of competing currency devaluations such as the economic warfare of the 1930s that helped generate World War II.

The problem is that shifting to System 2 is truly a leap from the frying pan into the fire. The national fiat blocs of the 1930s emerged out of the System 2 pound sterling standard in which other countries pyramided an inflation of their currencies on top of inflating pounds sterling, while Britain retained a nominal but phony gold standard. The 1930s system was itself replaced by Bretton Woods, a world dollar standard, in which other countries were able to inflate their own currencies on top of inflating dollars, while the United States maintained a nominal but phony gold standard at $35 per gold ounce.

Now the problems of the Friedmanite System 1 are inducing plans for some sort of return to a fixed exchange rate system. Unfortunately, System 2 is even worse than System 1, for any successful coordination permits a concerted world-wide inflation, a far worse problem than particular national inflations. Exchange rates among fiat moneys have to fluctuate, since fixed exchange rates inevitably create Gresham's Law situations, in which undervalued currencies disappear from circulation. In the Bretton Woods system, American inflation permitted world-wide inflation, until gold became so undervalued at $35 an ounce that demands to redeem dollars in gold became irresistible, and the system collapsed.

If System 1 is the Friedmanite ideal, then the Keynesian gold is the most pernicious variant of System 2. For what Keynesians have long sought, notably in the Bernstein and Triffin Plans of old, and in the abortive attempt to make

SDRs (special drawing rights) a new currency unit, is a World Reserve Bank issuing a new world paper-money unit, replacing gold altogether. Keynes called his suggested new unit the "bancor," and Harry Dexter White of the U.S. Treasury called his the "unita." Whatever the new unit may be called, such system would be an unmitigated disaster, for it would allow the bankers and politicians running the World Reserve Bank to issue paper "bancors" without limit, thereby engineering a coordinated world-wide inflation. No longer would countries have to lose gold to each other, and they could fix their exchange rates without worrying about Gresham's Law. The upshot would be an eventual world-wide runaway inflation, with horrendous consequences for the entire world.

Fortunately, a lack of market confidence, and inability to coordinate dozens of governments, have so far spared us this Keynesian ideal. But now, a cloud no bigger than a man's hand, an ominous trial balloon toward a World Reserve Bank has just been floated. In a meeting in Hamburg, West Germany, in late June of two hundred leading world bankers in an International Monetary Conference, bankers urged the elimination of the current volatile exchange rate system, and a move towards fixed exchange rates.

The theme of the Conference was set by its chairman, Willard C. Butcher, chairman and chief executive of Rockefeller's Chase Manhattan Bank. Butcher attacked the current system, and warned that it could not correct itself, and that a search for a better world currency system "must be intensified" (*New York Times*, June 23, 1987).

It was not long before Toyo Gyoten, Japan's vice-minister of finance for international affairs, spelled out some of the concrete implications of this accelerated search. Gyoten proposed a huge multinational financial institution, possessing "at least several hundred billion dollars," that would be empowered to intervene in world financial markets to reduce volatility.

And what is this if not the beginnings of a World Reserve Bank? Are Keynesian dreams at least beginning to come true?

Liberty and Property

Ludwig von Mises

The pre-capitalistic system of production was [based on] military conquest. The victorious kings had given the land to their paladins. These aristocrats were lords in the literal sense of the word, as they did not depend on the patronage of consumers buying or abstaining from buying on the market. On the other hand, they themselves were the main customers of the processing industries which under the guild system were organized on a cooperative basis.

This scheme was opposed to innovation. It forbade deviation from the traditional methods of production. The number of people for whom there were jobs even in agriculture or in the arts and crafts was strictly limited. Under these conditions, many a man, to use the words of Malthus, had to discover that at "nature's mighty feast there is no vacant cover for him," and that "she tells him to be gone." But some of these outcasts nevertheless managed to survive, begot children, and made the number of the destitute grow hopelessly more and more.

But then came capitalism.

It is customary to see the radical innovations that capitalism brought about as substitution of the mechanical factory for the more primitive and less efficient methods of artists and shops. This is a rather superficial view. The characteristic feature of capitalism, that distinguishes it from pre-capitalistic methods of production, was its new principle of marketing.

Capitalism is not simply mass production, but mass production to satisfy the needs of the masses. The arts and crafts of the good old days had catered almost exclusively to the wants of the well-to-do. But the factories produced cheap goods for the many. All that the early factories turned out was designed to serve the masses, the same strata that worked in the factories. They served them either by supplying them directly, or indirectly by exporting, and providing for them foreign food and foreign raw materials.

This principle of marketing was the signature of early capitalism as it is of present day capitalism. These employees themselves are the customers consuming the much greater part of all goods produced. They are the sovereign customers who are always right. Their buying or abstention from buying determines what has to be produced, in what quantity, and of what quality. In buying what suits best they made some enterprises profit and expand and made other enterprises lose money and shrink. Thereby they are continually shifting control of the factors of production into the hands of those businessmen who are most successful in filling their wants.

Under capitalism, private property of the factors of production is a social function. The entrepreneurs, capitalists, and land owners are mandatories, as it were, of the consumers, and their mandate is revocable. In order to be rich it is not sufficient to have once saved and accumulated capital. It is necessary to invest it again and again in those lines in which it best fills the wants of the consumers. The market process is a daily repeated plebiscite, and it ejects inevitably from the ranks of profitable people, those who do not employ their property according to the orders given by the public.

Big business, the target of fanatical hatred on the part of all contemporary governments and self-styled intellectuals, acquires and preserves bigness only because it works for the masses. The plans that cater to the luxuries of the few, never attain big size.

The shortcoming of 19th-century historians and politicians was that they failed to realize that the workers were the main consumers of the products of industry. In their view, the wage earner was a man toiling for the sole benefit of a parasitic leisure class. They labored under the delusion that the factories had impaired the lot of the manual workers. If they had paid any attention to statistics, they would have easily discovered the fallaciousness of their opinion. Infant mortality dropped. The average length of life was prolonged. The population multiplied, and the average common man enjoyed amenities of which even the well-to-do of earlier ages did not dream.

However this unprecedented enrichment of the masses was merely a by-product of the industrial revolution. Its main achievement was the transfer of economic supremacy from the owners of land to the totality of the population. The common man was no longer a drudge, who had to be satisfied with the crumbs that fell from the tables of the rich. The three pariah castes which were characteristic of the precapitalistic ages—the slaves, the serfs, and those people whom patristic and scholastic orders, as well as British legislation from the 16th through the 19th century, referred to as the poor—disappeared. Their scions became, in this new setting of business, not only free workers, but also customers. This radical change was reflected in the emphasis laid by business on markets. What business needs first of all, they repeated again and again, is markets and again markets. This was the watchword of capitalistic enterprise.

Markets mean patrons, buyers, consumers. There is under capitalism one way to wealth: to serve the consumers better and cheaper than other people do. But in the shop and factory, the owner—or in the corporations, the representative of the shareholders, the president—is the boss. The mastership is merely apparent and conditional. He is subject to the supremacy of the consumer. The consumer is king—the real boss—and the manufacturer is done for if he does not outstrip his competitors in best serving the consumers. It was this great economic transformation that changed the face of the world. . . .

What vitiates entirely the socialist economic critique of capitalism is its failure to grasp the sovereignty of the consumers in the market economy. They see only hierarchical organization of various enterprises and plans, and are at a loss to realize that the profit system forces business to serve the consumers.

In their dealings with their employers, the unions proceed as if malice and greed prevent what they call management from paying higher wage rates. Their shortsightedness does not see anything beyond the doors of the factory. They and their henchmen talk about the concentration of economic power, and do not realize that economic power is ultimately vested in the hands of the buying public, of which the employees themselves form the immense majority. Their inability to comprehend things as they are, is reflected in such inappropriate metaphors as industrial kingdoms and dukedoms. They are too dull to see the difference between a sovereign king or duke who could be dispossessed only by a more powerful conqueror, and the chocolate king who forfeits his kingdom as soon as the customers prefer to patronize another supplier.

This distortion is at the bottom of all socialist plans. If any of the socialist chiefs had tried to earn his living by selling hot dogs, he would have learned something about the sovereignty of the consumers. . . .

Socialism substitutes the sovereignty of the dictator, or committee of dictators, for the sovereignty of the consumers. . . . Freedom is indivisible. He who has not the faculty to choose among various brands of canned food or soap, is also deprived of the power to choose between various political parties and programs and to elect the office-holders. He is no longer a man; he becomes a form in the hands of the supreme social engineer. . . .

The socialists have engineered a semantic revolution in converting the meaning of terms into their opposite. . . . Freedom implies the right to choose between assent and dissent. But in Newspeak it means the duty to assent unconditionally, and the strict interdiction of dissent. This reversal of the traditional connotation of all words of the political terminology, is not merely a peculiarity of the language of the Russian communists, and their fascist and Nazi disciples. The social order that in abolishing private property deprives the consumers of their autonomy and independence, and thereby subjects every man to the arbitrary discretion of the central planning board, could not win the support of the masses if it were not to camouflage its main character.

The socialists would have never duped the voters if they had openly told them that their ultimate end is to cast them into bondage. For exoteric use, they were forced to pay lip-service to the traditional appreciation of liberty. It was different in the esoteric discussions among the inner circles of the great conspiracy. There the initiated did not dissemble their intentions concerning liberty. . . .

Freedom is to be found only in the sphere in which government does not interfere. Liberty is always freedom from the government. . . . In a free country nobody is prevented from acquiring riches by serving the consumers better than they are served already. What he needs is only brains and hard work. . . . Economic power, in the market economy, is in the hands of the consumers. . . . But the politicians and other would-be reformers see only the structure of industry as it exists today. They think that they are clever enough to snatch from business control of the plans as they are today, and to manage them by sticking to already established routine. But the ambitious newcomer, who will be the tycoon of tomorrow, is already preparing plans for things unheard of before. All they have in mind is to conduct affairs along tracks already beaten.

There's no record of an industrial innovation contrived and put into practice by bureaucrats. If one does not want to plunge into stagnation, a free hand must be left to those, the unknown men, who have the ingenuity to lead mankind forward on the way to more and more satisfactory conditions. . . . Private property of the material factors of production is not a restriction of the freedom of all other people to choose what suits them best. It is, on the contrary, the means that assigns to the common man, in his capacity as a buyer, supremacy in all economic affairs. It is the means to stimulate a nation's most enterprising men to exert themselves to the best of their abilities in the service of all of the people. . . .

It is a gratuitous pastime to belittle the material achievements of capitalism by observing that there are things that are more essential for mankind than bigger and speedier motorcars, and homes equipped with central heating, air conditioning, refrigerators, washing machines, and television sets. . . . It is not the fault of capitalism that the masses prefer a boxing match to a performance of Sophocles's *Antigone*, jazz music to Beethoven symphonies, and comics to poetry. But it is certain that by precapitalistic conditions, as they still prevail in the much greater part of the world, makes these goods things accessible only to a small minority of people. Capitalism gives to the many a favorable chance of striving after them. . . .

We are inaugurating tonight the ninth meeting of the Mont Pelerin Society. It is fitting to remember on this occasion that meetings of this kind in which opinions opposed to those of the majority of our contemporaries and to those of their governments are advanced, are possible only in the climate of liberty and freedom that is the most precious mark of Western civilization. Let us hope that this right to dissent will never disappear.*

*The Institute thanks Margit von Mises for her gracious permission to print excerpts from this 1957 talk. *ed.*

The Interest Rate Question

Murray N. Rothbard

The Marxists call it "impressionism": taking social or economic trends of the last few weeks or months and assuming that they will last forever. The problem is not realizing that there are underlying economic laws at work. Impressionism has always been rampant; and never more so than in public discussion of interest rates. For most of 1987, interest rates were inexorably high; for a short while after Black Monday, interest rates fell, and financial opinion turned around 180 degrees, and started talking as if interest rates were on a permanent downward trend.

No group is more prone to this day-to-day blowin' with the wind than the financial press. This syndrome comes from lack of understanding of economics and hence being reduced to reacting blindly to rapidly changing events. Sometimes this basic confusion is reflected within the same article. Thus, in the not-so-long ago days of double-digit inflation, the same article would predict that interest rates would fall because the Fed was buying securities in the open market, and *also* say that rates would be going *up* because the market would be expecting increased inflation. Nowadays, too, we read that fixed exchange rates are bad because interest rates will have to rise to keep foreign capital in the U.S., but also that *falling* exchange rates are bad because interest rates will have to rise for the same reason. If financial writers are mired in hopeless confusion, how can we expect the public to make any sense of what is going on?

In truth, interest rates, like any important price, are complex phenomena that are determined by several factors, each of which can change in varying, or even contradictory, ways.

As in the case of other prices, interest rates move inversely with the supply, but directly with the demand, for credit. If the Fed enters the open market to buy securities, it thereby increases the supply of credit, which will tend to lower interest rates; and since this same act will increase bank reserves by the same extent, the banks will now inflate money and credit out of thin air by a multiple of the initial jolt, nowadays about ten to one. So if the Fed buys one billion dollars of securities, bank reserves will rise by the same amount, and bank loans and the money supply will then increase by 10 billion dollars. The supply of credit has thereby increased further, and interest rates will fall some more.

But it would be folly to conclude, impressionistically, that interest rates are destined to fall indefinitely. In the first place, the supply and demand for credit are themselves determined by deeper economic forces, in particular the amount of their income that people in the economy wish to save and invest, as opposed to the amount they decide to consume. The more they save, the lower the interest rate; the more they consume, the higher. Increased bank loans may mimic an increase in genuine savings, yet they are very far from the same thing. Inflationary bank credit is artificial, created out of thin air; it does not reflect the underlying saving or consumption preferences of the public. Some earlier economists referred to this phenomenon as "forced" savings; more importantly, they are only temporary. As the increased money supply works its way through the system, prices and all values in money terms rise, and interest rates will then bounce back to something like their original level. Only a *repeated* injection of inflationary bank credit by the Fed will keep interest rates artificially low, and thereby keep the artificial and unsound economic boom going; and this is precisely the hallmark of the boom phase of the boom-bust business cycle.

But something else happens, too. As prices rise, and as people begin to anticipate further price increases, an inflation premium is placed on interest rates. Creditors tack an inflation premium onto rates because they don't propose to continue being wiped out by a fall in the value of the dollar; and debtors will be willing to pay the premium because they too realize that they have been enjoying a windfall. And this is why, when the public comes to expect further inflation, Fed increases in reserves will *raise*, rather than lower, the rate of interest. And when the acceleration of inflationary credit finally stops, the higher interest rate puts a sharp end to the boom in the capital markets (stocks and bonds), and an inevitable recession liquidates the unsound investments of the inflationary boom.

An extra twist to the interest rate problem is the international aspect. As a long-run tendency, capital moves from low-return investment (whether profit rates or interest rates) toward high-return investments until rates of return are equal. This is true within every country and also throughout the world. Internationally, capital will tend to flow from low-interest to high-interest rate countries, raising interest rates in the former and lowering them in the latter.

In the days of the international gold standard, the process was simple. Nowadays, under fiat money, the process continues, but results in a series of alleged crises. When governments try to fix exchange rates (as they did from the Louvre agreement of February 1987 until Black Monday), then interest rates cannot fall in the United States without losing capital or savings to foreign countries.

In the current era of a huge balance of trade deficit in the U.S., the U.S. cannot maintain a fixed dollar if foreign capital flows outward; the pressure for the dollar to fall would then be enormous. Hence, after Black Monday, the Fed decided to allow the dollar to resume its market tendency to fall, so that the Fed could then inflate credit and lower interest rates.

But it should be clear that that interest rate fall could only be ephemeral and strictly temporary, and indeed interest rates have already resumed their inexorable upward march. Price inflation is the consequence of the enormous monetary inflation pumped in by the Federal Reserve for several years before the spring of 1987, and interest rates are therefore bound to rise as well. Moreover, the Fed, as in many other matters, is caught in a trap of its own making; for the long-run trend to equalize interest rates throughout the world is a drive to equalize not simply money, or nominal, returns, but *real* returns corrected for inflation. But if foreign creditors and investors begin to receive dollars worth less and less in value, they will require higher money interest rates to compensate—and we will be back again, very shortly, with a redoubled reason for interest rates to rise.

In trying to explain the complexities of interest rates, inflation, money and banking, exchange rates and business cycles to my students, I leave them with this comforting thought: Don't blame *me* for all this, blame the government. Without the interference of government, the entire topic would be duck soup.

How the Market Creates Jobs and How the Government Destroys Them

Walter Block

The Creation of Jobs

If the media tell us that "the opening of XYZ mill has created 1,000 new jobs," we give a cheer. When the ABC company closes and 500 jobs are lost, we're sad. The politician who can provide a subsidy to save ABC is almost assured of widespread public support for his work in preserving jobs.

But jobs in and of themselves do not guarantee well-being. Suppose that the employment is to dig huge holes and fill them up again? What if the workers manufacture goods and services that no one wants to purchase? In the Soviet Union, which boasts of giving every worker a job, many jobs are just this unproductive. Production is everything, and jobs are nothing but a means toward that end.

Imagine the Swiss Family Robinson marooned on a deserted South Sea island. Do they need jobs? No, they need food, clothing, shelter, and protection from wild animals. Every job created is a deduction from the limited, precious labor available. Work must be rationed, not created, so that the market can create the most product possible out of the limited supply of labor, capital goods, and natural resources.

The same is true for our society. The supply of labor is limited. We must not allow government to create jobs or we lose the goods and services which otherwise would have come into being. We must reserve precious labor for the important tasks still left undone.

Alternatively, imagine a world where radios, pizzas, jogging shoes, and everything else we might want continuously rained down like manna from heaven. Would we want jobs in such a utopia? No, we could devote ourselves to other tasks—studying, basking in the sun, etc.—that we would undertake for their intrinsic pleasure.

Instead of praising jobs for their own sake, we should ask why employment is so important. The answer is, because we exist amidst economic scarcity and must work to live and prosper. That's why we should be of good cheer *only* when we learn that this employment will produce things people actually value, i.e., are willing to buy with their own hard-earned money. And this is something that can only be done in the free market, not by bureaucrats and politicians.

The Destruction of Jobs

But what about unemployment? What if people want to work, but can't get a job? In almost every case, government programs are the cause of joblessness.

Minimum Wage. The minimum wage mandates that wages be set at a government-determined level. To explain why this is harmful, we can use an analogy from biology: there are certain animals that are weak compared to others. For example, the porcupine is defenseless except for its quills, the deer vulnerable except for its speed.

In economics there are also people who are relatively weak. The disabled, the young, minorities, the untrained—all are weak economic actors. But like the weak animals in biology, they have a compensating advantage: the ability to work for lower wages. When the government takes this ability away from them by forcing up pay scales, it is as if the porcupine were shorn of its quills. The result is unemployment, which creates desperate loneliness, isolation, and dependency.

Consider a young, uneducated, unskilled person, whose productivity is $2.50 an hour in the marketplace. What if the legislature passes a law requiring that he be paid $5 per hour? The employer hiring him would lose $2.50 an hour.

Consider a man and a woman each with a productivity of $10 per hour, and suppose, because of discrimination or whatever, that the man is paid $10 per hour and the woman is paid $8 per hour. It is as if the woman had a little sign on her forehead saying, "Hire me and earn an extra $2 an hour." This makes her a desirable employee even for a sexist boss. But when an equal-pay law stipulates that she must be paid the same as the man, the employer can indulge his discriminatory tendencies and not hire her at all, at no cost to himself.

Comparable Worth. What if government gets the bright idea that nurses and truck drivers ought to be paid the same wage because their occupations are of "intrinsically" equal value? It orders that nurses' wages be raised to the same level, which creates unemployment for women.

Working Conditions. Laws which force employers to provide certain types of working conditions also create unemployment. For example, migrant fruit and vegetables pickers must have hot and cold running water and modern toilets in the temporary cabins provided for them. This is economically equivalent to wage laws because, from the point of view of the employer, working conditions are almost indistinguishable from money wages. And if the government forces him to pay more, he will have to hire fewer people.

Unions. When the government forces businesses to hire only union workers, it discriminates against non-union workers, causing them to be at a severe disadvantage or permanently unemployed. Unions exist primarily to keep out competition. They are a state-protected cartel like any other.

Employment Protection. Employment protection laws, which mandate that no one can be fired without due process, are supposed to protect employees. However, if the government tells the employer that he must keep the employee no matter what, he will tend not to hire him in the first place. This law, which appears to help workers, instead keeps them from employment. And so do employment taxes and payroll taxes, which increase costs to businesses and discourage them from hiring more workers.

Payroll Taxes. Payroll taxes like Social Security impose heavy monetary and administrative costs on businesses, drastically increasing the marginal cost of hiring new employees.

Unemployment Insurance. Government unemployment insurance and welfare cause unemployment by subsidizing idleness. When a certain behavior is subsidized—in this case not working—we get more of it.

Licensing. Regulations and licensing also cause unemployment. Most people know that doctors and lawyers must have licenses. But few know that ferret breeders, falconers, and strawberry growers must also have them. In fact, government regulates over 1,000 occupations in all 50 states. A woman in Florida who ran a soup kitchen for the poor out of her home was recently shut down as an unlicensed restaurant, and many poor people now go hungry as a result.

When the government passes a law saying certain jobs cannot be undertaken without a license, it erects a legal barrier to entry. Why should it be illegal for anyone to try their hand at haircutting? The market will supply all the information consumers need.

When the government bestows legal status on a profession and passes a law against competitors, it creates unemployment. For example, who lobbies for the laws which prevent just anyone from giving a haircut? The haircutting industry—not to protect the consumer from bad haircuts, but to protect themselves against competition.

Peddling. Laws against street peddlers prevent people from selling food and products to people who want them. In cities like New York and Washington, D.C., the most vociferous supporters of anti-peddling laws are established restaurants and department stores.

Child Labor. There are many jobs that require little training—such as mowing lawns—which are perfect for young people who want to earn some money. In addition to the earnings, working also teaches young people what a job is, how to handle money, and how to save and maybe even invest. But in most places, the government discriminates against teenagers and prevents them from participating in the free enterprise system. Kids can't even have a street-corner lemonade stand.

The Federal Reserve. By bringing about the business cycle, Federal Reserve money creation causes unemployment. Inflation not only raises prices, it also misallocates labor. During the boom phase of the trade cycle, businesses hire new workers, many of whom are pulled from other lines of work by the higher wages. The Fed subsidy to these capital industries lasts only until the bust. Workers are then laid off and displaced.

The Free Market. The free market, of course, does not mean utopia. We live in a world of differing intelligence and skills, of changing market preferences, and of imperfect information, which can lead to temporary, market-generated unemployment, which Mises called "catallactic." And some people choose unemployment by holding out for a higher paying job. But as a society, we can insure that everyone who wants to work has a chance to do so by repealing minimum wage law, comparable worth rules, working condition laws, compulsory union membership, employment protection, employment taxes, payroll taxes, government unemployment insurance, welfare, regulations, licensing, anti-peddling laws, child-labor laws, and government money creation. The path to jobs that matter is the free market.

The National Bureau and Business Cycles

Murray N. Rothbard

Not only is there confusion about whether or not a recession is imminent, but some economists think that we're already *in* one. Thus, Richard W. Rahn, chief economist for the U.S. Chamber of Commerce, recently declared: "The economic slowdown is not coming: it's here, and soon it will be gone." Not knowing whether or not we're in a recession is not as silly as it sounds. It takes a while for data to come in, and then to figure out if a decline is a mere glitch or if it constitutes a new trend. But the natural confusion is compounded by the thrall in which virtually all economists, statisticians, and financial writers have been held by the National Bureau of Economic Research.

Everyone waits for the National Bureau to speak; when the oracle finally makes its pronouncement, it is accepted without question. Thus, in 1966, the economy slowed down and receded to such an extent that I, for one, concluded that we were in a recession. But no, GNP had not declined quite long enough to meet the Bureau's definition of a recession, and that, unfortunately, was that. And since we were not in what the Bureau called a "recession," we by definition continued to be in a "boom." The reason is that, by the Bureau's peculiar and arbitrary standards and methods, the economy *cannot* be just sort of lolling along, in neither a boom nor a recession. It *has* to be in one or the other.

To say that the Bureau is fallible should go without saying; but instead, its pronouncements are taken as divine writ. Why is that? Precisely because the Bureau was cleverly designed, and so proclaimed, to be an allegedly value-free, purely "scientific" institution.

The Bureau is a private institution, supported by a large group of associations and institutions, business and union groups, banks, foundations, and scholarly associations, which confer upon it an almost painful respectability. Its numerous books and monographs are very long on statistics, short on text or interpretation. Its proclaimed methodology is Baconian: that is, it trumpets the claim that it *has no* theories, that it collects myriads of facts and statistics, and that its cautiously worded conclusions arise solely, Phoenix-like, out of the data themselves. Hence, its conclusions are accepted as unquestioned holy "scientific" writ.

And yet, despite its proclamations, the National Bureau's procedures themselves necessarily manipulate the data to arrive at conclusions. And these procedures are *not* free of theory, indeed they rest on faulty and questionable theoretical assumptions. Hence, the conclusions, far from being strictly "scientific," are skewed and misshaped to the extent that they are determined by the procedures themselves.

Specifically, the Bureau selects "reference cycles," of the general economy, and then examines "specific cycles" of particular prices, production, etc. and compares these with the reference cycles. Unfortunately, all depends on the Bureau's dating theory, that is, it picks out only the trough and peak months, first for the general cycles, and then for each specific cycle. But suppose, as in many cases, the curve is flat, or there are several peaks or troughs close to each other.

In these cases, the Bureau, purely arbitrarily, takes the *last month* of the plateau, or the multi-peak or trough period, and calls *that* the peak or trough month. There is no earthly economic reason for this; why not take the whole period as a peak or trough period, or average the data, or whatever? Instead, the Bureau takes *only* the last month and calls that the peak or trough, and then compounds that error by arbitrarily squeezing the distance between the designated "peak month" and "trough month" into three equal parts, and assuming that everything in between peak and trough is a straight line of expansion or contraction, boom or bust.

In other words, in the real world, any given time series, say copper prices, or housing starts in California, might have dawdled near the trough, gone quickly upward, and stayed at a plateau or multi-peak for many months. But on the Procrustean rack of National Bureau doctrine, the activity is squeezed into a single, one-month trough; a straight line expansion, divided into three parts by time; reaching a single-month peak; and then going down in a similar linear, jagged-line contraction. In short, National Bureau methods inevitably force the economy to look falsely like a series of jagged, sawtoothed, straight lines upward and downward. The triumphant conclusion that "life is a series of sawtooth lines" is imposed by the way the Bureau massages the data in the first place.

That massaging is bad enough. But then the Bureau compounds the error by averaging all the specific cycles, its leads and lags, etc. over numerous specific cycles, as far as the data will go back, say from the 1860s to the 1980s. It is from that averaging that the Bureau has developed its indices of "leading," "coincident," and "lagging" indicators, the first of which are supposed to (but not very successfully) forecast the future.

The problem with this averaging of cycle data over the decades is that it assumes a "homogeneous population," that is, it assumes that all these cycles, say for copper prices or housing starts in California, are the same thing, and operate in the same context over all these decades. But that is a whopping assumption; history means change, and it is absurd to assume that the underlying population of all this data remains constant and unchanging, and therefore can be averaged meaningfully.

When the National Bureau set forth this methodology in Arthur F. Burns and Wesley C. Mitchell, *Measuring Business Cycles* (National Bureau of Economic Research, 1946), it was correctly criticized by a distinguished econometrician for being "Measurement without Theory" in the *Journal of Political Economy*, but still it quickly swept the board to achieve oracular status.

Particularly irritating were the claims of the Bureau that those of us who held definite business cycle theories were partial and arbitrary, whereas the Bureau spoke only from the facts of hard, empirical reality. Yet the Bureau has had far less respect for empirical reality than have allegedly "anti-empirical" Austrians. Austrians realize that empirical reality is unique, particularly raw statistical data. Let that data be massaged, averaged, seasonals taken out, etc. and then the data necessarily falsify reality. Their Baconian methodology has not saved the Bureau from this trap; it has only succeeded in blinding them to the ways that they have been manipulating data arbitrarily.

2

Fiat Money and the Gold Standard

Confidence and Money

Llewellyn H. Rockwell, Jr.

In Ohio and Maryland, state-run savings and loan insurance schemes failed when depositors asked for their money. The crises came to an end, at least on the surface, with coverage from the Federal Savings and Loan Insurance Corporation.

The FSLIC was seen as a cure, not because of its assets—they cover less than .8% of deposits—but because of the Federal Reserve's implicit promise to print enough dollars to cover any FSLIC (or Federal Deposit Insurance Corporation) crisis. To stop just the Continental Illinois bank run, the Fed created \$3.5 billion to avoid draining the FDIC, which has assets covering less than .8% of deposits.

The S&L industry is shakier than ever before, thanks in part to real-estate and junk-bond speculation. The city of Washington, D.C., for example, has seven federally insured S&Ls. Only two meet the FSLIC's minimal requirement of a net worth equal to 3% of liabilities—and this is calculated using very liberal accounting standards. When you apply slightly stricter ones, two of the seven have a negative net worth.

This is true despite FSLIC gimmicks—such as "net-worth certificates"—designed to paper over S&L problems. Subtract these, and rate old mortgages at the market rather than the face value, and virtually the entire industry would be technically bankrupt.

"Technically" is the key word, however, because so long as the Fed stands ready to make cheap loans through the discount window—a subsidy S&Ls now share with banks—and to bail out the FSLIC, the industry will be kept afloat. (The value of the dollar will be another matter, however.)

In Ohio and Maryland, loss of confidence was blamed for the runs on the S&Ls. That is, depositors—after reading about fraud involving one state-insured institution—worried that their money might be at risk in all of them, and sought to withdraw it.

It's hard to imagine a similar problem in any other business. The computer industry, for example, couldn't go out of existence overnight because of fraud at one company causing a "loss of confidence." Of course, IBM doesn't pledge to have customers' property available on demand, while at the same time loaning it to others.

The dollar itself, thanks to the Fed, also depends on confidence, and as with the S&Ls, this can be lost overnight when the monetary and fiscal chickens come home to roost.

Justifiable confidence in the dollar, the S&Ls, and the banks will only come with a gold standard, and with savings and lending institutions built upon it: ones that would not—in the absence of federal subsidies—go belly up upon being asked to keep their word.

Bank Runs and Water Shortages

Murray N. Rothbard

It was a scene familiar to any nostalgia buff: all-night lines waiting for the banks (first in Ohio, then in Maryland) to open; pompous but mendacious assurances by the bankers that all is well and that the people should go home; a stubborn insistence by depositors to get their money out; and the consequent closing of the banks by government, while at the same time the banks were permitted to stay in existence and collect the debts due them by their borrowers.

In other words, instead of government protecting private property and enforcing voluntary contracts, it deliberately violated the property of the depositors by barring them from retrieving their own money from the banks.

All this was, of course, a replay of the early 1930s: the last era of massive runs on the banks. On the surface the weakness was the fact that the failed banks were insured by private or state deposit insurance agencies, whereas the banks that easily withstood the storm were insured by the federal government (FDIC for commercial banks; FSLIC for savings and loan banks).

But why? What is the magic elixir possessed by the federal government that neither private firms nor states can muster? The defenders of the private insurance agencies noted that they were technically in better financial shape than FSLIC or FDIC, since they had greater reserves per deposit dollar insured. How is it that private firms, so far superior to government in all other operations, should be so defective in this one area? Is there something unique about money that requires federal control?

The answer to this puzzle lies in the anguished statements of the savings and loan banks in Ohio and in Maryland, after the first of their number went under because of spectacularly unsound loans. "What a pity," they in effect complained, "that the failure of this one unsound bank should drag the sound banks down with them!"

But *in what sense* is a bank "sound" when one whisper of doom, one faltering of public confidence, should quickly bring the bank down? In what other industry does a mere rumor or frisson of doubt swiftly bring down a mighty and seemingly solid firm? What is there about banking that public confidence should play such a decisive and overwhelmingly important role?

The answer lies in the nature of our banking system, in the fact that both commercial banks and thrift banks (mutual savings and savings-and-loan) have been systematically engaging in fractional-reserve banking: that is, they have far less cash on hand than there are demand claims to cash outstanding. For commercial banks, the reserve fraction is now about 10%; for the thrifts it is far less.

This means that the depositor who thinks he has $10,000 in a bank is misled; in a proportionate sense, there is only, say, $1,000 or less there. And yet, both the checking depositor and the savings depositor *thinks* that he can withdraw his money at any time on demand. Obviously, such a system, which is considered fraud when practiced by other businesses, rests on a confidence trick: that is, it can only work so long as the bulk of depositors do not catch on to the scam and try to get their money out. The confidence is essential, and also misguided. That is why once the public catches on, and bank runs begin, they are irresistible and cannot be stopped.

We now see why private enterprise works so badly in the deposit insurance business. For private enterprise only works in a business that is legitimate and useful, where needs are being fulfilled. It is impossible to "insure" a firm, even less so an industry, that is inherently insolvent. Fractional reserve banks, being inherently insolvent, are uninsurable.

What, then, is the magic potion of the federal government? Why does everyone trust the FDIC and FSLIC even though their reserve ratios are lower than private agencies, and though they too have only a very small fraction of total insured deposits in cash to stem any bank run? The answer is really quite simple: because everyone realizes, and realizes correctly, that only the federal government—and not the states or private firms—can print legal tender dollars. Everyone knows that, in case of a bank run, the U.S. Treasury would simply order the Fed to print enough cash to bail out any depositors who want it. The Fed has the unlimited power to print dollars, and it is this unlimited power to inflate that stands behind the current fractional-reserve banking system.

Yes, the FDIC and FSLIC "work," but only because the unlimited monopoly power to print money can "work" to bail out any firm or person on earth. For it was precisely bank runs, as severe as they were that, before 1933, kept the banking system under check, and prevented any substantial amount of inflation.

But now bank runs—at least for the overwhelming majority of banks under federal deposits insurance—are over, and we have been paying and will continue to pay the horrendous price of saving the banks: chronic and unlimited inflation.

Putting an end to inflation requires not only the abolition of the Fed but also the abolition of the FDIC and FSLIC. At long last, banks would be treated like any firm in any other industry. In short, if they can't meet their contractual obligations they will be required to go under and liquidate. It would be instructive to see how many banks would survive if the massive governmental props were finally taken away.

Water *Not* Running

Most people agree that government is generally less efficient than private enterprise, but it is little realized that the difference goes far beyond efficiency. For one thing, there is a crucial difference in attitude toward the consumer. Private business firms are constantly courting the consumer, always eager to increase the sales of their products. So insistent is that courtship that business advertising is often criticized by liberal aesthetes and intellectuals as strident and unmannerly. But government, unlike private enterprise, is not in the business of seeking profits or trying to avoid losses. Far from eager to court the consumer, government officials invariably regard consumers as an annoying intrusion and as "wasteful" users of "their" (government's) scarce resources. Governments are invariably at war with their consumers.

This contempt and hostility toward consumers reaches its apogee in socialist states, where government's power is at its maximum. But a similar attitude appears in areas of government activity in all countries. Until a few decades ago, for example, water supplies to consumers in the United States were furnished by private companies. These were almost all socialized, so that government has come to monopolize water services.

In New York City, which shifted to a monopoly of government water several decades ago, there was never, in previous decades, any wailing about a "water shortage." But, recently, in a climate that is not conspicuously dry, a water shortage has reappeared every few years. This July water levels in the reservoirs supplying New York City were down to an unprecedented 55% of capacity, in contrast to the normal 94%. But surely, nature is not solely to blame, since neighboring New Jersey's water levels are still at a respectable 80%. It seems that the New York water bureaucrats must have carefully sought out nearby spots that particularly suffer from chronic drought. It also turns out that the New York pipelines were constructed too narrowly to increase water flow from wetter regions.

More important is New York's typical bureaucratic response to this, as well as to other periodic water crises. Water, as usual with government, is priced in an economically irrational manner. Apartment buildings, for example, pay a fixed water fee per apartment to the government. Since tenants pay nothing for water, they have no incentive to use it economically; and since landlords pay a fixed fee, regardless of use, they too couldn't care less.

Whereas private firms try to price their goods or services to achieve the highest profit—i.e. to supply consumer needs most fully and at least cost—government has no incentive to price for highest profit or to keep down costs. Quite the contrary. Government's incentive is to subsidize favored pressure groups or voting blocs; for government is pressured by its basic situation to price politically rather than economically.

Since government services are almost never priced so as to clear the market, i.e. equate supply and demand, it tends to price far below the market, and therefore bring about an artificial "shortage." Since the shortage is manifest in people not being able to find the product, government's natural despotic bent leads it invariably to treat the shortage by turning to coercive restraints and rationing.

Morally, government can then have its cake and eat it too: have the fun of pushing people around, while wrapping itself in the cloak of solidarity and universal "sacrifice" in the face of the great new emergency. In short, when the supply of water drops, governments almost never respond the way a business firm would: raise the price in order to clear the market. Instead, the price stays low, and restraints are then placed on watering one's lawn, washing one's car, and even taking showers. In this way, everyone is exhorted to sacrifice, except that priorities of sacrifice are worked out and imposed by the government, which happily decides how much lawn watering, or showering, may be permitted on what days in the face of the great crisis.

Several years ago, California water officials were loudly complaining about a water shortage and imposing local rationing, when suddenly an embarrassing event occurred: torrential rains all over the drought areas of the state. After lamely insisting that no one should be misled by the seeming end of the drought, the authorities finally had to end that line of attack, and then the title of the Emergency Office of Water Shortage was hastily changed to the Office of Flood Control.

In New York, this summer, Mayor Edward Koch has already levied strict controls on water use, including a ban on washing cars, and imposition of a minimum of 78 degrees for air conditioners in commercial buildings, plus the turning off of the conditioners for two hours during each working day (virtually all of these air conditioners are water-cooled). 78 degrees is tantamount to no air-conditioning at all, and will wreak great hardship on office workers, as well as patrons of movies and restaurants.

Air-conditioning has always been a favorite target for puritanical government officials; during the trumped-up "energy shortage" of the late 1970s, President Carter's executive order putting a floor of 78 degrees on every commercial air conditioner was enthusiastically enforced, even though the "energy saving" was negligible. As long as misery can be imposed on the consumer, why worry about the rationale? (What is now a time-honored custom in New York of reluctance to serve water to restaurant patrons originated in a long-forgotten water "shortage" of decades ago.)

There is no need for any of these totalitarian controls. If the government wants to conserve water and lessen its use, all it need do is raise the price. It doesn't have to order an end to this or that use, set priorities, or decide who should be allowed to drink more than three glasses a day. All it has to do is clear the market, and let people conserve each in his own way and at his own pace.

In the longer run, what the government should do is privatize the water supply, and let water be supplied, like oil or Pepsi-Cola, by private firms trying to make a profit and to satisfy and court consumers, and not to gain power by making them suffer.

The World Currency Crisis

Murray N. Rothbard

I: Keynesians and Fixed Exchange Rates, 1944-73

The world is in permanent monetary crisis, but once in a while, the crisis flares up acutely, and we noisily shift gears from one flawed monetary system to another. We go back and forth from fixed paper rates to fluctuating rates, to some inchoate and aborted blend of the two. Each new system, each basic change, is hailed extravagantly by economists, bankers, the financial press, politicians, and central banks, as the final and permanent solution to our persistent monetary woes.

Then, after some years, the inevitable breakdown occurs, and the Establishment trots out another bauble, another wondrous monetary nostrum for us to admire. Right now, we are on the edge of another shift.

To stop this shell game, we must first understand it. First, we must realize that there are three coherent systems of international money, of which only one is sound and non-inflationary. The sound money is the genuine gold standard; "genuine" in the sense that each currency is defined as a certain unit of weight of gold, and is redeemable at that weight.

Exchange rates between currencies were "fixed" in the sense that each was defined as a given weight of gold; for example, since the dollar was defined as one-twentieth of a gold ounce and the pound sterling as .24 of a gold ounce, the exchange rate between the two was naturally fixed at their proportionate gold weight, i.e., £1=$4.87.

The other two systems are the Keynesian ideal, where all currencies are fixed in terms of an international paper unit, fluctuating independent fiat-paper moneys. Keynes wanted to call his new world paper unit the *bancor* while U.S. Treasury official (and secret Communist) Harry Dexter White wanted to name it the *unita*. *Bancor* or *unita*, these new paper tickets would ideally be issued by a World Reserve Bank and would form the reserves of the various central banks. Then, the World Reserve Bank could inflate the *bancor* at will, and the *bancor* would provide reserves upon which the Fed, the Bank of England, etc. could pyramid a multiple expansion of their respective national fiat currencies.

The whole world would then be able to inflate together, and therefore not suffer the inconvenience of inflationary countries losing either gold or income to sound-money countries. All the countries could inflate in a centrally-coordinated fashion, and we could suffer manipulation and inflation by a world government-banking elite without check or hindrance. At the end of the road would be a horrendous world-wide hyper-inflation, with no way of escaping into sounder or less inflated currencies.

Fortunately, national rivalries have prevented the Keynesians from achieving their goal, and so they had to settle for "second best," the Bretton Woods system that the U.S. and Britain foisted on the world in 1944, and which lasted until its collapse in 1971. Instead of the *bancor*, the dollar served as the international reserve upon which other currencies could pyramid their money and credit. The dollar, in turn, was tied to gold in a mockery of a genuine gold standard, at the prewar par of $35 per ounce. In the first place, dollars were not redeemable in gold coins, as they had been before, but only in large and heavy gold bars, which were worth many thousands of dollars. And secondly, only foreign governments and central banks could redeem their dollars in gold even on this limited basis.

For two decades, the system seemed to work well, as the U.S. issued more and more dollars, and they were then used by foreign central banks as a base for their own inflation. In short, for years the U.S. was able to "export inflation" to foreign countries without suffering the ravages itself. Eventually, however, the ever-more inflated dollar became depreciated on the gold market, and the lure of high priced gold they could obtain from the U.S. at the bargain $35 per ounce led European central banks to cash in dollars for gold. The house of cards collapsed when President Nixon, in an ignominious declaration of bankruptcy, slammed shut the gold window and went off the last remnants of the gold standard in August 1971.

With Bretton Woods gone, the Western powers now tried a system that was not only unstable but also incoherent: fixing exchange rates without gold or even any international paper money with which to make payments. The Western powers signed the ill-fated Smithsonian Agreement on December 18, 1971, which was hailed by President Nixon as "the greatest monetary agreement in the history of the world." But if currencies are purely fiat, with no international money, they become goods in themselves, and fixed exchange rates are then bound to violate the market rates set by supply and demand.

At that time the inflated dollar was heavily overvalued in regard to Western European and Japanese currencies. At the overvalued dollar rate, there were repeated scrambles to buy European and Japanese moneys at bargain rates, and to get rid of dollars. Repeated "shortages" of the harder moneys resulted from this maximum price control of their exchange rates. Finally, panic selling of the dollar broke the Smithsonian system apart in March 1973. With the collapse of Bretton Woods and the far more rapid disintegration of the "greatest monetary agreement" in world history, both the phony gold standard and the fixed paper exchange rate systems were widely and correctly seen to be inherent failures. The world now embarked, almost by accident on a new era: a world of fluctuating fiat paper moneys. Friedmanite monetarism was to have its day in the sun.

II: Monetarists and Fluctuating Fiat Monies, 1973-?

The Friedmanite monetarists had now come into their own, replacing the Keynesians as the favorites of the financial press and of the international monetary establishment. Governments and central banks began to hail the soundness and permanence of fluctuating exchange rates as fervently as they had once trumpeted the eternal virtues of Bretton Woods. The monetarists proclaimed the ideal international monetary system to be freely fluctuating exchange rates between different moneys, with no government intervention to try to stabilize or even moderate the fluctuations. In that way, exchange rates would reflect, from day to day, the fluctuations of supply and demand, just as prices do on the free market.

Of course, the world *had* suffered mightily from fluctuating fiat money in the not too distant past: the 1930s, when every country had gone off gold (a phony gold standard preserved for foreign central banks by the United States). The problem is that each nation-state kept fixing its exchange rates, and the result was currency blocs, aggressive devaluations attempting to expand exports and restrict imports, and economic warfare culminating in World War II. So the monetarists were insistent that the fluctuations must be absolutely free of all government intervention.

But, in the first place, the Friedmanite plan is *politically* so naive as to be almost impossible to put into practice. For what the monetarists do, in effect, is to make each currency fiat paper issued by the national government. They give total power over money to that government and its central bank, and then they issue stern admonitions to the wielders of absolute power: "Remember, use your power wisely, *don't* under any circumstances interfere with exchange rates." But inevitably, governments will find many reasons to interfere: to force exchange rates up or down, or stabilize them, and there is nothing to stop them from exercising their natural instincts to control and intervene.

And so what we have had since 1973 is an incoherent blend of "fixed" and fluctuating, unhampered and hampered, foreign currency markets. Even Beryl W. Sprinkel, a dedicated monetarist who served as Undersecretary of Treasury for Monetary Policy in the first Reagan Administration, was forced to backtrack on his early achievement of persuading the Administration to decontrol exchange rates. Even he was compelled to intervene in "emergency" situations, and now the second Reagan Administration is moving insistently in the direction of refixing exchange rates.

The problem with freely fluctuating rates is not only political. One virtue of fixed rates, especially under gold but even to some extent under paper, is that they keep a check on national inflation by central banks. The virtue of fluctuating rates—that they prevent sudden monetary crises due to arbitrarily valued currencies—is a mixed blessing, because at least those crises provided a much-needed restraint on domestic inflation. Freely fluctuating rates mean that the only damper on domestic inflation is that the currency might depreciate. Yet countries often *want* their money to depreciate, as we have seen in the recent agitation to soften the dollar and thereby subsidize exports and restrict imports—a back-door protectionism. The current refixers have one sound point: that worldwide inflation only became rampant in the mid and late 1970s, after the last fixed-rate discipline was removed.

The refixers are on the march. During November 1985, a major, well-publicized international monetary conference took place in Washington, organized by Representative Jack Kemp and Senator Bill Bradley, and including representatives from the Fed, foreign central banks, and Wall Street banks. this liberal-conservative spectrum agreed on the basic objective: refixing exchange rates. But refixing is no solution; it will only bring back the arbitrary valuations, and the breakdowns of Bretton Woods and the Smithsonian. Probably what we will get eventually is a world-wide application of the current "snake," in which Western European currencies are tied together so that they can fluctuate but only within a fixed zone. This pointless and inchoate blend of fixed and fluctuating currencies can only bring us the problems of both systems.

When will we realize that only a genuine gold standard can bring us the *virtues* of both systems and a great deal more: free markets, absence of inflation, and exchange rates that are fixed not arbitrarily by government but as units of weights of a precious market commodity, gold?

Understanding the Austrian Theory of the Business Cycle

Mark Skousen

One of the highlights of my professional career occurred recently when I had the opportunity to talk with Professor F. A. Hayek at his vacation home in the Austrian Alps. It was an unforgettable experience. Since the death of Ludwig von Mises in 1973, Professor Hayek has been the acknowledged dean of the "Austrian" school of economics, which teaches individualism, laissez-faire economics, and the gold standard. He is now 86 years old, but sharp and alert, and still working hard on a number of projects.

Professor Hayek is the oldest living member of the Austrian school, which began in Vienna with Carl Menger in the 1870s, and continued with Eugen von Böhm-Bawerk, Ludwig von Mises, and Murray N. Rothbard, among others. In 1974, Professor Hayek won the Nobel Prize in Economics for his work on the Mises-Hayek theory of the business cycle.

Of all the many contributions of the "Austrians," their theory of the business cycle is one of the most valuable. Economists and Wall Street analysts have known for decades that the markets are highly volatile. There is a business cycle in national output, interest rates, and inflation, creating bull and bear markets in stocks, bonds, gold, and so on. And Austrian theory is the only satisfactory explanation of this business cycle.

The first thing to understand is that the principle source of economic disruption and the business cycle is irresponsible government policy. The business cycle, inflation, and high nominal interest rates are not caused by the free market, but by government's monetary and fiscal policies.

Without government intervention, the free-market economy would reflect:

1) Stable interest rates, probably in the 2%-3% range, as in the 1950s.

2) No inflation. In fact, historically, average prices have tended to decline slightly with a free market and gold standard.

3) Low unemployment. No minimum wage laws and forced collective bargaining, which keep wages artificially high during a recession.

4) High savings rate. Contrary to standard Keynesian doctrine, high personal savings rates are good for economic growth.

5) Economic growth without recessions or depressions.

But as long as government is ubiquitous, and controls the supply of money, it will appear that "capitalism" is inherently unstable, as the Marxists say. Only the wise student of history and economic science knows that government policy, not the free market, is responsible for economic instability.

The key to understanding the economic cycle is what the Austrians call the "structure of production." Unlike the Keynesians and Monetarists, the Austrians look at the economy not as a whole, but as a collection of individual parts—not "macroeconomics," but "microeconomics."

The easiest way to understand the "structure of production" is to see how the economy exists at a single moment, as if a snapshot were taken. If the whole economy were suddenly frozen, what would you see? You would see some products and services completed, such as cars coming off the assembly line ready to sell to consumers. Other products would be half finished, and still others would be just starting production.

In other words, there is an order to the production of goods and services in an economy. The "higher" order or stages of production are "capital goods," which include tools, machinery, raw materials, trucks, and other goods necessary to produce final consumer goods, which include automobiles, food, clothing, and so on.

This distinction is very important in understanding the inflationary boom-bust cycle. As the Austrians point out, the central bank (the Federal Reserve) expands the money supply in a way that affects certain industries more than others. Historically, because the Fed expands the money supply primarily through the credit markets, the capital-goods investor has been more affected than the consumer-goods market.

There are essentially four states to the business cycle:

First, the inflationary boom. The Fed expands the money supply by purchasing Treasury securities from banks. Profits in capital-intensive industries tend to rise, and because the stock market is highly capital-intensive, the stock market goes through a bull market. However, at the later stages of the inflationary boom, consumer prices start catching up, the stock market loses its luster, and the bull market ends. Also, at the end of the inflationary cycle, gold and silver and other inflation hedges move up sharply.

Second, the credit crunch. Once consumer prices start rising sharply, and interest rates start edging up, the Fed usually puts on the brakes and causes a credit crunch. Interest rates rise rapidly as capital industries scramble for funds to escape bankruptcy.

Third, recession. Production of capital goods falls more sharply than consumer goods. Gross National Product declines, and stocks continue to fall. Interest rates start dropping as demand for credit declines. Prices for commodities and capital goods tend to fall more sharply than consumer goods, which sometimes continue to rise ("inflationary recession").

Fourth, economic recovery. The recession in capital goods ends as the economy returns to stability. The Austrians are the only school with satisfactory answers to two questions facing economics today: 1) how it is possible to have low inflation in the face of double-digit increases in the money supply, and 2) inflationary recession.

The "low-inflation" environment continues, despite 10% annual increases in the money supply, because of the previous "malinvestments" in the capital goods industries. When companies are on their backs, it requires a greater increase in credit than the previous cycle to achieve a return to previous levels of economic prosperity. After the economy has gone through a major recession and the inflationary psychology has been broken, the government must expand the money supply at a higher rate than the previous cycle in order to achieve the same level of economic activity and price inflation. Note, however, that under President Reagan, the money supply has grown at the same rate as under President Carter, but not more—therefore, we would expect, under Austrian theory, the inflation rate to fall below the double-digit rates of the 1970s. Indeed it has.

I believe the money supply must expand at a 15% to 20% annual rate in order to rekindle double-digit price inflation this time around. So far it hasn't happened, although lately M1 has been growing at a 14% rate. At some point, of course, price inflation will catch up, but it's too early to tell when this will happen.

During the inflationary stage of the business cycle, production and prices for capital goods and raw commodities tend to rise much more than for final consumer goods. Only at the later stages of the inflationary boom do consumer goods (as measured by the Consumer Price Index) begin to rise.

Look, for example, at the production of automobiles. During an inflationary boom, the price of iron, steel, aluminum, and other producer goods used in building cars may increase substantially, perhaps doubling in value. But the price of an automobile in the showroom may increase only 5% to 10%.

During a recession, just the opposite occurs. Prices for producers' goods and raw commodities drop sharply, compared to consumer goods. In the case of cars, steel may fall sharply in price. Meanwhile, the price of finished cars may fall only slightly, or, as has occurred recently, continue to rise.

Thus, consumer goods always tend to rise in a recession relative to capital goods. If you look at the statistics of any recession, you'll note that the raw commodities price index and the wholesale price index fell by a greater amount than consumer prices. Consumer prices also tended to fall, but not by the same amount. In other words, consumer prices rose in relation to wholesale and commodity prices.

The relationship still holds even today during a recession, except that now in absolute terms, consumer prices are rising instead of falling. This is because the magnitude of monetary inflation is much greater than in past cycles. So, relative to capital goods, all recessions are "inflationary recessions." It's just that such a relationship didn't become obvious until the Consumer Price Index continued to rise in the 1973-1975 recession and the 1980-1981 recession.

If you want to learn more about this aspect of Austrian economics, I recommend the following books, all available from the Institute: *What Has Government Done to Our Money?*, by Murray N. Rothbard ($5), *America's Great Depression* also by Rothbard ($20), *An Introduction to Austrian Economics* by Thomas C. Taylor ($6), and *The Austrian Theory of the Trade Cycle* by Ludwig von Mises and others ($5); shipping charge: $2.75 with each order.

All show that the only way that we can escape from the business cycle is through the establishment of sound money (i.e., a gold standard and no central bank) and the free market. If we are ever able to do so, the Austrian school of economics will deserve the credit.

Money Inflation and Price Inflation

Murray N. Rothbard

In the last few months, the Reagan administration seems to have achieved the culmination of its "economic miracle" of the last several years: while the money supply has skyrocketed upward in double digits, the consumer price index has remained virtually flat. Money cheap and abundant, stock and bond markets booming, and yet prices remaining stable: what could be better than that? Has the president, by inducing Americans to feel good and stand tall, really managed to repeal economic law? Has soft soap been able to erase the need for "root-canal" economics?

In the first place, we have heard that song before. During every boom period, statesmen, economists, and financial writers manage to find reasons for proclaiming that now, *this time*, we are living in a new age where old-fashioned economic law has been nullified and cast into the dust bin of history. The 1920s is a particularly instructive decade, because then we had expanding money and credit, and a stock and bond market boom, while prices remained constant. As a result, all the experts as well as the politicians announced that we were living in a brand "new era," in which new tools available to government had eliminated inflations and depressions.

What were these marvelous new tools? As Bernard M. Baruch explained in an optimistic interview in the spring of 1929, they were (a) expanded cooperation between government and business; and (b) the Federal Reserve Act, "which gave us coordinated control of our financial resources and . . . a unified banking system." And, as a result, the country was brimming with "self-confidence." But, also as a result of these tools, there came 1929 and the Great Depression. Unfortunately both of these mechanisms are with us today in aggravated form. And great self confidence, which persisted in the market and among the public into 1931, didn't help one whit when the fundamental realities took over.

But the problem is not simply history. There are very goods reasons why monetary inflation cannot bring endless prosperity. In the first place, *even if there were no price inflation*, monetary inflation is a bad proposition. For monetary inflation is counterfeiting, plain and simple. As in counterfeiting, the creation of new money simply diverts resources from producers, who have gotten their money honestly, to the early recipients of the new money—to the counterfeiters, and to those on whom they spend their money.

Counterfeiting is a method of taxation and redistribution—*from producers to counterfeiters* and to those early in the chain when counterfeiters spend their money and the money gets respent. Even if prices do not increase, this does not alleviate the coercive shift in income and wealth that takes place. As a matter of fact, some economists have interpreted price inflation as a desperate method by which the public, suffering from monetary inflation, tries to recoup its command of economic resources by raising prices at least as fast, if not faster, than the government prints new money.

Secondly, if new money is created via bank loans to business, as much of it is, the money inevitably distorts the pattern of productive investments. The fundamental insight of the "Austrian," or Misesian, theory of the business cycle is that monetary inflation via loans to business causes overinvestment in capital goods, especially in such areas as construction, long-term investments, machine tools, and industrial commodities. On the other hand, there is a relative underinvestment in consumer goods industries. And since stock prices and real estate prices are titles to capital goods, there tends as well to be an excessive boom. It is not necessary for consumer prices to go up, and therefore to register as price inflation. And this is precisely what happened in the 1920s, fooling economists and financiers unfamiliar with Austrian analysis, and lulling them into the belief that no great crash or recession would be possible. The rest is history. So, the fact that prices have remained stable recently does not mean that we will not reap the whirlwind of recession and crash.

But why didn't prices rise in the 1920s? Because the enormous increase in productivity and the supply of goods offset the increase of money. This offset did not, however, prevent a crash from developing, even though it did avert price inflation. Our good fortune, unfortunately, is not due to increased productivity. Productivity growth has been minimal since the 1970s, and real income and the standard of living have barely increased since that time.

The offsets to price inflation in the 1980s have been very different. At first, during the Reagan administration, a severe depression developed in 1981 and continued into 1983, of course dragging down the price inflation rate. Recovery was slow at first, and in the last few years, three special factors have held down price inflation. An enormous balance of trade deficit of $150 billion was eagerly enhanced by foreign investors in American dollars, which kept the dollar unprecedentedly high, and therefore import prices low, despite the huge deficit.

Secondly, and unusually, a flood of cash dollars stayed overseas, in hyperinflating countries of Asia and Latin America, to serve as underground money in place of the increasingly worthless domestic currency. And thirdly, the well-known collapse of the OPEC cartel at last brought down oil and petroleum product prices to free-market levels. But all of these offsets are obviously one-shot, and are rapidly coming to an end. In fact, the dollar has already declined in value, compared to foreign currencies, by about 30% since last September.

We are left with the fourth offset to price inflation, the increased willingness by the public to hold money rather than spend it, as the public has become convinced that the Reagan administration has discovered the secrets to an economic miracle in which prices will never rise again. But the public has not been *deeply* convinced of this, because real interest rates (interest rates in money minus the inflation rate) are at the highest level in its history. And interest rates are strongly affected by people's expectations of future price inflation; the higher the expectation, the higher the interest rate.

We may therefore expect a resumption of price inflation before long, and, as the public begins to wake up to the humbug nature of the "economic miracle," we may expect that inflation to accelerate.

First Step Back to Gold

Murray N. Rothbard

September 1986 is an historic month in the history of United States monetary policy. For it is the first month in over fifty years—thanks to the heroic leadership of Ron Paul during his four terms in Congress—that the United States Treasury has minted a genuine gold coin.

Gold coins were the standard money in the United States until Franklin Roosevelt repudiated the gold standard and confiscated the gold coins Americans possessed in 1933. Not only were these gold coins confiscated, under cover of the depression emergency, but possession not only of gold coins but of all gold (with the exception of designated amounts grudgingly allowed to collectors, dentists, jewelers, and industrial users) was prohibited.

During the 1970s, Congress made possession of gold by Americans legal, and now the Treasury itself acknowledges at least some monetary use by minting its own gold coins. We have come a long way, in only a decade, from total outlawry to Treasury minting.

It is true that the political motives for the new coin were not all of the purest. Some of it was a way of trying to attract the gold coin business from the South African krugerrands, which somehow have acquired a taint of apartheid by their mere production in South Africa. But the important thing is that gold is at least partially back in monetary use, and also that the public will have a chance to see, look at, and invest in gold coins.

One of the ways by which government was able to weaken the gold standard, even before 1933, was to discourage its broad circulation as coins, and to convince the public that all the gold should be safely tucked away in the banks, in the form of bullion, rather than in general use as money in the form of coins. Since Americans were not using coins directly as money by 1933, it was relatively easy for the government to confiscate their coins without raising very much of an opposition.

The new American Eagle coin is a very convenient one for possible widespread use in the future. It usefully weighs exactly one troy ounce, and the front of the coin bears the familiar Saint-Gaudens design for the goddess Liberty that had been used on American gold coins from 1907 until 1933.

But while the minting of the new American Eagle coin is an excellent first step on the road back to sound money, much more needs to be done. It is important not to rest on our laurels.

For one thing, even though gold coins are now legal, the U.S. government has never relinquished its possession of the confiscated coins, nor given it back to its rightful owners, the possessors of U.S. dollars. So it is vitally important to denationalize the U.S. gold stock by returning it to private hands.

Secondly, there is what can only be considered a grisly joke perpetrated on us by the U.S. Treasury. The one-ounce gold coin is designated, like the pre-1933 coins, as "legal tender," but only at $50. In other words, if you owe someone $500, you can legally pay your creditor in ten one-ounce coins. But of course you would only do so if you were an idiot, since on the market gold is now worth approximately $420 an ounce. At the designated rate, who would choose to pay their creditors in $4,200 of gold to discharge a $500 debt?

The phony, artificially low gold price, is of course so designed by the U.S. Treasury so as to make sure that no one would use these gold coins as money, that is, to make payments and discharge debt. Suppose, for example, that the government designated the one-ounce coin at a bit higher than the market price, say at $500. Then, everyone would rush to exchange their dollars for gold coins, and gold would swiftly replace dollars in circulation.

All this is a pleasant fantasy, of course, but even this superior system would not solve the major problem: what to do about the Federal Reserve and the banking system.

To solve that problem, it would not be enough merely to find a way to get the gold out of the hands of the Treasury. For that gold is technically owned by the Federal Reserve Banks, although kept in trust for the Fed by the Treasury at Fort Knox and other depositories. Furthermore, the Federal Reserve has the absolute monopoly on the printing of dollars, and that monopoly would remain even if people began to trade in dollars for Treasury gold coins.

It is indeed important to denationalize gold—to get it out of Fort Knox and into the hands of the people. But it is just as, if not more, important to denationalize the dollar—that is, to tie the name "dollar" firmly and irretrievably to a fixed weight of gold. Every piece of gold at Fort Knox would be tied to the dollar, and then, and only then, the Federal Reserve System could be swiftly abolished, and the gold poured back into the hands of the public at the fixed dollar weights. To accomplish this task, those who wish to return the gold of the nation and the dollar from the government to the people will have to agree on the fixed weight.

It is best to pick the initial definition of the gold dollar at the most convenient rate. Certainly $50 an ounce of gold is not it. There are good arguments for the current market price, for higher than the current price, and for a price sufficiently high (or a dollar weight sufficiently low) so as to enable the Fed, upon liquidation, to pay off not only its own debts but also all bank demand deposits one-for-one in gold (which would require a gold price of approximately $1,600 per ounce). But within those parameters, it almost doesn't matter what price is chosen, so long as these reforms are effected as soon as possible, and the country returns to sound money.

Sound Money: Gold or Denationalized?

Llewellyn H. Rockwell, Jr.

Hard-money advocates in American politics, from Thomas Jefferson to Ron Paul, have always favored a specie standard: that is, the dollar defined as a weight of precious metal.

In Austrian economics, the tradition has been the same. Carl Menger and Eugen von Böhm-Bawerk advocated a gold standard as politicians and as professors. (They were both cabinet ministers as well as scholars.) Ludwig von Mises, the greatest exponent of the Austrian school, was the first fully to apply Austrian theory to money. He too advocated a gold standard as well as the abolition of central banking and the establishment of 100%-reserve, non-inflationary free banking.

Building on Menger, Mises showed—in his famous regression theorem—that money *must* originate on the market as a useful commodity. The most liquid (i.e., the most readily acceptable) commodity becomes money. From the dawn of civilization, this has been gold, with silver playing a useful subsidiary role.

But, like many other truths, this idea is unpopular in mainstream economics, where fiat-paper money, central banking, commercial bank privilege, and inflation are considered scientific. In response to this, there is growing popularity for a monetary theory that threatens neither the academic nor the banking establishment.

That theory (and the resulting policy prescriptions) has four parts: 1) Forget gold. Keynes called it a "barbarous relic," and so it is; 2) Ignore the Federal Reserve. It can be circumvented, and besides, it may even be a "market institution" (huh?); 3) Criticize legal-tender laws as the central problem; 4) Encourage banks to issue their own unbacked paper money, which would then outcompete the Fed's dollars.

Point one is answered by theory and history, as shown by Mises. Point two: the Federal Reserve was created and is sustained by the government's police power. It is perhaps the most anti-market institution in America, as well as the Politburo of our monetary enemy. Its predecessor was called the "Monster" by Andrew Jackson, and that is still a good name for this unconstitutional giant of state control and banking privilege.

Point three is irrelevant and a policy dead-end. Legal-tender laws, which require us to accept Federal Reserve Notes, are unconstitutional restraints on our freedom and should be repealed. But as Murray N. Rothbard has shown, this is not enough to allow private, non-dollar competitors to succeed. Mises's regression theorem proves that people, having used the dollar for two centuries, will not switch to Chase Manhattan "Rockies" (or whatever the banks' currencies would be called). Even at the height of the great German or Chinese inflations, with monetary depreciation in thousands of percent, people still clung to marks and yen.

These currencies, like the dollar, the pound, and the franc, originated on the market as useful commodities, and were then nationalized by government. Only monies that originate on the market as useful commodities can win acceptance. That's why #4 is, as Professor Rothbard points out, an entrepreneurial scheme masquerading as theory, although he is happy to allow the market to decide its fate.

Only the denationalization of the *dollar*, not money generically, will end the tyranny of inflation and the business cycle, and of the transfers of wealth from the working and middle classes to the government-connected rich that go with them.

That means fixing the dollar permanently as a weight of gold: probably about 1/2,000 of an ounce, which would back the entire money supply with the gold held by the U.S. government, and the U.S. gold held by the International Monetary Fund. This gold would then be disgorged to the American people in return for their notes and deposits. Just as important, the central bank would be abolished, and banks required to adhere to the same standards of non-fraudulent behavior as other businesses. They would get no government license to inflate.

This is a very long-run cause, of course, and it is criticized as unrealistic by the would-be mainstreamers. But it is their strategy that is actually impractical.

Great change must originate in the world of ideas. But we will never bring about a monetary revolution without mobilizing the people. And great popular movements cannot be built on repealing legal tender. Gold and anti-central banking, as our own history shows, *are* mobilizing issues. They also have the not-inconsiderable virtue of being true.

When we do establish sound money, and gold coins circulate, Morgan Guaranty will be free to print up its irredeemable "Trilats." Just don't ask me to accept them.

Alan Greenspan: A Minority Report on the New Fed Chairman

Murray N. Rothbard

The press is resounding with acclaim for the accession to Power of Alan Greenspan as chairman of the Fed; economists from right, left, and center weigh in with hosannas for Alan's greatness, acumen, and unparalleled insights into the "numbers." The only reservation seems to be that Alan might not enjoy the enormous power and reverence accorded to his predecessor, for he does not have the height of a basketball player, is not bald, and does not smoke imposing cigars.

The astute observer might feel that anyone accorded such unanimous applause from the Establishment couldn't be all good, and in this case he would be right on the mark. I knew Alan thirty years ago, and have followed his career with interest ever since.

I found particularly remarkable the recent statements in the press that Greenspan's economic consulting firm of Townsend-Greenspan might go under, because it turns out that what the firm *really* sells is not its econometric forecasting models, or its famous numbers, but Greenspan himself, and his gift for saying absolutely nothing at great length and in rococo syntax with no clearcut position of any kind.

As to his eminence as a forecaster, he ruefully admitted that a pension-fund managing firm he founded a few years ago just folded for lack of ability to apply the forecasting where it counted: when investment funds were on the line.

Greenspan's real qualification is that he can be trusted never to rock the Establishment's boat. He has long positioned himself in the very middle of the economic spectrum. He is, like most other long-time Republican economists, a conservative Keynesian, which in these days is almost indistinguishable from the liberal Keynesians in the Democratic camp. In fact, his views are virtually the same as Paul Volcker, also a conservative Keynesian. Which means that he wants moderate deficits and tax increases, and will loudly worry about inflation as he pours on increases in the money supply.

There is one thing, however, that makes Greenspan unique, and that sets him off from his Establishment buddies. And that is that he is a follower of Ayn Rand, and therefore "philosophically" believes in laissez-faire and even the gold standard. But as the *New York Times* and other important media hastened to assure us, Alan only believes in laissez-faire "on the high philosophical level." *In practice*, in the policies he advocates, he is a centrist like everyone else because he is a "pragmatist."

As an alleged "laissez-faire pragmatist," at no time in his prominent twenty-year career in politics has he ever advocated anything that even remotely smacks of laissez-faire, or even any approach toward it. For Greenspan, laissez-faire is not a lodestar, a standard, and a guide by which to set one's course; instead, it is simply a curiosity kept in the closet, totally divorced from his concrete policy conclusions.

Thus, Greenspan is only in favor of the gold standard if all conditions are right: if the budget is balanced, trade is free, inflation is licked, everyone has the right philosophy, etc. In the same way, he might say he only favors free trade if all conditions are right: if the budget is balanced, unions are weak, we have a gold standard, the right philosophy, etc. In short, *never* are one's "high philosophical principles" applied to one's actions. It becomes almost piquant for the Establishment to have this man in its camp.

Over the years, Greenspan has, for example, supported President Ford's imbecilic Whip Inflation Now buttons when he was Chairman of the Council of Economic Advisers. Much worse is the fact that this "high philosophic" adherent of laissez-faire saved the racketeering Social Security program in 1982, just when the general public began to realize that the program was bankrupt and there was a good chance of finally slaughtering this great sacred cow of American politics. Greenspan stepped in as head of a "bipartisan" (i.e. conservative and liberal centrists) Social Security Commission, and "saved" the system from bankruptcy by slapping on higher Social Security taxes.

Alan is a long-time member of the famed Trilateral Commission, the Rockefeller-dominated pinnacle of the financial-political power elite in this country. And as he assumes his post as head of the Fed, he leaves his honored place on the board of directors of J. P. Morgan & Co. and Morgan Guaranty Trust. Yes, the Establishment has good reason to sleep soundly with Greenspan at our monetary helm. And as icing on the cake, they know that Greenspan's "philosophical" Randianism will undoubtedly fool many free market advocates into thinking that a champion of their cause now perches high in the seats of power.

Fiat Paper Money: Tyranny's Credit Card

J. Tucker Alford

In the 20th century, the American dollar has a grim history. It has only about 9% of its 1913 value, because Federal Reserve inflation has caused consumer prices to increase more than eleven-fold.

During the same time, the power of the central bank has increased enormously, as has the presence of the federal government in the economy. Compared to the previous 113 years, the difference is startling. Then, prices generally fell, and prosperity was always on the rise.

The crucial difference between then and now is the quality of the dollar. Today's dollar is created out of thin air by the U.S. government, and there is virtually no restraint on the Federal Reserve's power. But when there is no Fed and money is a real commodity like gold, as during the 19th century, money is more likely to maintain its quality and purchasing power.

Money has not always been in the claws of the government. In fact, as Carl Menger theorized, money very likely came about through the process of the market. Ludwig von Mises went even further and proved that the free market was the only place money could develop. Government coercion never has and never will be able to impose a new institution of money on the economy.

Even so, money has been the victim of brutal attacks by the government. In the Middle Ages, monarchs found that raising taxes was a risky way to raise revenue. It often provoked violent revolution, and kings didn't relish the risk of meeting the executioner's ax. Instead, they found a discreet and underhanded way to extract wealth from the public: debasement of coinage. The king would call in coins for reissue, melt them down, and redistribute them with slightly less gold content, but with the same face value. The "excess" gold would pay off the kings debts, and while the value of the circulating coins would drop, the public outcry was limited.

Paper money first came into use to save the cost of physically transporting bullion. People felt uncomfortable carrying around large quantities of gold. They placed their gold with a goldsmith, and he issued a paper receipt for the deposit, guaranteeing the bearer payment of the gold on demand. The depositor could then use his receipt for the purchase of goods and services. Goldsmiths, soon called banks, began redeeming one another's gold receipts, and paper receipts became accepted as substitutes for money.

The goldsmiths, however, quickly recognized an opportunity to make more profits. They began printing up phony gold receipts and spending them for their own use. They could even lend them out and charge interest, knowing all depositors wouldn't call for redemption at once. This counterfeiting is today hailed as the basis of our banking system: fractional reserve banking.

Always hanging over the head of the banker-goldsmith, however, was the threat that too many of his depositors would redeem their notes for gold on the same day. His bank, like all modern banks, was inherently broke, but its bankruptcy became apparent only in the event of a bank run. If he couldn't meet his depositors' demands, he would likely be hanged.

Governments, of course, found paper money to their liking. In the New World, paper money was first used in Massachusetts in 1690. After several failed pillaging expeditions into Canada, the colonial government issued irredeemable paper to pay the troops. Back then, no one would accept a simple piece of paper in exchange for real goods, so the government had to promise to redeem in specie at a certain date in the future. It also promised that there would be only one such issue. But the government's promise was as thin as its paper, and many more such issues followed when the government found itself short on money.

The people of colonial America learned to distrust paper money. During the Revolutionary War, Congress issued paper notes called Continentals, which were not backed in gold. They were issued in great quantities, and thus depreciated until they were worth next to nothing. People knew the true cause of the depreciation of the Continental. It wasn't aliens, speculators, slackers, hoarders, or jobbers. It was the government defrauding the people with its printing presses. That's why they wrote gold and silver into the Constitution.

Today, however, the banking and central banking system is so complex that few know why the dollar continues to lose value. The Fed doesn't help much with its confusing array of money stock and liquid asset definitions (Ms). Much better is

Professor Murray N. Rothbard's True Money Supply (TMS). It combines selected components of the different Ms according to Austrian theory, and provides a more accurate accounting of the total outstanding medium of exchange at any given time.

The first step in the establishment of a 100% gold standard money must be to define the U.S. dollar as a weight of gold, with 100% redeemability insured. The dollar was once 1/20 an ounce of gold. It was then devalued to 1/35 an ounce of gold. What would it be now if the dollar were again tied to gold? To approximate the answer we only need to know the government's gold stock, the current money supply, and some simple mathematics.

Using the Federal Reserve's M1 as money (cash, checking accounts, and travelers checks), the dollar would be defined as 1/2837 of an ounce gold. This would value the government's gold stock at $749.3 billion and enable all of M1 to be back by gold at 100%.

Using Rothbard's broader definition of money, TMS, the most recent figures show the dollar would be defined as 1/7340 an ounce of gold. (Just think what the Fed has done: the pre-1934 dollar was 1/20 ounce!) This would allow the government's gold to cover all of TMS. The Federal Reserve's assets could then be sold, and the whole ugly system dismantled.

Though there are few dedicated individuals who remain champions of hard, honest money, the mainstream lambastes the gold standard advocates as archaic, reactionary, anachronistic, loony, and Neanderthal.

The record speaks for itself. Even under an imperfect gold standard, from the end of the American Civil War to World War I, the world experienced unprecedented prosperity and improvement in living standards. Since the "Progressives" destroyed the dollar in 1913, there has been worldwide inflation, the impoverishment of the developing world, the decline of Western prosperity, and a rise of totalitarianism, both right and left. It is anti-gold statists who are pointing us toward the despotism and barbarism of a new Neanderthal era.

Hard money is free money, and it goes hand in hand with liberty and democracy. Fiat paper money is tyranny's credit card. One can only hope that circumstances need not get worse before they get better. Perhaps someday our nine-cent paper ticket will give way to a genuine, honest gold dollar.

Back to Fixed Exchange Rates: Another "New Economic Order"

Murray N. Rothbard

Hold on to your hats: the world has now embarked on yet another "new economic order"—which means another disaster in the making. Ever since the abandonment of the "classical" gold coin standard in World War I [by the United States in 1933], world authorities have been searching for a way to replace the peaceful world rule of gold by the coordinated, coercive rule of the world's governments.

They have searched for a way to replace the sound money of gold by an internationally coordinated inflation which would provide cheap money, abundant increases in the money supply, increasing government expenditures, and prices that do not rise too wildly or too far out of control, and with no embarrassing monetary crises or excessive declines in any one country's currency. In short, governments have tried to square the circle, or, to have their pleasant inflationary cake without "eating" it by suffering decidedly unpleasant consequences.

The first new economic order of the 20th century was the New Era dominated by Great Britain, in which the world's countries were induced to ground their currencies on a phony gold standard, actually based on the British pound sterling, which was in turn loosely based on the dollar and gold. When this recipe for internationally coordinated inflation collapsed and helped create the Great Depression of the 1930s, a new and very similar international order was constructed at Bretton Woods in 1944. In *this* case, another phony gold standard was created, this time with all currencies based on the U.S. dollar, in turn supposedly redeemable, *not* in gold coin to the public, but in gold bullion to foreign central banks and governments at $35 an ounce.

In the late 1920s, governments of the various nations could inflate their currencies by pyramiding on top of an inflating pound; similarly in the Bretton Woods system, the U.S. exported its own inflation by encouraging other countries to inflate on top of their expanding accumulation of dollar reserves. As world currencies, and especially the dollar, kept inflating, it became evident that gold was undervalued and dollars overvalued at the old $35 par, so that Western European countries, reluctant to continue inflationary policies, began to demand gold for their accumulated dollars [in short, Gresham's Law, that money overvalued by the government will drive undervalued money out of circulation, came into effect]. Since the U.S. was not able to redeem its gold obligations, President Nixon went off the Bretton Woods standard, which had come to its inevitable demise in 1971.

Since that date, or rather since 1933, the world has had a fluctuating fiat standard, that is, exchange rates of currencies have fluctuated in accordance with supply and demand on the market. There are grave problems with fluctuating exchange rates, largely because of the abandonment of one world money [i.e. gold] and the shift to international barter. Because there is no world money, every nation is free to inflate its own currency at will— and hence to suffer a decline in its exchange rates. And because there is no longer a world money, fluctuating uncertain exchange rates create a double uncertainty on top of the usual price system—creating, in effect, multi-price systems in the world. The inflation and volatility under the fluctuating exchange rate regime has caused politicians and economists to try to resurrect a system of fixed exchange rates—but this time, without even the element of the gold standard that marked the Bretton Woods era. But without a world gold money, this means that nations are fixing exchange rates arbitrarily, without reference to supply and demand, and on the alleged superior wisdom of economists and politicians as to what exchange rates should be.

Politicians are pressured by conflicting import and export interests, and economists have made the grave error of mistaking a long-run *tendency* (of exchange rates on a fluctuating market to rest at the proportion of purchasing-powers of the various currencies) for a *criterion* by which economists can correct the market. This attempt to place economists above the market overlooks the fact that the market properly sets exchange rates on the basis, not only of purchasing power proportions, but also expectations of the future, differences in interest rates, differences in tax policy, fears of future inflation of confiscation, etc. Once again, the market proves wiser than economists.

This new coordinated attempt to fix exchange rates began two years ago in a hysterical reaction against the high dollar. The Group of Seven nations [the U.S., Britain, France, Italy, West Germany, Japan, and Canada] helped drive down the value of the dollar, and then, in their wisdom, in February 1987, decided that the dollar was now somehow at a perfect rate, and coordinated their efforts to keep the dollar from falling further.

In reality, the dollar was high until early 1986 because foreigners had been unusually willing to invest in dollars—government bonds as well as others assets. While this happy situation continued, they were willing to finance Americans in buying cheap imports. After early 1987, this unusual willingness disappeared, and the dollar began to fall in order to equilibrate the U.S. balance of payments. Artificially propping up the dollar in 1987 has led the other countries of the Group of Seven to purchase billions of dollars with their own currencies—a short-sighted effort which cannot last forever, especially because West Germany and Japan have fortunately not been willing to inflate their own currencies and lower their interest rates further, to divert capital from themselves toward the U.S.

Instead of realizing that this coordination game is headed toward inevitable crisis and collapse, Secretary of Treasury James Baker, the creator of the new system, proposes to press ahead to a more formal New Order. In his September speech to the IMF and World Bank, Secretary Baker proposed a formal, coordinated regime of fixed exchange rates, in which—as a sop to public sentiment for gold—gold is to have an extremely shadowy, almost absurd, role. In the course of fine tuning the world economy, the central banks and treasuries of the world, in addition to looking at various "indicators" on their control panels—price levels, interest rates, GNP, unemployment rates, etc.—will also be consulting a new commodity price index of their own making which, by *secret* formula, would also include gold.

Such a ludicrous substitute for genuine gold money will certainly fool no one, and is an almost laughable example of the love of central bankers and treasury officials for secrecy and mystification for its own sake, so as to bewilder and bamboozle the public. I do not often agree with J. K. Galbraith, but he is certainly on the mark when he calls this new secret index a "marvelous exercise in fantasy and obfuscation."

Politically, the secret index embodies a new ruling alliance within the Reagan Administration between such conservative Keynesians as Secretary Baker and such supply-siders as Professor Robert Mundell and Congressman Jack Kemp (who have both hailed the scheme as a glorious step in the right direction). The supply-siders have long desired the restoration of a Bretton Woods-type system that would allow coordinated world cheap money and inflation, *coupled* with a phony gold standard as camouflage, so as to build unjustified confidence in the new scheme among the pro-gold public.

The conservative Keynesians have long desired a new Bretton Woods, based eventually on a new world paper unit issued by a World Central Bank. Hence the new alliance. The alliance was made politically possible by the disappearance from the Reagan Administration of the Friedmanite monetarists, such as former Undersecretary of Treasury for Monetary Policy Beryl W. Sprinkel and Jerry Jordan, spokesmen for fluctuating exchange rates. With monetarism discredited by the repeated failures of their monetary predictions over the last several years, the route was cleared for a new international fixed rates system.

Unfortunately, the only thing worse than fluctuating exchange rates is fixed exchange rates based on fiat money and international coordination. Before rates were allowed to fluctuate, and after the end of Bretton Woods, the U.S. government tried such an order, in the international Smithsonian Agreement of December 1971. President Nixon hailed this agreement as "the greatest monetary agreement in the history of the world." This exercise in international coordination lasted no more than a year and a half, foundering on monetary crises brought about by Gresham's Law and overvaluation of the dollar.

How long will it take this new, New Order, along with its puerile secret index, to collapse as well?

Monetary Crises

Llewellyn H. Rockwell, Jr.

Since the 1690s, America has undergone more than 20 monetary crises. Some have led to genuine reform, others to increased government power.

The fitful fiat-money inflation of the colonial governments had its culmination in the much worse inflation engineered by the continental Congress. "Why should we consent to load our constituents with taxes," said one Member, "when we can send to the printer for a whole wagonload of money, and pay for it with but one quire's worth?"

The Americans managed to win the Revolution, despite the Congress, but the inflationary burden fell heaviest on the patriots. The Tories, Pelatia Webster reports, refused to have anything to do with the new money, and would accept only gold and silver. But many of those fighting for American freedom and independence accepted the Continental paper currency. As a result, they were wiped out when the Continental fell, because of the printing press, to one tenth of one percent of its original value. Webster, probably America's first economist, said the whole experience was summed up for him by the sight of a drunken sailor dressed in a suit made entirely of Continental money.

But the debacle of government fiat money led, not to authoritarianism as is usually the case, but to restrictions on state power and the establishment of the classical gold standard. The American gold standard was never perfect. The government and its attendant banking interests were still able to manipulate it, which led to recurrent crises, but the damage was always limited. Until the establishment of the Federal Reserve System in 1913.

The Fed's bank credit inflation of the 1920s led directly, in the Austrian business cycle, to the Great Depression, which gave Franklin D. Roosevelt the excuse to violate the Constitution and end the domestic gold standard. The international gold standard was killed by Richard Nixon on August 15, 1971, when he also imposed price and wage controls.

We've seen prices go up more than 350% since that day, with the inevitable busts. Since the depression of 1981-82, the Fed has increased the money supply by more than 100%. We saw the effects, as in the 1920s, in stock market and other booms. Since the crash of October, the media keep nervously asking if we're facing a recession. The answer is, of course, yes. That was made inevitable by the inflation of 82-87. The question is what we do with it.

The government, as in previous crises, will try to use the coming troubles as an excuse for more of the poison that caused the troubles to begin with. But the climate of ideas really has changed.

Americans are much more suspicious of politicians and their nostrums than they were in the 1930s. There are signs that today, as in the 19th century, money can again become a political issue.

Thanks to Ron Paul and others, tens of millions of Americans own gold today, and know that its value is independent of government. Many know about, and approve of, the idea of a gold standard. In the academic world, thanks to Murray N. Rothbard and others, the intellectual case for the gold standard is being made with a logical brilliance unseen since the glory days of hard money, and it is buttressed as well with Ludwig von Mises's Austrian business cycle theory, which shows the hidden damage wrought by inflation.

For those of us who believe an individual liberty and sound money, these are days of opportunity. There is chance for real reform. If we grasp it.

The Real Secrets of the Temple

Llewellyn H. Rockwell, Jr.

The Federal Reserve—the U.S. government's central bank—was schemed at a secret meeting in 1910 at J. P. Morgan's hunting club on Jekyll Island, Georgia.

The participants—who claimed, as they boarded a private railroad car in New York City, to be going on a hunting trip—were, in addition to Morgan himself: Senator Nelson W. Aldrich (R-RI), John D. Rockefeller's son-in-law; A. Piatt Andrew, Assistant Secretary of the Treasury in the Taft administration; Henry P. Davison, the "political partner" (i.e., lobbyist) for J. P. Morgan's banking house; Paul Warburg of Kuhn Loeb & Co., a German political partner brought to the U.S. specifically to help establish a central bank; and Frank A. Vanderlip of New York's National City Bank (today's Citibank).

Three years later the U.S. had a central bank, after a propaganda campaign using the Big Lie. Americans were told that major bankers—whom they heartily distrusted—were opposed to the Fed. In fact, the Fed was set up to cartelize the banking industry, doing for it what the ICC had done for big railroads and the FTC for other big businesses. Before 1913, market forces prevented any one bank or group of banks from expanding the money supply too egregiously. The Fed changed all that by enabling big banks to inflate together while protecting them from competition.

In its origins and its operations, the Federal Reserve is the most secretive of American political institutions. After his briefings before the first presidential debate with Ronald Reagan in 1984, Walter Mondale exclaimed to his campaign manager: "For the first time I understand the Federal Reserve!"

Like Mondale, a U.S. senator for many years and then vice president, we are told almost nothing about what the Fed does and why. All we hear—from political leaders, bankers, pundits, and kept economists—is that it ensures prosperity and prevents depressions, that its officials know exactly what they're doing, and that no one in his right mind could possibly question its existence.

Like virtually all of the official line, this is the reverse of the truth.

William Greider—one of America's best political reporters—set out to examine all of this in *Secrets of the Temple: How the Federal Reserve Runs the Country* (Simon and Schuster, 1987). But the man who has exposed the charades of government in so many other areas does not do a similar job on the government's great inflation machine.

To his credit, Greider has changed the way journalists think about the Fed. Even his old paper, the *Washington Post*, no longer automatically defers to the central bank, where once it ran its pronouncements as fact. Also to his credit, Greider has angered financiers and bankers by telling the truth: that the Fed is the most powerful policy-making institution in America and maybe the world. (Those who profit from what Andrew Jackson used to call the Monster prefer to continue operating in the dark.)

Greider criticizes the Fed, but for all the wrong reasons. For example, he claims it isn't inflationary enough! And he calls for high, sustained inflation to create prosperity and justice. Inflation will resolve the eternal conflict between the rich and the poor, says Greider, in favor of the poor.

There is a seemingly eternal conflict, but it's between those who use the government to get rich, and the rest of us who are thereby made poorer.

In his chapter on the founding of the Fed, Greider mentions the idea of the Fed as cartel, but he never brings it up again. His own position is that the Fed came about through popular demand, stimulated by political movements for higher farm prices and an end to bank panics. In fact, these groups provided only a political opportunity and an ideological excuse for the Morgan-Rockefeller forces—in cahoots with the politicians—to seize control of the dollar by establishing the Fed.

Greider claims that deflation, not inflation, benefits bankers, and says that the Fed seeks to promote "the virtual elimination of dollar inflation." But the central bank was established only to circumvent the strictures of the gold standard. That is, it was founded to inflate.

The constituents of Fed Chairman Alan Greenspan are commercial bankers and the government, not depositors or citizens, and the Fed's actions are primarily motivated by the interests of Washington and the big money-center banks.

Inflation benefits the Fed and its constituents as counterfeiting benefits a counterfeiter and his gang. The private counterfeiter, however, is a relatively minor criminal; the Fed does exactly what the counterfeiter does, but massively and on a world-wide scale. As in so many other areas, what is (rightly) condemned in the private sector is lauded in the public.

Greider calls inflation "a promising model for social equity." "Many poor people" benefit since they don't have to bear the rising costs of medical care and housing with "Medicaid and public housing." Similarly, the "elderly" are "partially protected" from inflation because Social Security is "indexed to the inflation rate."

The government, politicians, bureaucrats, banks, government contractors, and other interests profit, since they get the new money first, and can spend it before prices go up, thereby transferring wealth to themselves from the people who get it last.

Average taxpayers are harmed in at least five ways: first, since they receive new Fed money last, they can spend it only after prices have gone up; second, they pay a hidden tax of currency debasement on their dollar-denominated savings; third, they pay a direct tax for the salaries and perks of the bureaucrats, politicians, and welfare recipients whose incomes are indexed to inflation; fourth, they suffer the consequences of inflation-caused recessions and depressions; and five, they lose some of their liberty, since inflation strengthens the government at the expense of individual freedom.

The poor, despite Greider, are harmed especially. The inflation-fueled growth of government creates more hungry and homeless by decreasing general prosperity and opportunity. Then, only the smart, well-educated, and healthy can get ahead. Those most in need of a charitable helping hand are instead kicked in the teeth by Washington, D.C.

Inflation also increases the costs to the poor of becoming independent from the dole. However, like so many negatives for the people, this is a benefit for the government. By enlarging the dependent class, inflation justifies even more "poverty" programs actually designed to benefit bureaucrats, social workers, Medicaid doctors, D.C. consultants, public housing builders, etc.: the whole welfare industry.

Inflation, by illegitimately transferring wealth to the government-connected, also helps cement present social stratifications in place. The bigger government is, the fewer Horatio Algers there are. People who get to the top through force and fraud prefer it that way.

Inflation can help debtors (by stealing from savers)—one of its great advantages, according to Greider—but it mainly aids the greatest debtor of them all, big government, which is always and everywhere the enemy of the poor.

Then there is the business cycle, which even a little inflation will cause. In the free market, interest rates are determined by consumer preferences for savings over consumption. In the days of a real U.S. gold standard, this meant that corporations could issue 30-year bonds paying 3%.

The Austrian theory of the business cycle, developed by Ludwig von Mises, shows that when the Fed artificially lowers interest rates by injecting credit into the banking system, it gives businessmen the same signal as if people decided to save more of their incomes. In response, companies invest in processes to produce goods for later purchase by consumers with their larger savings.

But when businessmen seek to market these goods, they find the demand isn't there. Consumers haven't saved enough, and the investments were what Mises called "malinvestments"—those unjustified by real economic conditions. The result is a bust.

Any amount of new Fed money and credit will lead to these malinvestments, despite the claim of Greider (and of Milton Friedman) that recessions only occur when the Fed steps on the brakes. The monetarist notion of increasing the money supply every year by 3-5% "to keep up with GNP" is damaging for this very reason. Only zero inflation will do.

By the way, despite Friedman, there is nothing wrong with the Fed's stopping the flow of money and credit to end the boom, as happened in 1929. The wrong was the inflation that took place during the 1920s, and the Hoover-Roosevelt policies that prevented a recovery for over a decade. The original culprit, of course, was the existence of an institution able to cause all this trouble.

Greider hates deflation, but it is the natural, healthy condition of the market. With the money supply relatively stable under a gold standard and the production of goods and services increasing, the dollar buys more. Prices gently fall (imagine the VCR situation extended to the whole market) and real wages increase. That's what happened to our country in the 19th century, and it brought about the greatest economic growth in history.

Greider, good journalist that he is, does provide compelling accounts of the Fed's Continental Illinois and Mexican debt bailouts, and new evidence that "Arthur Burns . . . deliberately manipulated monetary policy . . . to help re-elect his old friend Richard Nixon." He quotes Fed Governors admitting that they consciously pursued a monetarist policy from 1979-1982 (something Friedman would like us to forget), shows how "Volcker stared down U.S. Senators and presidential advisers" during the recessions of the early 80s, and tells how the officers of Volcker's old employer, Rockefeller's Chase Manhattan Bank, persuaded him to loosen the money supply.

Greider criticizes the quantity theory of money as a "simple answer to bewildering complexities," and cites money supply statistics from the 1970s and 1980s that use M-1 as a base. But the "money supply" in these years can hardly be summarized by M-1 because of financial deregulation (and the Fed's propensity to keep changing its statistical bases to hide its activities). A much more accurate monetary statistic is the True Money Supply (TMS) constructed at the request of the Mises Institute by Murray Rothbard and Joseph Salerno on Austrian economic principles.

Greider does have one point, however: most economists do oversimplify the quantity theory of money. An increase in the money supply raises relative prices, but what mainstream economists call the "price level" is a fiction. As relative prices increase, different sectors of the economy are affected in different ways. Prices have risen, but far more important, the price structure has changed.

Greider rebukes Congressional Democrats for voting for the deregulation of interest rates in the Monetary Control Act of 1980. This aspect of the bill merely recognized something the market had already accomplished through money market funds. But he glosses over, or does not mention, other important provisions, which: centralized even more power in the Fed, removed all collateral from U.S. notes, enabled the Fed to reduce bank reserve requirements to zero, empowered the president to declare bank holidays, and allowed the Fed to monetize foreign debt (including nearly worthless Third World debt held by the money-center banks). Only Ron Paul, then a Congressman from Texas, understood what the bill really meant, and waged a courageous and single-handed fight against it.

The Secrets of the Temple serves an important purpose by shining a bright light on an institution for too long hidden in obfuscation and propaganda. But the real secrets of the temple are that: the Federal Reserve is an unconstitutional and illegitimate enterprise; it serves a narrow elite of bankers, government officials, and connected businessmen; it ensures prosperity for these insiders at the expense of the rest of us; it causes economic disasters; its officials are arrogant bumblers; and great statesmen and economists—from Andrew Jackson to Ron Paul, from Ludwig von Mises to Murray N. Rothbard—have wanted it or similar operations wiped from the face of the earth.

A central bank is incompatible with a free society. For the sake of our economy and our liberty, and of simple justice, we should abolish the Monster, and sow salt in the earth where it stood. In its place we need a real gold standard and non-fraudulent free banking, as Ludwig von Mises outlined, and as the Founding Fathers intended.

3

FREE TRADE AND PROTECTIONISM

The Case for Free Trade

Congressman Ron Paul

In 1981, the *Federal Register* published a declaration from President Reagan: "I determine that it is in the national interest for the Export-Import Bank of the United States to extend a credit in the amount of $120.7 million to the Socialist Republic of Romania (for) the purchase of two nuclear steam turbine generators."

This loan carried an interest rate of 7¾% for ten years, but the first payment wasn't due until July, 1989.

Not too long before this announcement, the administration had made public its "voluntary" restraints on the number of cars Japan can export to the United States.

These two items—subsidization of trade and its restriction—are all too typical of our present trade policy.

Although we think of ourselves as a free-trading nation, it takes more than 700 pages just to list all the tariffs on imported goods, and another 400 to inventory all the non-tariff restraints, such as quotas and "orderly marketing agreements."

A tariff is a tax levied on a foreign good, to help a special interest at the expense of American consumers.

A trade restraint or marketing agreement—on the number of inexpensive Taiwanese sneakers than Americans can buy, for example—achieves the same goal, at the same cost, in a less forthright manner.

And all the trends are towards more subsidies for U.S. exporters, and more prohibitions and taxes on imports.

Trade is to be subsidized or restrained, not left to the voluntary actions of consumers and producers.

In 1930, Congress passed the Smoot-Hawley tariff bill, imposing heavy tariffs on imports, with the avowed motive of "protecting" U.S. companies and jobs. Within one year, our 25 major trading partners had retaliated with their own tariffs on American goods. World trade declined sharply, and the depression was made world-wide and longer-lasting.

Today the policy of protectionism is again gaining favor in Congress, and in other countries. But it must be fought with all our strength.

Not only does protectionism make everyone poorer—except certain special interests—but it also increases international tensions, and can lead to war.

"If a foreign country can supply us with a commodity cheaper than we ourselves can make it," wrote Adam Smith in 1776, "better buy it of them with some part of the produce of our own industry employed in a way in which we have some advantage. The general industry of the country will not therefore be diminished . . . but only left to find out the way in which it can be employed to the greater advantage."

An important economic principle is called the division of labor. It states that economic efficiency, and therefore growth, is enhanced by everyone doing what he does best.

If I had to grow my own food, make my own clothes, build my own house, and teach my own children, our family's living standard would plummet to a subsistence, or below-subsistence, level.

But if I practice medicine, and allow others with more talent as farmers, builders or tailors to do what they do best, we are all better off. Precious capital and labor are directed to the areas of most productivity, and through voluntary trading, we all benefit.

This principle works just as effectively on a national and world-wide scale, as Adam Smith pointed out.

It may be that Japan can make cars more efficiently than Detroit, at least certain kinds of cars, and that the capital and labor in parts of the U.S. auto industry could be better employed in other areas. With quotas, however, we will never find out. We will only increase the price of those Japanese cars that do get through, and of U.S. cars as well, since competitive pressures will be taken off General Motors and Ford.

Free trade at all levels makes for more prosperity, as the Founding Fathers knew. That's why they gave Congress power to remove barriers to interstate commerce.

During the period of the Confederation—after our independence but before the adoption of the Constitution—some of the states erected tariff barriers against imports from their neighbors. The resulting economic stagnation and antagonism threatened the unity of our country, and led to the adoption of the interstate commerce clause by the Constitutional convention. The removal of all trade barriers—and not meddling in the economy—was the purpose of the clause.

As a result, we, as Americans, are free to trade with all other Americans, so that resources are put to their most efficient use in our giant domestic market. This happy consequence is no small contributor to our wealth.

Without this constitutional prohibition, state legislatures would listen to lobbyists for special interests, and enact protection against "unfair" out-of-state competition.

Knowing how similar situations come about, we could bet that someone in Minnesota, with idle greenhouses, would lobby the state legislature, pointing out that farmers in Florida, California, and Texas have too easy a time growing oranges. To protect Minnesota farmers, and create jobs, they would call for a heavy tax on out-of-state citrus, so greenhouse growing of oranges would become economic in Minneapolis.

As a result, oranges would drastically increase in price, and the quality would be lower. Minnesotans who like orange juice would be able to afford less, and what they could get would not be as good. But some would reap windfall profits, at the expense of the consumer. And pressure in orange-growing states would grow it retaliate against Minnesota products, to the detriment of everyone in the country. And we could bet that interstate antagonisms would increase as well. International trade barriers work no differently.

But because our Constitution forbids such domestic barriers, a company in Laredo, Texas, can trade freely, easily, and profitably with a firm in Oregon, thousands of miles away. (It's important to remember that both parties to a non-coerced, non-fraudulent trade benefit from the exchange, or hope to benefit, or the exchange would not take place.)

But let that Laredo firm seek to trade with a Mexican company only a mile away, and tremendous impediments spring up, thanks to government regulations on both sides. "The motive of all these regulations," wrote Adam Smith, "is to extend our own manufactures, not by their own improvements, but by putting an end, as much as possible, to the troublesome competition of such disagreeable rivals.

No one worries about the balance of trade between Oregon and Texas. That between Mexico and Texas should be of no consequence either. It is a problem only to government planners.

Dr. Murray Rothbard, who lives in New York City, has said that he's delighted the federal government doesn't keep interborough trade statistics. "We'd have the Bronx and Brooklyn worried about balance of trade!"

"Nations," notes Dr. Rothbard, "may be important politically and culturally, but economically they appear only as a consequence of government intervention."

But doesn't protection save U.S. jobs? Yes, it can save the jobs of some, but it costs jobs overall, and harms consumers.

Limiting Japanese car imports, for example, does protect the jobs of high-seniority members of the United Auto Workers, who earn twice the average U.S. industrial wage. But it takes away any incentive to correct government-caused productivity problems.

Diverting resources into uneconomic uses takes them away from other, more productive areas and costs jobs. Some jobs are lost; others are never created. The uneconomic effects of protectionism benefit a few—usually well-to-do—at the expense of the great majority, including the poor.

Protectionism cannot be justified on economic or moral grounds. As Frederic Bastiat wrote, tariffs are "legalized plunder." The law is used to steal.

By what right does the U.S. government tell an American citizen he cannot buy a foreign product? Such action is reprehensible on every ground imaginable, and is totally incompatible with individual freedom. Also inexcusable on any ground is the vast network of U.S. trade subsidies.

The taxpayers subsidize companies through the Export-Import Bank, the Department of Commerce, and the Overseas Private Investment Corporation, to name only three.

Such programs contribute to inflation, high taxes, "crowding out" in the capital markets, higher prices, and misallocation of resources.

Exports are only useful economically when they are profitable. Otherwise they represent a net loss.

But don't we need our own subsidies because other countries have theirs? If the government of France wishes to help impoverish their own citizens to send us cheap products, why should we impoverish ours as well? We can, and should, oppose those policies for France as well as the United States, but we have no right to take away buying opportunities from our own consumers.

Notes the Council for a Competitive Economy: we should consider what would happen if a foreign country decided to give us free cars, TVs, steel, and other products. Would this hurt the American people? To ask the question is to answer it.

Every economic intervention in trade, domestic or foreign, should be abolished, for practical and moral reasons.

Even if other countries maintain tariffs or subsidies, we would be helped, not hurt, by unilaterally ending ours.

We would improve our productivity, shift resources to those areas where we have an advantage, grow more prosperous, and make a greater variety of less-expensive goods available to our people.

And we would serve the cause of peace and set a good example for the world to emulate.

"When people and goods cross borders," Ludwig von Mises used to quote, "armies do not." Free and extensive trade, unsubsidized, between the peoples of the Earth lowers tensions and makes us all better off. It is, morally and economically, the only proper policy.

Turgot and Iacocca

Llewellyn H. Rockwell, Jr.

After we won our War of Independence—fought partly over English trade restrictions—the 13 former colonies adopted the Articles of Confederation. Despite later criticism, this pact had much to recommend it, but it did have one incapacitating flaw: the lack of any provision for internal free trade.

As a result, politically powerful merchants succeeded in getting state legislatures to place tariff taxes on competing goods from other states. These were attempts to make buying out-of-state goods seem unpatriotic, and the inevitable results were increasing hostility between the states, and decreasing prosperity.

The nation faced commercial paralysis, and this was one of the major factors leading to the adoption of the Constitution.

The famous interstate commerce clause was designed to outlaw interstate trade restrictions, and although that clause has been perverted by the courts to justify many federal interventions in the economy, we still have open state borders.

There are no customs police patrolling the line between Massachusetts and Connecticut—as under the Articles of Confederation—and no one thinks a Virginian disloyal for buying something made in New Hampshire.

We are all much better off, in amity and economics, because of this internal free trade. In fact, it was essential to the growth of American prosperity.

The relative free trade that exists internationally benefits us all as well. Anti-free trade legislation, such as the high tariffs of the 1930s, devastated world trade and thereby helped deepen and lengthen the Great Depression. They also increased international tensions.

The many retreats on free trade over the past few years have been disheartening, but the recent non-renewal of the "voluntary" import ceiling on Japanese cars was an important improvement.

The great French economist A. R. J. Turgot (1727-1781) was the first to point out that attempts to restrict international trade are based not just on intellectual error, but on the search by some businesses for special privilege.* And that such privileges harm domestic consumers more than foreign competitors.

Free international trade, he noted, follows necessarily from the principle of free exchange. That is, parties benefit from any non-fraudulent economic transaction. An American buying a Chrysler is no different in this sense from an American buying a Toyota. He also noted that it is economically ridiculous to try to sell to foreigners while not buying anything in return.

Each branch of industry in France, he noted, seemed to want free markets for everyone else and controlled markets for itself, resulting in "a war of reciprocal oppression which government lends its authority to all against all," with everyone losing.

Recently Lee Iacocca, head of Chrysler Corporation, made one of his frequent attacks on free trade before a closed meeting of Democratic Congressmen. His remarks made the news, however, because some of the audience thought his tone was racist. Mr. Iacocca, who might have stepped out of one of Turgot's examples, denounced the non-renewal of the car quotas, and said the U.S. had more to fear from Japanese attacks than Soviet ones.

The restriction on imports has had—like all government interventions in the economy—costs and benefits. The majority, who have borne the undeserved costs, are American car buyers (and would-be car buyers). The unearned benefits have accrued to highly paid auto workers and executives.

With an import ceiling artificially decreasing the supply, but demand increasing, Japanese car makers sent more of their most expensive, option-loaded vehicles. And U.S. car makers faced fewer competitive pressures, enabling them to raise their prices.

As a result, U.S. consumers have had fewer inexpensive cars to buy, and the cars that are available—domestic and foreign—cost an estimated $800-1400 more per vehicle.

Mr. Iacocca, who succeeded in getting heavy credit subsidies from the federal government for Chrysler, made it possible for average Americans to support $35-an-hour unionized auto workers (and $1,000-an-hour auto company chairmen). And now he's campaigning for American consumers to keep paying through more restrictions on imports.

A. R. J. Turgot came from a free-market family, and his grandfather was a close friend of Thomas La Gendre, one of the most successful merchants of the 17th century. A free-market champion at a time when most businessmen sought special favors from the king, his ships were constantly harassed by the royal trade bureaucrats because of his principled stand.

When asked by Jean-Baptiste Colbert, the king's finance minister, what the government should do for business, La Gendre answered laissez-faire—allow people to do as they choose.

Three hundred years later, that is still the proper answer.

**I am indebted to Dr. Murray N. Rothbard for this material.*

The Crusade Against South Africa

Murray N. Rothbard

For many years, America's campuses have been sunk in political apathy. The values of the 1950s are supposed to be back, including concentration on one's career and lack of interest in social or political causes.

But now, suddenly, it begins to seem like a replay of the late 1960s: demonstrations, placards, even sit-ins on campus. The issue is apartheid in South Africa, and the campaign hopes to bring down apartheid by pressuring colleges and universities to disinvest in South Africa. Coercion against South Africa is also being pursued on the legislative front, including drives to embargo that country as well as prohibit the importation of Krugerrands.

I yield to no one in my abhorrence of the apartheid system, but it must never be forgotten what the road to Hell is paved with. Good intentions are scarcely enough, and we must always be careful that in trying to do good, we don't do harm instead.

The object of the new crusade is presumably to help the oppressed blacks of South Africa. But what would be the impact of U.S. disinvestment?

The demand for black workers in South Africa would fall, and the result would be loss of jobs and lower wage rates for the oppressed people of that country. Not only that: presumably the U.S. firms are among the highest-paying employers in South Africa, so that the impact on black wages and working conditions would be particularly severe. In short: the group we are most trying to help by our well-meaning intervention will be precisely the ones to lose the most. As on so many other occasions, doing good *for* becomes doing harm *to*.

The same result would follow from the other legislative actions against South Africa. Prohibition of Krugerrands, for example, would injure, first and foremost, the black workers in the gold mining industry. And so on down the line.

I suppose that demonstrating and crusading against apartheid gives American liberals a fine glow of moral righteousness. But have they really pondered the consequences? Some American black leaders are beginning to do so. A spokesman for the National Urban League concedes that "We do not favor disinvestment. . . . We believe that the workers would be the ones that would be hurt." And Ted Adams, executive director of the National Association of Blacks Within Government, warns that disinvestment would "come down hard on black people," and could wind up "throwing the baby out with the bath water."

But other black leaders take a sterner view. A spokesman for Chicago Mayor Harold Washington admits "some concern that the most immediate effect of disinvestment may be felt by the laborers themselves," but then adds, on a curious note, "that's never an excuse not to take action." Michelle Kourouma, executive director of the National Conference of Black Mayors, explains the hard-line position: "How could it get any worse? We have nothing to lose and everything to gain: freedom."

The profound flaw is an equivocation on the word "we," a collective term covering a multitude of sins. Unfortunately, it is not Ms. Kourouma or Mr. Washington or any American liberal who stands to lose by disinvestment; it is only the blacks in South Africa.

It is all too easy for American liberals, secure in their well-paid jobs and their freedom in the United States, to say, in effect, to the blacks of South Africa: "We're going to make you sacrifice for your own benefit." It is doubtful whether the blacks in South Africa will respond with the same enthusiasm. Unfortunately, they have nothing to say in the matter; once again, their lives will be the pawns in other people's political games.

How can we in the United States help South African blacks? There is no way that we can end the apartheid system. But one thing we can do is the exact opposite of the counsel of our misled crusaders.

During the days of the national grape boycott, the economist Angus Black wrote that the only way for consumers to help the California grape workers was to buy as many grapes as they possibly could, thereby increasing the demand for grapes and raising the wage rate and employment of grape workers. Similarly, all we can do is to encourage as much as possible American investment in South Africa and the importation of Krugerrands. In that way, wages and employment, in relatively well-paid jobs, will improve for the black laborers.

Free-market capitalism is a marvelous antidote for racism. In a free market, employers who refuse to hire productive black workers are hurting their own profits and the competitive position of their own company.

It is only when the state steps in that the government can socialize the costs of racism and establish an apartheid system.

The growth of capitalism in South Africa will do far more to end apartheid than the futile and counterproductive grandstanding of American liberals.

We the People vs. the Loot Seekers

Mark D. Hughes

We, the loot-seekers of the United States, in order to form more perfectly protected monopolies, impose injustices, insure domestic servitude, provide for our common defense against competition, promote our own welfare by securing the coercive powers of the state for ourselves and our posterity, do ordain and establish this Constitution for the United Special Interest Groups of America."

Those were not the words penned by the Founding Fathers, but who could tell from today's America? Over the last two centuries, we have seen our civil and economic liberties thwarted, despite the clear intent of the Founders. They sought to prevent the concentration of power in the hands of a privileged few. But regulatory legislation has enabled loot-seeking special interests to use the coercive powers of the state against the rest of us.

Ludwig von Mises called this a "caste system":

> Our age is full of serious conflicts of economic group interests. But these conflicts are not inherent in the operation of an unhampered capitalist economy. They are the necessary outcome of government policies interfering with the operation of the market. They are not conflicts of Marxian classes. They are brought about by the fact that mankind has gone back to group privileges and thereby to a new caste system. . . .
>
> In a free-market society . . . there are neither privileged nor underprivileged. There are no castes and therefore no caste conflicts. There prevails the full harmony of the rightly understood interests of all individuals and of all groups. . . .

One example of caste privilege began in 1937 when a few large New York dairies successfully lobbied the legislature for protective licensing. Under the law, still in effect, new licenses could be issued only if they do not cause "destructive competition."

There is, of course, no such thing as destructive competition for the consumer. Competition means lower prices, higher quality, and better service. To be sure, competition may be a nuisance for inefficient, established dairies. But it is not an annoyance to the milk-consuming public.

While the 1937 licensing law does not openly forbid the entry of new dairies into New York, that was its intent and effect. Until this January, the market was controlled by five large dairies. As a result, New York City consumers have traditionally paid a considerably higher price for milk than any other metropolitan area with a similar supply. In November 1986 the average price of a gallon of milk in New York City (except Staten Island) was $2.42. Philadelphia consumers paid $1.93.

Then in December 1985, after trying for seven years to gain access to the New York market, Farmland Dairies of Wallington, New Jersey, was reluctantly granted a license to serve Staten Island. The average price immediately dropped 40 cents per gallon and consistently remained about 30 cents cheaper than milk sold in the rest of New York City.

The New Jersey dairy spent the next year unsuccessfully trying to gain access to the rest of the city. On December 11, 1986, Agricultural Commissioner Gerace rejected Farmland's request because "it would tend to destructive competition . . . and would not be in the public interest."

The Commissioner's decision immediately became the topic of angry editorials throughout the state. Even statist politicians like New York's Mayor Ed Koch, recognizing the mood of the city's consumers, jumped on the band wagon.

New York Governor Cuomo claimed that he would like to see increased competition among milk dealers, but said he would not intervene in the Commissioners "quasi-judicial" decision.

The Governor had received $58,700 in campaign contributions from the dairy cartel. But the dairies' licensed overcharges have earned them more than $50 million a year, so it is not hard to understand the incentive for such donations, nor Governor Cuomo's decision not to intervene.

Although it is a relatively small example of state intervention, the New York dairy licensing law reflects the isolationist mentality indicative of all loot-seeking interests. It is no different from those seeking tariffs on foreign automobiles, restrictions on foreign investment, or business licensing for entrepreneurs.

The economic isolationists claim that restricting entry into a market will "save jobs." They argue that added competition from an external source will force local producers out of business and thereby cause irreparable damage to the economy of the region (whether a city, state, or nation). But clearly they know nothing of a market economy. As Henry Hazlitt wrote in his great *Economics in One Lesson*:

> This is the persistent tendency of men to see only the immediate effects of a given policy, or its effects only on a

special group, and to neglect to inquire what the long-run effects of that policy will be not only on that special group but on all groups. It is the fallacy of overlooking secondary consequences.

The secondary consequence of economic isolationism is simple—it reduces the actual and potential wealth of the community involved. By preventing competition in the New York dairy industry, the milk licensing law allows the dairy cartel to charge a higher price for milk than would exist in a free market. This is money the consuming public would spend on other goods and services in the community. It is true that added competition might force some of the inefficient dairies out of the market and some dairy workers would then be unemployed. However, contrary to what the economic isolationists claim, the story does not stop there, since more than $50 million a year of added consumer spending translates into *new* jobs in other businesses.

Even if the new jobs created just replace the old ones lost (probably not the case), the wealth of the community is still increased. After the price of milk is reduced, the consumer can do one of two things: 1) purchase the same amount of milk as usual for less money and spend what's left on other goods and services, or 2) spend the same amount of money on milk and take more milk home. Regardless of the choice, the amount of goods and services consumed by the public will increase even though the amount spent by each consumer did not change.

Someone understood at least part of this, however. On January 8, 1987, Federal Judge Leonard D. Wexler held that the decision to prohibit Farmland Dairies from distributing milk in all of New York City was unconstitutional. "It is clear," he said, "from Gerace's report that this decision to deny Farmland's license application was based on economic protectionism."

Farmland started delivering milk to seven supermarkets in the city on January 9. Each immediately lowered the price it charged the consumer by 20 cents a gallon. By January 17, prices had dropped between 30 and 71 cents per gallon.

Unfortunately, Judge Wexler did not declare the law itself unconstitutional, although he did say that this "would not be without foundation." The judge suggested this be left "to the discretion of the State Legislature."

So, despite the court's ruling, the New York City dairy market is still not free. New York has seen the price of milk drop, but we will never know how much more it will drop until the milk licensing law is repealed and all who want to compete are allowed to try.

The economic and civil liberty we still have in America exists not because legislators are concerned for the welfare of "We the people." Our liberty, and the chance we have to expand it, exists only because a heroic few refuse to stand aside while special interests impose a new two-caste system—the state privileged vs. the rest of us.

The Myth of the Trade Deficit

Sam Wells

Almost daily we read and hear demands from leaders of industry and demagogic politicians to increase restrictions on foreign imports because of the "unfavorable balance of trade" that America is supposed to have with other countries. Although the Reagan administration has paid lip service to free trade, it has drastically increased political obstructions to foreign imports. In 1981, approximately 25% of all goods imported into the United States were subject to some kind of U.S. government restrictions. Today, that figure has risen to 40%.

And now the president has sent to Congress legislation to stiffen restrictions on imports and pile another layer of controls on top of the bunch we already have. Since 1982 the administration has, through government-to-government negotiations and arm-twisting, secured 18 agreements that limit steel exports to the United States. Last year, the administration pressured Japan and Taiwan into agreeing to limit their exports of machine tools to the U.S. for the next five years. After failing to secure "voluntary" trade restraints from Switzerland and Germany, the administration set new quotas which rolled back exports from those countries. Also last year, it used threats to obtain agreements with South Korea, Hong Kong, and Japan that limited the growth in the quantity of textiles they could export to the U.S. to only 1% or less per year. And these are only a few examples of increasingly prevalent protectionism.

In ominous tones, we are told that the United States has incurred a "trade deficit" and that this means disaster. In late January, the government—from whom all such numbers flow—revealed that the trade deficit for 1986 had amounted to $169.8 billion, a record level. Gosh! But what does it mean? Was the president right when he referred to us as "trade patsies"? Are Americans being taken advantage of by the opportunity to buy low-priced, foreign-made products? Are the trade policies of the Japanese "cheating" us? The answer is a clear No.

The great Ludwig von Mises, writing in 1946, showed how free trade works to the benefit of all parties:

> Under free trade the Swiss watchmakers would expand their sales on the American market and the sales of their American competitors would shrink. But this is only a part of the consequences of free trade. Selling and producing more, the Swiss would earn and buy more. It does not mat-

> ter whether they themselves buy more of the products of other American industries or whether they increase their domestic purchases and those in other countries, for instance, in France. Whatever happens, the equivalent of the additional dollars they earned must finally go to the United States and increase the sales of some American industries. If the Swiss do not give away their products as a gift, they must spend these dollars in buying.

So, in the long run, trade can never take jobs away, but only add them to the American economy as a whole.

Moreover, artificially trying to prop up inefficient industries through protectionist trade policies hurts us all by driving up prices and holding down quality. These policies also hurt other, efficient U.S. industries by tying up resources and capital in the protected sectors, which would otherwise flow to more efficient uses and satisfy consumer needs less expensively. How many Americans have any notion of the high costs imposed by auto import restraints? Despite its laudable free-market rhetoric, the current administration pushed for "voluntary" restraints on the number of Japanese automobiles sold to Americans. This had the effect of narrowing the alternatives from which American consumers could choose—and hiked the price by nearly $2,000 per car. That's a total cost to American consumers of more than $250,000 for each U.S. auto-industry job supposedly saved. If you multiply that example by the number of other "protected" U.S. industries and jobs, the total burden to U.S. consumers amounts to $30-40 billion. And neo-mercantilist policies invite similar measures in retaliation from foreign governments whose leaders are also deluded by mercantilist myths.

Stepped-up protectionism in the U.S. Congress just in the last two years has already resulted in some very harmful foreign reprisals. While all American (and foreign) consumers are hurt by this war between governments, the American farmer has been especially hard hit. An editorial in *USA Today* noted:

> A typical wheat, soybean, or cotton farmer gets fifty percent of his income from foreign sales. And recent U.S. efforts to protect specialty steel, textiles, and other industries have led to heavy retaliation by other countries against our grain exports. We've lost farm sales worth many times what we saved in the protected industries.

When Americans choose to buy lower-cost imports, they have more money to spend or invest in other ways. This means they have more of their wants and needs satisfied for a given income.

The freedom of Americans to buy goods made in other countries gives them a wider choice, and that's all to the good. Not only has buying Japanese products not hurt Americans, but the money earned by the Japanese from their sales to us of VCRs, cars, stereos, cameras, and computer chips has come back to us in the form of Japanese investments.

If it were not for the inflow of this foreign capital (from Europe as well as Japan and elsewhere), the "crowding out" of domestic borrowers in our credit markets by big government's gargantuan budget deficits would have slammed us into a deep repression long before now. So, it has given us a little more precious time to put our own house in order. Instead of expressing gratitude for this salutary consequence, our demagogic politicians are trying to make the Japanese and other foreigners the scapegoats for ills which the politicos themselves created.

What about "dumping" (selling goods to Americans at prices allegedly "below the cost of production") or the Japanese keeping out U.S. goods? Japan is actually less protectionist than is the United States. And nobody can sell his products at below-cost for long without going out of business—much less making any profit. Besides, costs can only be subjectively determined, and they cannot be aggregated between or among industries, let alone countries. If "dumping" does occur, it is a great boon to Americans who take advantage of such bargains. (Why, by the way, isn't Safeway attacked by Giant for dumping when it sells ketchup at a nominal loss to attract customers?)

But what if the Japanese government subsidizes some of its exporting companies so they can increase their American market share by selling at below-cost prices? Since consumption is the end of production, and since consumers clearly benefit by such a good deal, why should we care? If foreigners are foolish enough to allow their governments to tax them to subsidize their exporting companies, we should take full advantage of their generosity. It won't last forever! (The only thing that apparently lasts forever is the U.S. government's massive subsidization of our exporting companies through the Export-Import Bank and other examples of corporate welfare.)

One of the most important notions underlying the calls for stifling foreign imports is the "balance of trade" concept and the idea that a "trade deficit" (your country imports more goods than it exports) is bad and that a "trade surplus" (your country exports more than it imports) is good. This is pure superstition and goes back to the mercantilist days of the 17th century.

The terms "deficit" and "surplus" are accounting terms that apply to budgets. But they have been misappropriated from the context in which they have meaning and used to describe international trade. A "trade surplus" means a "favorable balance of trade" (exports greater than imports), while a "trade deficit" is supposed to denote an "unfavorable balance of trade" (imports greater than exports). This is what we are told by the modern mercantilists and Keynesians. But this notion is as false as it is widespread in current discussions on international economics. Although this fallacy was refuted by the great French economist Richard Cantillon 275 years ago, many have not learned the lesson.

There is no reason why trade should "balance out" between countries at any specific moment—any more than it should balance out between individuals or companies doing business with each other. If you walk into a supermarket and buy a loaf of bread by exchanging money for it, you don't expect that particular supermarket to turn around and buy an equal amount of goods from you. It may take the money you gave for the bread and buy goods from somebody else, like a supplier or a truck farmer; but there's no reason that goods should balance out in trade between two parties. The buyer gives up money for goods, and the seller gives up goods for money. Both sides benefit. The same applies to people or firms living in different countries.

When Americans buy imports, they are simply accepting payment for the goods they export (sell) to foreigners. Imports pay for exports and exports pay for imports. There is no reason they should always balance. Taking a statistical snapshot of the flow of goods between countries at any single time and calling that the "balance of trade" is artificial, misleading, and irrelevant. We don't have to be concerned about it since it has no real bearing on the status or health of the economy. Yet, judging from all the media hype, we are supposed to fear a national "trade deficit" (which isn't even a real deficit at all) more than the very real and definitely harmful federal budget deficit!

Americans who wish to preserve and expand their liberty, and maximize their choices in the market, should work to repeal existing restrictions and taxes on imported goods, and vigorously oppose efforts in Congress to impose still more protectionist legislation. Despite what we hear from the politicians, there is no conflict between the principles of freedom and patriotism: free trade is in the best interests of Americans and America. Instead of clamoring for more political intrusions on our freedom to buy and sell, those genuinely concerned about the struggling sectors of U.S. industry should demand abolition of the taxes and controls which the U.S. government has clamped on our domestic industries. Let

American consumers have the freedom to choose to buy Sony and Honda. And liberate American producers from government.

Another Federal Crime Against Consumers

Llewellyn H. Rockwell, Jr.

The Reagan administration has verbally championed free trade while imposing more protectionism than any other administration since World War II. In 1981, about 25% of our imports were restricted in some way by the feds. Today, the figure is over 40%. And now we have an attack on American consumers in the name of retaliation against Japanese computer chips.

Because Japanese companies make these chips—the silicon hearts of computers—more economically than domestic producers, the administration has sought to protect inefficient U.S. firms at the expense of American consumers (and efficient U.S. firms).

The Japanese crime is "dumping": selling products below cost. But there is no way to tell if dumping is taking place. Austrian economics shows us that the notion of cost is necessarily a subjective and changing one. No government bureaucrat can tell what a company's cost is.

Even if dumping takes place, why should the police powers of the state be used to impede it? It can't be bad for consumers, and as Ludwig von Mises taught, it is from the standpoint of consumers that all economics and economic policy must be judged.

Even if true and taking place, why outlaw this consumer-enhancing process only internationally? Why not prevent

Safeway from selling ketchup at a loss to lure customers into its stores? Isn't "ketchup dumping" unfair to the A&P?

Because Japanese companies benefit American consumers by selling us computer chips at prices we want to pay, the president is levying 100% tariffs on some Japanese electronic goods. This punishes U.S. consumers with higher prices to benefit inefficient but politically influential U.S. corporations.

Trade restrictions are wrong on at least three counts:

1) *Moral.* By what right does the U.S. government seek to benefit special interests by telling Americans what consumer products we can or can't buy?

2) *Economic.* Protectionism, like all government interventions into the economy, rewards political pull at the expense of economic efficiency, and thus makes us all poorer.

3) *Political.* It is no coincidence that trade wars usually precede shooting wars. Why increase international tensions to pay off unsuccessful (but well-compensated) executives?

The collectivism that accompanies protectionism is off-putting as well: "Japan is harming 'us' by ________________ (fill in the blank)." What "us"? I have a lot more in common with a free-market Japanese businessman than I do with a protectionist and statist like Lee Iacocca, whether we share the same citizenship or not.

There's a big trade fight in Washington these days. But no one seems to care about the consumer. The battle instead is over whether the White House or the Congress will get political credit for protectionist rip-offs. Mises called capitalism the system of consumer sovereignty. Anything that inhibits that sovereignty makes us all poorer—and less free.

Economic Warfare Hurts Us More Than Them

Robert Higgs and Charlotte Twight

During the past decade the United States has repeatedly waged war, not with guns, missiles, and bombs, but with economic sanctions restricting the international transactions and travel of Americans.

Economic warfare—prohibitions of travel and commercial and financial dealings imposed selectively in order to alter the behavior of other governments—has been waged at one time or another since 1979 against Iran, Libya, Nicaragua, South Africa, and Syria as well as various communist countries.

Sanctions usually fail to attain their ostensible objective: they do not alter the conduct of other governments. But they do have significant domestic consequences. Americans suffer economic losses, both short-term and long-term. In effect, sanctions impose the costs of U.S. foreign policy on Americans interested in certain international commercial and financial deals or travel to certain countries.

Sanctions imposed after the Iranians took American hostages in Tehran in 1979 illustrate the erratic and arbitrary character of this instrument of foreign policy. President Carter first blocked all Iranian property in the United States and forbade most commercial and financial dealings with Iran. Then, as part of the deal to gain freedom for the hostages, Carter rescinded the sanctions, nullified attachments of Iranian property issued by federal courts, and suspended the legal claims of Americans against Iran. An Iran-United States Claims Tribunal was established in the Netherlands, and Americans were forbidden to press their claims in U.S. courts.

This extraordinary setting-aside of the judicial system by the president was challenged in an important 1981 Supreme Court case, *Dames & Moore V. Regan*. The Court's decision gave broad scope to the president's powers under the International Emergency Economic Powers Act, sustaining his nullification of courts' attachments of Iranian property. Moreover, the Court held that, even without explicit statutory authority, the president has constitutional power to suspend American claims in federal courts because of "a history of congressional acquiescence" in similar instances. Whatever Executive action Congress has never overtly disapproved, it has implicitly approved—a doctrine that would have astonished the Founding Fathers.

In making regulations to implement sanctions, the bureaucrats of the Treasury's Office of Foreign Assets Control (OFAC) have extraordinary discretion—the power to act arbitrarily and capriciously. Licenses may be denied, granted, or revoked at will. OFAC is not bound by the Administrative Procedure Act with regard to notice of proposed rule making, opportunity for public participation, or delay in effective date. OFAC officials may, and sometimes do, abruptly alter the rules solely at their pleasure. They often create loopholes for privileged parties, such as wholly-owned foreign subsidiaries of American oil companies that continue business as usual with Libya, notwithstanding the president's order that Americans cease operations in that country. Administrative officials may, as in the Iranian case, set aside the protections normally afforded private property rights by the U.S. judicial system.

Economic warfare rarely promotes the national interest effectively. Rather, it is a costly form of political theater. Only governmental officials, especially the president, normally benefit from it; and even that benefit is fleeting.

A president wages economic warfare because it enhances his popularity, if only momentarily. It diverts attention from intractable domestic problems and creates an image that he is strong, that he is "doing something" to defend or promote American interests beyond our borders.

The image has little substance. The governments of Iran, Libya, Nicaragua, South Africa, and Syria have not been visibly moved by U.S. sanctions against them. But American citizens have been hurt. Although some firms have found ways to circumvent the sanctions, important business has been lost—computer sales to South Africa, aircraft sales to Syria, all exports to Nicaragua. American reputations for reliable service have suffered in the world market, where alternative foreign suppliers are usually happy to take on the business denied Americans by their own government.

More importantly, economic warfare has shifted rights from private hands into the hands of governmental officials who are free to exercise their newly acquired powers with virtually unchecked discretion. Nothing of genuine public importance has been gained; bad political and legal precedents have become established; a little more liberty has been lost. As Ludwig von Mises pointed out in *The Free and Prosperous Commonwealth*: "Nationalist policies, which always begin by aiming at the ruination of one's neighbor, must, in the final analysis, lead to the ruination of all."

Protectionism and the Destruction of Prosperity

Murray N. Rothbard

Protectionism, often refuted and seemingly abandoned, has returned, and with a vengeance. The Japanese, who bounced back from grievous losses in World War II to astound the world by producing innovative, high-quality products at low prices, are serving as the convenient butt of protectionist propaganda. Memories of wartime myths, mixed with discrete anti-Oriental racism, can prove a heady brew, as protectionists warn about this new "Japanese imperialism," even "worse than Pearl Harbor." This "imperialism" turns out to consist of selling Americans wonderful Sony TV sets, autos, microchips, etc. at prices more than competitive with backward and lumbering American firms.

Is this "flood" of Japanese products really a menace, to be combated by the U.S. government? Or is the new Japan a godsend to American consumers?

In taking our stand on this issue, we should recognize that all government action means coercion, so that calling upon the U.S. government to intervene means urging it to use force and violence to restrain peaceful trade. One trusts that the protectionists are not willing to pursue their logic of force to the ultimate in the form of another Hiroshima and Nagasaki.

Keep Your Eye on the Consumer

As we unravel the tangled web of protectionist argument, we should keep our eye on two essential points: 1) protectionism means force in restraint of trade; and 2) the key is what happens to the consumer. Invariably, we will find that the protectionists are out to cripple, exploit, and impose severe losses not only on foreign consumers but especially on Americans. And since each and every one of us is a consumer, this means that protectionism is out to mulct all of us for the benefit of a specially privileged, subsidized few—and an inefficient few at that: people who cannot make it in a free and unhampered market.

Take, for example, the alleged Japanese menace. All trade is mutually beneficial to both parties—in this case Japanese producers and American consumers—otherwise they would not engage in the exchange. In trying to stop this trade, protectionists are trying to stop American consumers from enjoying high living standards by buying cheap and high-quality Japanese products. Instead, we are to be forced by government to return to the inefficient, higher-priced products we have already rejected. In short, inefficient producers are trying to deprive all of us of products we desire so that we will have to turn to inefficient firms. American consumers are to be plundered.

How To Look at Tariffs and Quotas

The best way to look at tariffs or import quotas or other protectionist restraints is to forget about political boundaries. Political boundaries of nations may be important for other reasons, but they have no economic meaning whatever. Suppose, for example, that each state of the United States were a separate nation. Then we would hear a lot of protectionist bellyaching that we are now fortunately spared. Think of the howls by inefficient, high-priced New York or Rhode Island textile manufacturers who would then be complaining about the "unfair," "cheap labor" competition from various low-type "foreigners" from Tennessee or North Carolina, or vice versa.

Fortunately, the absurdity of worrying about the balance of payments is made evident by focusing on interstate trade. For nobody worries about the balance of payments between New York and New Jersey, or, for that matter, between Manhattan and Brooklyn, because there are no customs officials recording such trade and such balances.

If we think about it, it is clear that a call by New York firms for a tariff against North Carolina is a pure ripoff of New York (as well as North Carolina) consumers, a naked grab for coerced special privilege by inefficient business firms. If the 50 states were separate nations, the protectionists would then be able to use the trappings of patriotism, and distrust of foreigners, to camouflage and get away with their looting the consumers of their own region.

Fortunately, interstate tariffs are unconstitutional. But even with this clear barrier, and even without being able to wrap themselves in the cloak of nationalism, protectionists have been able to impose interstate tariffs in another guise. Part of the drive for continuing increases in the federal minimum wage law is to impose a protectionist device against lower-wage, lower-labor-cost competition from North Carolina and other southern states against their New England and New York competitors.

During the 1966 Congressional battle over a higher federal minimum wage, for example, the late Senator Jacob Javits (R-NY) freely admitted that one of his main reasons for supporting the bill was to cripple the southern competitors of New York textile firms. Since southern wages are generally lower than in the north, the business firms (and the workers struck by unemployment) hardest hit by an increased minimum wage will be located in the south.

Another way in which interstate trade restrictions have been imposed has been in the fashionable name of "safety." Government-organized state milk cartels in New York, for example, have prevented importation of milk from nearby New Jersey under the patently spurious grounds that the trip across the Hudson would render New Jersey milk "unsafe."

If tariffs and restraints on trade are good for a country, then why not indeed for a state or region? The principle is precisely the same. In America's first great depression, the Panic of 1819, Detroit was a tiny frontier town of only a few hundred people. Yet protectionist cries arose—fortunately not fulfilled—to prohibit all "imports" from outside of Detroit, and citizens were exhorted to "buy only Detroit." If this nonsense had been put into effect, general starvation and death would have ended all other economic problems for Detroiters.

So why not restrict and even prohibit trade, i.e. "imports," into a city, or a neighborhood, or even on a block, or, to boil it down to its logical conclusion, to one family? Why shouldn't the Jones family issue a decree that from now on, no member of the family can buy any goods or services produced outside the family house? Starvation would quickly wipe out this ludicrous drive for self-sufficiency.

And yet we must realize that this absurdity is inherent in the logic of protectionism. Standard protectionism is just as preposterous, but the rhetoric of nationalism and national boundaries has been able to obscure this vital fact.

The upshot is that protectionism is not only nonsense, but dangerous nonsense, destructive of all economic prosperity. We are not, if we were ever, a world of self-sufficient farmers. The market economy is one vast latticework throughout the world, in which each individual, each region, each country, produces what he or it is best at, most relatively efficient in, and exchanges that product for the goods and services of others. Without the division of labor and the trade based upon that division, the entire world would starve. Coerced restraints on trade—such as protectionism—cripple, hobble, and destroy trade, the source of life and prosperity. Protectionism is simply a plea that consumers, as well as general prosperity, be hurt so as to confer permanent special privilege upon groups of inefficient producers, at the expense of competent firms and of consumers. But it is a peculiarly destructive kind of bailout, because it permanently shackles trade under the cloak of patriotism.

The Negative Railroad

Protectionism is also peculiarly destructive because it acts as a coerced and artificial increase in the cost of transportation between regions. One of the great features of the Industrial Revolution, one of the ways in which it brought prosperity to the starving masses, was by reducing drastically the cost of transportation. The development of railroads in the early 19th century, for example, meant that for the first time in the history of the human race, goods could be transported cheaply over land. Before that, water—rivers and oceans—was the only economically viable means of transport. By making land transport accessible and cheap, railroads allowed interregional land transportation to break up expensive inefficient local monopolies. The result was an enormous improvement in living standards for all consumers. And what the protectionists want to do is lay an axe to this wonderous principle of progress.

It is no wonder that Frederic Bastiat, the great French laissez-faire economist of the mid-19th century, called a tariff a "negative railroad." Protectionists are just as economically destructive as if they were physically chopping up railroads, or planes, or ships, and forcing us to revert to the costly transport of the past—mountain trails, rafts, or sailing ships.

"Fair" Trade

Let us now turn to some of the leading protectionist arguments. Take, for example, the standard complaint that while the protectionist "welcomes competition," this competition must be "fair." Whenever someone starts talking about "fair competition" or indeed, about "fairness" in general, it is time to keep a sharp eye on your wallet, for it is about to be picked. For the genuinely "fair" is simply the voluntary terms of exchange, mutually agreed upon by buyer and seller. As most of the medieval scholastics were able to figure out, there is no "just" (or "fair") price outside of the market price.

So what could be "unfair" about the free-market price? One common protectionist charge is that it is "unfair" for an American firm to compete with, say, a Taiwanese firm which needs to pay only one-half the wages of the American competitor. The U.S. government is called upon to step in and "equalize" the wage rates by imposing an equivalent tariff upon the Taiwanese. But does this mean that consumers can never patronize low-cost firms because it is "unfair" for them to have lower costs than inefficient competitors? This is the same argument that would be used by a New York firm trying to cripple its North Carolina competitor.

What the protectionists don't bother to explain is why U.S. wage rates are so much higher than Taiwan. They are not imposed by Providence. Wage rates are high in the U.S. because American employers have bid these rates up. Like all other prices on the market, wage rates are determined by supply and demand, and the increased demand by U.S. employers has bid wages up. What determines this demand? The "marginal productivity" of labor.

The demand for any factor of production, including labor, is constituted by the productivity of that factor, the amount of revenue that the worker, or the pound of cement or acre of land, is expected to bring to the brim. The more productive the factory, the greater the demand by employers, and the higher its price or wage rate. American labor is more costly than Taiwanese because it is far more productive. What makes it productive? To some extent, the comparative qualities of labor, skill, and education. But most of the difference is not due to the personal qualities of the laborers themselves, but to the fact that the American laborer, on the whole, is equipped with more and better capital equipment than his Taiwanese counterparts. The more and better the capital investment per worker, the greater the worker's productivity, and therefore the higher the wage rate.

In short, if the American wage rate is twice that of the Taiwanese, it is because the American laborer is more heavily capitalized, is equipped with more and better tools, and is therefore, on the average, twice as productive. In a sense, I suppose, it is not "fair" for the American worker to make more than the Taiwanese, not because of his personal qualities, but because savers and investors have supplied him with more tools. But a wage rate is determined not just by personal quality but also by relative scarcity, and in the United States the worker is far scarcer compared to capital than he is in Taiwan.

Putting it another way, the fact that American wage rates are on the average twice that of the Taiwanese, does not make the cost of labor in the U.S. twice that of Taiwan. Since U.S. labor is twice as productive, this means that the double wage rate in the U.S. is offset by the double productivity, so that the cost of labor per unit product in the U.S. and Taiwan tends, on the average, to be the same. One of the major protectionist fallacies is to confuse the price of labor (wage rates) with its cost, which also depends on its relative productivity.

Thus, the problem faced by American employers is not really with the "cheap labor" in Taiwan, because "expensive labor" in the U.S. is precisely the result of the bidding for scarce labor by U.S. employers. The problem faced by inefficient U.S. textile or auto firms is not so much cheap labor in Taiwan or Japan, but the fact that other U.S. industries are efficient enough to afford it, because they bid wages that high in the first place.

So, by imposing protective tariffs and quotas to save, bail out, and keep in place inefficient U.S. textile or auto or microchip firms, the protectionists are injuring the American consumer. They are also harming efficient U.S. firms and industries, which are prevented from employing resources now locked into incompetent firms, and who would otherwise be able to expand and sell their efficient products at home and abroad.

"Dumping"

Another contradictory line of protectionist assault on the free market asserts that the problem is not so much the low costs enjoyed by foreign firms, as the "unfairness" of selling their products "below costs" to American consumers, and thereby engaging in the pernicious and sinful practice of "dumping." By such dumping they are able to exert unfair advantage over American firms who presumably never engage in such practices and make sure that their prices are always high enough to cover costs. But if selling below costs is such a powerful weapon, why isn't it ever pursued by business firms within a country?

Our first response to this charge is, once again, to keep our eye on consumers in general and on American consumers in particular. Why should it be a matter of complaint when consumers so clearly benefit? Suppose, for example, that Sony is willing to injure American competitors by selling TV sets to Americans for a penny apiece. Shouldn't we rejoice at such an absurd policy of suffering severe losses by subsidizing us, the American consumers? And shouldn't our response be: "Come on, Sony, subsidize us some more!" As far as consumers are concerned, the more "dumping" that takes place, the better.

But what of the poor American TV firms, whose sales will suffer so long as Sony is virtually willing to give their sets away? Well, surely, the sensible policy for RCA, Zenith, etc. would be to hold back production and sales until Sony drives itself into bankruptcy. But suppose that the worst happens, and RCA, Zenith, etc. are themselves driven into bankruptcy by the Sony price war? Well, in that case, we the consumers will still be better off, since the plants of the bankrupt firms, which would still be in existence, would be picked up for a song at auction, and the American buyers at auction would be able to enter the TV business and outcompete Sony because they now enjoy far lower capital costs.

For decades, indeed, opponents of the free market have claimed that many businesses gained their powerful status on the market by what is called "predatory price-cutting," that is, by driving their smaller competitors into bankruptcy by selling their goods below cost, and then reaping the reward of their unfair methods by raising their prices and thereby charging "monopoly prices" to the consumers. The claim is that while consumers may gain in the short-run by price wars, "dumping," and selling below costs, they lose in the long-run from the alleged monopoly. But, as we have seen, economic theory shows that this would be a mug's game, losing money for the "dumping" firms, and never really achieving a monopoly price. And sure enough, historical investigation has not turned up a single case where predatory pricing, when tried, was successful, and there are actually very few cases where it has even been tried.

Another charge claims that Japanese or other foreign firms can afford to engage in dumping because their governments are willing to subsidize their losses. But again, we should still welcome such an absurd policy. If the Japanese government is really willing to waste scarce resources subsidizing American purchases of Sony's, so much the better! Their policy would be just as self-defeating as if the losses were private.

There is yet another problem with the charge of "dumping," even when it is made by economists or other alleged "experts" sitting on impartial tariff commissions and government bureaus, there is no way whatever that outside observers, be they economists, businessmen, or other experts, can decide what some other firm's "costs" may be. "Costs" are not objective entities that can be gauged or measured. Costs are subjective to the businessman himself, and they vary continually, depending on the businessman's time horizon or the stage of production or selling process he happens to be dealing with at any given time.

Suppose, for example, a fruit dealer has purchased a case of pears for $20, amounting to $1 a pound. He hopes and expects to sell those pears for $1.50 a pound. But something has happened to the pear market, and he finds it impossible to sell most of the pears at anything near that price. In fact, he finds that he must sell the pears at whatever price he can get before they become overripe. Suppose he finds that he can only sell his stock of pears at 70 cents a pound. The outside observer might say that the fruit dealer has, perhaps "unfairly," sold his pears "below costs," figuring that the dealer's costs were $1 a pound.

"Infant" Industries

Economists agree on very little. But economists agree virtually unanimously on one thing: their oppostion to protectionism. Classically, they made one unfortunate exception, an exception which the specially privileged were able to use and magnify to become an enormous hole in the free-trade case. This argument held that the government should provide a temporary protective tariff to aid, or to bring into being, an "infant industry." Then, when the industry was well established, the government would and should remove the tariff and toss the now "mature" industry into the competitive swim.

The theory was fallacious, and the policy proved disastrous in practice. For there is no more need for government to protect a new, young, industry from foreign competition than there is to protect it from domestic competition.

In the last few decades, the "infant" plastics, television, and computer industries made out very well without such protection. Any government subsidizing of a new industry will funnel too many resources into that industry as compared to older firms, and will also inaugurate distortions that may persist and render the firm or industry permanently inefficient and vulnerable to competition. As a result, "infant-industry" tariffs have tended to become permanent, regardless of the "maturity" of the industry. The proponents were carried away by a misleading biological analogy to "infants" who need adult care. But a business firm is not a person, young or old.

Older Industries

Indeed, in recent years, older industries that are notoriously inefficient have been using what might be called a "senile-industry" argument for protectionism. Steel, auto, and other outcompeted industries have been complaining that they "need a breathing space" to retool and become competitive with foreign rivals, and that this breather could be provided by several years of tariffs or import quotas. This argument is just as full of holes as the hoary infant-industry approach, except that it will be even more difficult to figure out when the "senile" industry will have become magically rejuvenated. In fact, the steel industry has been inefficient ever since its inception, and its chronological age seems to make no difference. The first protectionist movement in the U.S. was launched in 1820, headed by the Pennsylvania iron (later iron and steel) industry, artificially force-fed by the War of 1812 and already in grave danger from far more efficient foreign competitors.

The Non-Problem of the Balance of Payments

A final set of arguments, or rather alarms, centers on the mysteries of the balance of payments. Protectionists focus on the horrors of imports being greater than exports, implying that if market forces continued unchecked, Americans might wind up buying everything from abroad, while selling foreigners nothing, so that American consumers will have engorged themselves to the permanent ruin of American business firms. But if the exports really fell to somewhere near zero, where in the world would Americans still find the money to purchase foreign products? The balance of payments, as we said earlier, is a pseudo-problem created by the existence of customs statistics.

During the day of the gold standard, a deficit in the national balance of payments was a problem, but only because of the nature of the fractional-reserve banking system. If U.S. banks, spurred on by the Fed or previous forms of central banks, inflated money and credit, the American inflation would lead to higher prices in the U.S., and this would discourage exports and encourage imports. The resulting deficit had to be paid for in some way, and during the gold standard era this meant being paid for in gold, the international money. So as bank credit expanded, gold began to flow out of the country, which put the fractional-reserve banks in even shakier shape. To meet the threat to their solvency posed by the gold outflow, the banks eventually were forced to contract credit, precipitating a recession and reversing the balance of payment deficits, thus bringing gold back into the country.

But now, in the fiat-money era, balance of payments deficits are truly meaningless. For gold is no longer a "balancing item." In effect, there is no deficit in the balance of payments. It is true that in the last few years, imports have been greater than exports by $150 billion or so per year. But no gold flowed out of the country. Neither did dollars "leak" out. The alleged "deficit" was paid for by foreigners investing the equivalent amount of money in American dollars: in real estate, capital goods, U.S. securities, and bank accounts.

In effect, in the last couple of years, foreigners have been investing enough of their own funds in dollars to keep the dollar high, enabling us to purchase cheap imports. Instead of worrying and complaining about this development, we should rejoice that foreign investors are willing to finance our cheap imports. The only problem is that this bonanza is already coming to an end, with the dollar becoming cheaper and exports more expensive.

We conclude that the sheaf of protectionist arguments, many plausible at first glance, are really a tissue of egregious fallacies. They betray a complete ignorance of the most basic economic analysis. Indeed, some of the arguments are almost embarrassing replies of the most ridiculous claims of 17th-century mercantilism: for example, that it is somehow a calamitous problem that the U.S. has a balance of trade deficit, not overall, but merely with one specific country, e.g. Japan.

Must we even relearn the rebuttals of the more sophisticated mercantilists of the 18th century: namely, that balance with individual countries will cancel each other out, and therefore that we should only concern ourselves with the overall balance? (Let alone realize that the overall balance is no problem either.) But we need not reread the economic literature from Adam Smith to the present-day to realize that the impetus for protectionism comes not from preposterous theories, but from the quest for coerced special privilege and restraint of trade at the expense of efficient competitors and consumers.

In the host of special interests using the political process to repress and loot the rest of us, the protectionists are among the most venerable. It is high time that we get them, once and for all, off our backs, and treat them with the righteous indignation they so richly deserve.

4

GREAT ECONOMISTS

A Call to Activism

Margit von Mises

Thank you, Mr. Rockwell, for your most generous and gracious remarks. Thank you all who came here tonight, for without you, I would not be here. And thank you especially for your kind welcome. I know, of course, that this welcome is really meant for my husband, in whose name I gladly and gratefully accept it.

People often ask me, "Aren't you proud about what you have done?" I can only say, "no." I really am not. I am happy that the ideas of my husband get more and more recognition, but I am not proud. I did only what I *had* to do. It was an inner "must."

Perhaps you will be interested to learn how this book,

which you will all receive through the kindness of Mr. Rockwell, came into being.

When my husband died on October 10, 1973, I could not even cry. I was like a stone. It took two months until the first tears came into my eyes. My daughter, Gitta, and Don, my son-in-law, who live and work in London, insisted that I come and stay with them for a while. They suggested that I make a reservation on the Queen Elizabeth, which at that time still regularly crossed the Atlantic. They knew how much I loved the sea. And so I got my reservation for the month of February 1974. The sailing was rough, but I loved every minute of it. Most of the time I spent on deck, where I was pretty much alone. It was so stormy and cold that most passengers preferred the warmth of the staterooms. But a friendly steward kept a chair for me facing the water. He covered me with blankets, and I could watch the seagulls following the boat from morning to night, shrieking, their wings fluttering, always moving. Dark clouds covered the sky. Sometimes the wind was so strong that water came over the railing. But I was safe and warm, watched over by this kind steward.

I tried to read, but I couldn't. Always I thought of my husband, the years we spent together, but suddenly, it was as if a thunderbolt struck me. "Why don't you write about him? Why don't you put down on paper everything you know?" And I decided to do so.

I did not even have a notebook or pencil with me when my mind started to work. But in my thoughts I divided the book into eleven chapters. I decided on all their titles, and I never changed a single one of them. For example, I knew I had to write one chapter about *Human Action*. People had to know how my husband suffered about this, his greatest work.

The boat landed one day late, and I stayed with my children and started writing, never telling anyone a word. It took me two years to finish the book. Often I rewrote a chapter four or five times, but I never changed the table of contents. (Except for the second edition, which has two new chapters.) All research was done carefully, and every word I wrote is true.

If I told you before that I am not proud of the work I have done, then I must tell you now that there is something I *am* proud of. And that is that all of my husband's former students, from the Vienna seminar as well as the New York seminar—with very few exceptions—became, since my husband's death, *my* friends also. They stayed by my side all the time, all the way, and helped me when I needed help.

I want to mention first of all my very dear friend Professor Fritz Machlup, who died on January 30, 1983, of a heart attack. Since his student days in Vienna, he had been especially devoted to my husband, even though they did not agree in all their economic views. But it was as if—after my husband's death—he wanted to prove his great admiration for his beloved teacher by helping and advising me. It was on his advice that I wrote the new chapter about the Vienna seminar. He guided and supervised and helped me, in his wonderfully kind and charming way, and I shall never forget him.

I also want to give special thanks to Professor Israel Kirzner, who helped me put the material together for a chapter on Austrian economics. Here is another example of a famous man who has helped me because of his devotion to his great teacher. Another one of these famous pupils who has always most willingly helped is Nobel Prize winner Friedrich von Hayek, about whom I wrote so much in *My Years With Ludwig von Mises.*

But now I have to come back to the story of how the book came to life. I had already finished five chapters, and still no one knew anything about it.

Let me first tell you about a good friend of mine, Nellie Erickson. Nellie is the creator of the famous bronze bust of my husband, with copies now in so many different parts of the world. One day Nellie and her husband George invited me to join them on a Sunday trip on their yacht on Long

Island Sound. With them were Ilo and George Koether, our mutual friends. It was a beautiful day. The sun was hot and the sea glittered like gold. I was sitting on a winch when George Koether joined me and said, "You know, Margit, I thought so much about you. I wonder why you don't write a book about your husband." It was then that I could no longer keep my secret. The words poured out of me, and I told him everything.

He was enthusiastic about the news, and immediately offered all the help he could give. I asked him to keep silent about it, and told him I would accept gladly—but I wanted no ghost writing. The story was absolutely mine. He promised, and from that moment he became one of the best advisors and helpers I could have found. Always ready to do something for me, he never let me down.

When I finished the book, George Koether showed the manuscript to Neil McCaffrey, then president of Arlington House, Publishers, and one day later the book was accepted. No other publisher had ever seen it.

What happened afterward came without my asking for it: one work followed another. And so these ten years went by, and it still seems as if my husband died only yesterday.

Those who have read my book will remember much about my husband that the general public does not know. But there was one aspect of his life that I did not describe in my book, and this is an appropriate occasion on which to emphasize it.

Professor Hayek once called my husband "a great radical, an intelligent and rational radical, but nonetheless a radical on the right lines." This was correct, but Ludwig von Mises was also an *activist*—an *activist of the mind*. Not only did he write scholarly books containing great wisdom—he also promoted the free market in speeches, articles, lectures, and seminars. And he worked hard as an *activist* at his desk in the solitude of his study.

He did not confine his interest and time to writing and to contact with scholars only—although the brilliant scholars who developed out of his teachings, the professors Hayek, Haberler, Morgenstern, Machlup, and many more, could justifiably have claimed all his attention. He also had the time and interest for others: businessmen, journalists, and members of many professions other than teaching. To all of those people with whom he came in contact he was an *activist of the mind*. He stimulated the interest, and then the understanding of all the people he met. And he did even more. He stimulated them to *action*.

Think, for example, of Professor Murray Rothbard, who has written, and is still writing, brilliant books extending the influence of Austrian economics, and who—with some friends—founded the Center for Libertarian Studies which works to foster libertarian scholarship, following in economics solely the ideas of Ludwig von Mises.

Think of Antony Fisher, whose Atlas Economic Research Foundation has brought about the creation of nineteen institutes in twelve countries throughout the world, always mentioning Ludwig von Mises and quoting Weaver, "Ideas have consequences."

Think of Leonard Read, the late founder of the Foundation for Economic Education, who—after meeting my husband and reading all of his books—gave students as well as teachers the opportunity to learn about individual freedom and the free market. Out of this foundation came great men like Baldy Harper, who founded the Institute for Humane Studies, and George Roche, who is now president of Hillsdale College, which shelters the Ludwig von Mises Library, and who heads his own Shavano Institute in Colorado, never asking for help from the government.

And last, but certainly not least, think of Lew Rockwell and the Ludwig von Mises Institute, which in a very short time has attracted 14,000 contributors, begun an extensive teaching, fellowship, and publications program, held a very successful conference on the gold standard in Washington, D.C., and become integrated with Auburn University. Never before has a university and an institute of this kind entered into a partnership.

Yes, Ludwig von Mises was an activist, whose influence has reached—and is still reaching—far over the world. Imagine how much better our world would be today if all those "activists" who chant for womens' rights, for gay rights, for tenants' rights, for minorities' rights, were working to correct the *true* cause of our social problems! Imagine how much better off we would be if those who blame the West for the plight of the so-called underdeveloped nations could be taught the economic facts of life as demonstrated by Ludwig von Mises!

They *can* be taught, if all of us become activists of the mind. If each of us will do this—in his or her own way—we may accomplish more than we now imagine. And we will do it, not like mindless sports fans cheering for their hero, but out of dedication to those principles of truth and freedom for which my husband fought. We *must* do it—not simply out of admiration for a man like Ludwig von Mises. We must do it because we are dedicated to the principles which he elaborated so well in his many great works.

Is it idle—now, in these dark days when the shadows of Communist dictatorship reach over more than half the world—to dream of a day when knowledge instead of ignorance, respect instead of hate, peace instead of war, freedom instead of force, will reign over the world? Not if we spread the truth as my husband did.

I can see a day when *every* great university will have in its economics department a bust of Ludwig von Mises, when all of his writings will be combined in one grand edition available in every library of any size.

I can see a day when economics will be taught as human action—including every subject that those words imply—and not broken up into courses that produce mathematicians instead of economists.

I can see the day when more and more followers of my husband's thoughts will produce book after book and paper after paper elaborating on the fundamental ideas contained in his works. (And this day has arrived already.)

I can see an anthology of my husband's thoughts published in a series of books dealing with specific issues that are getting attention in the daily press. The special edition of the *Freeman* magazine that appeared on the 100th anniversary of my husband's birthday indicates the possibilities I see in this direction.

I can see more universities asking the Ludwig von Mises Institute for assistance in choosing professors to teach the economics of the free market. And I can see, as an activity of the Institute, establishment of fellowships to permit young journalists to enjoy a full year of study in Austrian economics to further their understanding and ability to better report events in the daily press.

I could go on and on—but many of you will have even more ideas than those I have just mentioned. In order to achieve *anything*, however, we must *all* become activists. We have no choice. As Ludwig von Mises said many years ago, in words I once quoted at Hillside:

"Everyone carries a part of society on his shoulders; no one is relieved of his share of responsibility by others. And no one can find a safe way for himself if society is sweeping towards destruction. Therefore everyone, in his own interests, must thrust himself vigorously into the intellectual battle. No one can stand aside with unconcern: the interests of everyone hang on the result. Whether he chooses or not, every man is drawn into the great historical struggle, the decisive battle into which our epoch has plunged us."

I feel confident that the Ludwig von Mises Institute will do much more than "carry its part of society on its shoulders."

We have the intellectual leadership, the managerial expertise, and the burning desire to succeed. And, happily for us, we have the truth on our side.

If anyone doubts that, let him or her look at all the calamities, the miseries, the cruelties, and the stupidities of every form of collectivism and interventionism. With truth on our side we cannot, we must not, we *will not* fail!

Thank you. Thank you very much for listening to me.

Mrs. Mises delivered this speech in February 27, 1984 at the Mises Institute dinner in her honor in New York City.

Ludwig von Mises: Hero

Llewellyn H. Rockwell, Jr.

When Ludwig von Mises died in New York City in 1973 at the age of 92, the liberals hardly noticed. There was no front page obituary in the *New York Times* and Walter Cronkite didn't mention it on the CBS Evening News. But libertarians and conservatives knew that a giant had fallen, for Mises had the greatest mind of our time, and he had employed it in a life-long, uncompromising, and effective fight for freedom.

Today, his influence is more widespread than ever before. And his ideas remain the core of the movement for a free market, sound money, private property, and individual liberty. As his great student Murray N. Rothbard pointed out, "If the world is ever to get out of its miasma of statism, it will have to move to the high ground that Mises developed for us."

Ludwig von Mises was born in 1881 in the Austro-Hungarian Empire city of Lemberg, the son of a successful engineer. At the age of 19, he entered the University of Vienna, and received his doctorate at 27.

At this time, the university was the world center of free-market economics, and Mises studied under its two greatest teachers, Carl Menger and Eugen von Böhm-Bawerk. These two founders of the Austrian school of economics were responsible for a revolution in economics that successfully refuted Marxism—something the followers of Adam Smith had been unable to do.

Smith could not understand why, for example, diamonds should be more expensive than food, since food is so much more useful. This "value paradox" could never be solved, he said. All value that could be understood, however, came from the labor that went into production. Followers of Smith agreed, and said that diamonds must have a higher "exchange" value while food had a higher "use" value. They also saw a class conflict, claiming that if wages went up, profits would have to go down, and vice versa.

Karl Marx, building on these errors, preached class war, and said that profit must therefore be "surplus value" stolen from the workers, and that the only just system was production for "use" rather than profit.

The Austrian economists solved the problem by focusing on the individual, and not on classes. They built their theories on the actions of consumers in the real world, and saw that each of us makes decisions based on our own personal preferences, and that business people are constantly trying to serve those preferences. Therefore, economic value cannot be inherent in products; it is only conferred by consumer desires.

I might spend an entire week making a giant mud pie, but a product that has no value to consumers has no economic worth, no matter how much labor goes into it.

And, yes, all the foods in the world is more valuable than all the diamonds, but we are never forced to make that choice. Instead, we make our economic valuations "at the margin." That is, the greater the number of units of a desired economic good, the less we will value any given unit, and vice versa. That's why a canteen of water has so much more value in the desert than in your kitchen sink.

The Austrians also showed that capital—and its share of production, i.e. profit—was as necessary as labor, and that in a free market, they work together to satisfy consumers. The only "conflict" is between competitors, not between owners and employees, and that conflict is over who can best satisfy consumers.

The classical economists—Smithian and Marxian—also did not understand the role of interest. The Austrians, again looking at individuals, saw that people would rather consume now than in the future. All other things being equal, we would rather take a vacation this year than next. Thus "time-preference" is the reason for interest: the payment for deferring consumption.

Investors who put up capital to start a business are also deferring consumption (whereas employees get paid immediately), and their payment is called profit. In fact, the "normal" rate of profit in a free market is the interest rate.

In this stimulating atmosphere the young Ludwig von Mises studied, and in the honored tradition of scholarship, went on to surpass his teachers. For, as great as the founders of the Austrian school were, there were serious gaps and errors in their theories. Mises filled the gaps, corrected the errors, and went on to rebuild the entire science of economics on a sound free-market basis.

This would have been a magnificent and enduring achievement had Mises, like his teachers, been able to work in peace. His great work is all the more incredible because it was accomplished at great personal cost and despite unceasing opposition from academic leftists in Europe and the U.S.

After receiving his Ph.D., the young Mises set to work on *The Theory of Money and Credit*, his first great work published in 1912. The earlier Austrians, mimicking one of Smith's mistakes, had put money in a separate category from the rest of the economy. Mises repaired this split, showing that just as the price of any commodity is determined by supply and demand, so is the "price" of money, its purchasing power. The demand for money is determined by the desire of consumers to hold cash rather than something else.

Some of the classical economists, especially David Ricardo, had seen that an increase in the supply of money causes prices to increase. But Mises showed that this increase is not proportional. When the government increases the money supply, the "price level" doesn't rise by that amount. The amount and speed of price increases depend on the people's desire to hold cash. That's why, during an inflation, prices can increase faster or slower than the money supply.

Mises also showed that inflation, through relative price changes, brings about a redistribution of wealth, from savers and earners to the banking system and the government and related special interests. Even more damaging, he showed, are the misinvestments that inflation brings about.

When government inflates, it lowers the interest rate below what it would otherwise have been. This encourages bad business and investment decisions during the inflationary boom. When the inflation slows or stops, these mistakes are seen for what they are, and the result is bankruptcies and unemployment. That is, government is the cause of the business cycle. Through inflation, it brings about recessions and depressions.

In this pathbreaking book, Mises also showed that the institution of money originated in the market as a valuable commodity, and was only later nationalized (and debauched) by government. He also demonstrated that gold is the best monetary commodity, and that only a gold standard could prevent inflation. A central bank (like the Federal Reserve to be established the next year), he noted, would inevitably bring recessions, depressions, and suffering for the majority, although a small minority would benefit from its depredations.

The publication of *The Theory of Money and Credit* made the 31-year old Mises one of the top economists in Europe, but World War I was soon to end the gold standard and relative laissez-faire of the previous century, and renew the ancient evils of statism and inflation.

The new atmosphere was, of course, much less conducive to a man like Ludwig von Mises, and as a result he never received the academic rewards that were his due. Although he was appointed a professor of economics at the University of Vienna, it was to an unsalaried position. His income, from 1909 until 1934 when he left Austria, came from his position as economic advisor to the Austrian Chamber of Commerce, a government body roughly equivalent to the U.S. Department of Commerce. This was also where he established the prestigious Austrian Institute for Business Cycle Research.

Among his duties, he had to write economic analyses of proposed government actions, and he managed almost single-handedly to keep Austria from following Germany into hyperinflation during the early 1920s.

His famous Mises seminar in these years attracted the best minds in Europe, and produced many great economists including Nobel-prize winner F. A. Hayek. In addition to his unpaid teaching and his government work, Mises continued his writing and research. His next major work came in 1922: *Socialism*.

This book demonstrated that socialism could not function in an industrial economy. Since they have no free-market price system, socialist planners are incapable of calculating costs or rationally planning production. The result of any socialist system, he predicted, would be economic chaos.

And, just as important, he showed that semi-socialism or government interventionism cannot function efficiently either. So, he noted, if total or partial government planning cannot work, we are left with the free market.

Not content with being the leading champion of the free market, Mises also set to work on the foundation of economics —its "methodology." Mises saw that economics was increasingly coming under the sway of the nihilistic "institutionalism" which virtually denies economics altogether, and of the pseudo-scientific "positivism," which apes physics and treats people as mere consciousless objects.

Mises's answer was the science of "praxeology," which bases economics on the deductive logic that human beings are unique individuals, each with their own purposes and their own ideas about how to achieve them. His major works here were *Epistemological Problems of Economics* and especially the later *Theory and History* and *Ultimate Foundation of Economic Science*.

Mises saw that positivism, which has since swept the non-Austrian portions of the economics profession, was especially dangerous. Not only was it scientifically invalid, but by treating people as inanimate objects to be manipulated, it gave would-be social engineers the perfect intellectual framework and justification for their destructive activities.

Despite all the early opposition, Mises, during this time, saw a quickening of interest in his ideas, although it was only a temporary spring. When other economists were proclaiming the new age of perpetual prosperity in the 1920s, Mises was the only one to predict the Great Depression. In the early 1930s, many important economists became Misesians, but after the publication of John Maynard Keynes's *General Theory* swept the academic world, Mises's followers—with the shining exception of F.A. Hayek—became Keynesians.

Undaunted, and in exile in Geneva from fascist Austria, Mises next set about to reconstruct the whole of economics upon the individualistic foundation he had built. He did it in his monumental *Nationalokönomie*, published in 1940 and instantly forgotten in the turmoil of World War II. It was this work, later expanded and translated into English as the 900-page *Human Action*, that was his crowning achievement.

In Geneva came another milestone in Mises's life; he married the beautiful Margit Sereny—after warning her that while he would write much about money, he would never have much of it—and in 1940 they immigrated to the United States.

At a time when every left-wing professor was given a high academic post in the United States, Mises was refused any job—a permanent blot on American universities. Finally, with the help of Henry Hazlitt and Lawrence Fertig, Mises secured a visiting professorship at New York University's Graduate School of Business. His salary was paid by business people and foundations, and he was never a regular member of the faculty.

Treated as a second-class citizen by the university, whose business school dean lobbied good students not to take his classes (which were relegated to the basement and scheduled at inconvenient times), Mises was neither bitter nor resentful. With gentle brilliance, he carried on the fight for Austrian economics and freedom. "We well knew," wrote Professor Rothbard, "that in the very aura and person of Ludwig von Mises that we were seeing an embodiment of the Old Vienna of a far nobler and more charming day. Those of us privileged to attend his seminar at NYU could well understand how Mises was a great teacher as well as a great economist."

When he retired in 1969, a spry 87, Ludwig von Mises had been the oldest active professor in the United States. He could look back on a lifetime of teaching and writing—25 books and more than 250 scholarly articles—and of incredible achievements for liberty. His students Wilhelm Roepke and Ludwig Erhard had turned West Germany towards freedom and the resulting "economic miracle." In Italy, Mises's student Luigi Einaudi had, as president, led the successful fight against postwar Communism. In France, his student Jacques Rueff—as economic advisor to General DeGaulle—led the fight for the gold standard and pushed back many statist economic controls. In the United States, Mises produced—

despite his circumstances—such students as Murray N. Rothbard and Israel Kirzner.

Sadly, he did not live to see the renaissance of interest in his work, which began with F. A. Hayek's Nobel prize in 1974, granted for the Mises-Hayek theory of the business cycle.

Since Mises's death, the center of this new interest has been his widow. She has been, in Murray Rothbard's words, "a one-woman Mises industry," supervising the reprinting, translation, and new editions of his works, and chairing the Ludwig von Mises Institute. She has also written her own moving memoirs, *My Years with Ludwig von Mises*.

Socialism and its variants still control most of the world, but, notes Dr. Rothbard, "everywhere, in all spheres of thought and action, the modern statism that Ludwig von Mises combatted all his life, is coming under a swelling drumfire of criticism and disillusion." This resurrection of the spirit of freedom—and our work to encourage it—is the only appropriate monument to the life and thought of a great and noble man.

Memories of Ludwig von Mises

William H. Peterson

I look back with special pleasure and deep respect on that giant of our age, Ludwig von Mises (1881-1973). How he shone in his students' lives and minds, gently schooling us in the meaning of human action and the free market.

Today we glory in the truth of Misesian economics, and marvel at his lonely and courageous struggle against heavy odds. As the 20th century's uncompromising defender of laissez-faire economics and human liberty, and as the leader of the Austrian school, his spirit is still very much alive—and growing more influential day by day.

I was privileged to take three courses from Lu Mises at New York University's Graduate School of Business Administration in the early 1950s: "Socialism and the Profit System," "Government Control and the Profit System," and "Seminar in Economic Theory." So eye-opening were they that I continued to participate in his seminar even after graduating and joining the faculty myself.

In these courses he developed a theory of individual action and the indispensability of freedom in the marketplace. He focused on social cooperation springing from individual action, which came from the human condition of subjective valuations and limited means.

Man is a unique being, Mises said, because he alone has a vision of the future, possesses abstract reasoning power, integrates thought and action, and acts with particular purposes in mind. Simplistic notions like *Homo Economicus* miss the richness of Misesian economics.

Mises's seminar, first held in the Wall Street area and later on Washington Square, always attracted his great students like Murray N. Rothbard, Henry Hazlitt, Lawrence Fertig, Israel Kirzner, Ralph Raico, Hans Sennholz, Leonard Liggio, and many others. Sometimes a graduate student would ask a less-than-intelligent question, but Mises would always respond with kindness and understanding. One such question in the 1960s followed his discussion of the inflationary implications of deficit finance, in which a student asked why President Johnson couldn't have both "guns and butter." Mises smiled and replied: "Ah, President Johnson can have both," but added with a twinkle in his eye, "if he is willing to pay for them."

Because of Mises's uncompromising stand for liberty, the rest of the business school faculty and NYU itself isolated him. They dismissed him as an ideologue and an iconoclast. But Mises was always a very tolerant and courageous man.

Although attacked by other people in the department and in the profession, Mises continued to read, study, teach, and write—quite content all the while.

Sometimes Lu and Margit would invite my wife Mary and me, and sometimes our children, to dinner at their warm and lovely apartment on West End Avenue. There we enjoyed the company of the Fertigs, Hazlitts, Reads, Petros, and others. The parties were always sparkling affairs, graced with the enchanting beauty of Margit and the courtly charm of Lu.

When the Mont Pelerin Society met, Mises's students were always among those attending, including F. A. Hayek, Gottfried Haberler, Fritz Machlup, and Wilhelm Roepke. Also attending were scholars who had read and admired Mises's writings—men like James Buchanan, W. H. Hutt, George Stigler, Gordon Tullock, Warren Nutter, and many others.

Mises's courage and integrity showed at one meeting when he expressed concern that some of Mont Pelerin members were becoming infected with the virus of interventionism, approving of state ownership of transport, government social insurance, minimum wage laws, countercyclical policy, and other interventions.

One member asked, "But what would you do if you were in the position of our French colleague, Jacques Rueff," who was present at the meeting and responsible for the fiscal administration of Monaco. "Suppose there were widespread unemployment and hence famine and revolutionary discontent in the principality. Would you advise the government to limit its activities to police action for the maintenance of order and protection of private property?"

Mises stood fast: "If the policies of nonintervention prevailed—free trade, freely fluctuating wage rates, no form of social insurance, etc.—there would be no acute unemployment. Private charity would suffice to prevent the absolute destitution of the very restricted hard-core of unemployables."

The academic world did not take kindly to Ludwig von Mises. Many economists felt he was too impolitic, too adamant, too pure, too uncompromising. Then, like now, the conventional wisdom was in fashion.

Because of his staunch adherence to liberty, Mises never held a regular professorship at the University of Vienna. And it was no different in America. He was a "visiting professor" at New York University for 24 years, with his modest salary paid not by the university but by foundations and friends.

His prolific writings and magnificent contributions to economics were largely ignored by the profession. Among these contributions, he pulled together monetary theory and the theory of marginal utility, proved that socialism cannot calculate rationally and therefore couldn't work, and systematically developed the science of economics as a major subset of the science of human action, praxeology.

Mises set an example for us. He held that it is the duty of everyone to read, think, and speak about the importance of freedom. The preservation of civilization depends upon it. Lu Mises would be happy to know that the torch he lit is burning brighter than ever.

Mises vs. the Green-Eyed Monster

Bradley Miller

A truism among free-marketeers is that collectivism is flawed because it flies in the face of human nature. But many writers on our side also ignore a key aspect of human nature. They write about politics and economics as if they were logic or mechanics. Pull lever X for output Y. Disseminate the evidence of capitalism's success and collectivism's failures, and the capitalist paradise, in time, will come.

Most true-believing collectivists—and frauds increasingly swell the ranks—underestimate the force of self-interest. But many capitalist thinkers underestimate the force of envy, and in this regard are far more naive than collectivists. Lenin never tired of stressing that his goal was to make class envy flare into revolutionary hatred.

Capitalist thinkers continue tabulating collectivism's follies and savageries, and capitalism's virtues—tabulations that at this stage of history shouldn't seriously be disputed—while watching indignantly and incredulously as collectivism claims more and more ground even in the very citadel of capitalism, the United States, where six and a half years into the reign of the supposedly most free-market president since the 1920s, federal spending is at an all-time high. Why?

Ludwig von Mises showed 31 years ago in *The Anti-capitalistic Mentality* that reason, evidence, and humaneness have about as much impact on public policy as an Oral Roberts sermon would have on Nietzsche. As too few contemporary economists do, Mises realized that for libertarian economists to have a practical as well as scholarly impact, they must understand the non-rational factors that breed hostility to capitalism:

> In a society of equality under the law the inequality of men with regard to intellectual abilities, will power and application becomes visible. The gulf between what a man is and achieves and what he thinks of his own abilities and achievements is pitilessly revealed. Daydreams of a "fair" world which would treat him according to his "real worth" are the refuge of all those plagued by a lack of self-knowledge.
>
> The more sophisticated sublimate their hatred into . . . the philosophy of anti-capitalism, in order to render inaudible the inner voice that tells them that their failure is entirely their own fault. Their fanaticism in defending their critique of capitalism is precisely due to the fact that they are fighting their own awareness of its falsity.

The anti-capitalism of intellectuals tends to be greater than that of common men because, Mises wrote, the latter tend to associate with other common men, and so have mere abstractions—e.g. Wall Street, the plutocracy—as objects of their envy and resentment. These can't rouse nearly as much hatred as direct contact with people, and intellectuals often have daily contact with colleagues far wealthier and more prominent than they are.

This happens far more today than in 1956, when *The Anti-capitalistic Mentality* was written. Today's obscure prof in Pine Bluff, Arkansas, with a break or two, *could* become tomorrow's darling of the publishing house, think tanks, talk shows, and lecture circuits, while his ex-colleagues remain obscure and rage against the system that catapulted him to the top. To rage at him directly not only would be bad form, but also would reveal small, ungenerous souls. So they rage at the Unjust Capitalist System. Should the prof actually be a capitalist—a rarity but not yet illegal in America—no obloquy and punishment would be too severe.

Thus do the envious find scapegoats and, more important, project images of sophistication and rebelliousness. Average Americans in their parochialism and philistinism actually admire the rich and famous—intellectuals sneer—being blind to the system's tawdriness and injustice. Only they are worldly enough to see the truth and daring enough to call attention to it.

Mises found these attitudes to be even more pronounced among intellectuals in America than in Europe, since intellectuals have far more contact with businessmen here. The greedy, philistine businessman is likely the most common stereotype in American literature, not to mention television and movies. I don't dispute that plenty of Americans are serious when they ask, "If you're so smart why ain't you rich?" But then, as Mises says, most intellectuals who ignorantly disparage business as too vulgar to bother learning about, show less intellectual capacity than businessmen.

Some business *is* vulgar. Some get rich pushing products that have no more moral, cultural, or aesthetic worth than

Christian Marxism. "Nobody ever contended," Mises said, "that under unhampered capitalism those fare best who, from the standpoint of eternal standards of value, ought to be preferred." What capitalism ensures is the dictatorship of consumers: in other words, the populism Marx thought would ultimately accompany *destruction* of property.

Anti-capitalists blame capitalism for all the vulgar and vacuous products that enchant the masses. They might have at least a small point if (1) they were themselves fit to decide what the masses should buy, (2) noncapitalist nations had higher levels of culture, or (3) the vulgarities and vacuities of capitalism prevented quality from being produced.

In fact, in countries where capitalism has been crippled or eliminated, citizens are lucky if they can afford the bare necessities of daily living, let alone culture, and in communist countries being a mere spectator of *true* culture, which requires intellectual freedom, is illegal. In Czechoslovakia forming a jazz club lands you in jail. But filthy-rich capitalists often underwrite high art. Pictures of nude beauties bring Hugh Hefner the wealth with which he commissions award-winning journalism. Such examples are endless.

Successful capitalism means satisfying the very masses in whose name anti-capitalists push their pishposh. Market forces may take a while to take effect, but soon enough an entrepreneur must shut down if his products aren't popular (assuming he's not rich enough to keep operating in the red).

Anti-capitalists' chief delusion is that *X*'s wealth causes Y's poverty. Greed does run amok from time to time in capitalist societies, and not always to society's benefit. But what's remarkable under capitalism is how individual greed usually enhances the commonwealth.

The fact is that only in the ignorant, envy-fueled hallucinations of anti-capitalists is capitalist greed all-consuming. For every jackass obsessed with upping his annual income from seven figures to eight, there are millions who care nothing for yachts and Rolls Royces, and want only to be comfortable and have "the-heck-with-you" money, i.e., enough to be able to say "the heck with you" if asked to do demeaning or dishonorable work. Indeed, the hallucinations to the contrary richly suggest that it is not capitalists but anti-capitalists who are obsessed with money.

Perhaps, indeed, the ideal of most anti-capitalists is former Soviet General Secretary Leonid Brezhnev, who owned, among other delights of Veblenian conspicuousness, 25 Western cars, including two Rolls Royce limos, a Lincoln Continental, and a Mercedes Benz. As many Western socialists prove as well, cornucopian can be the blessings that flow from a life of selfless striving to free the working class from its chains.

Hazlitt, Hutt, and Rothbard: Three Economists Who Are National Treasures

Llewellyn H. Rockwell, Jr.

To most Americans, economists don't leap instantly to mind as treasures, let alone national treasures. Whether making arrogant and fallacious mathematical predictions; filling the minds of college students with Keynesian and socialist buncombe; or giving a theoretical cover to state inflation, taxation, regulation, and spending—the typical economist is not a friend of liberty.

But all this is a perversion of real economics as exemplified by the Austrian school and its greatest exponent, the late Ludwig von Mises. Professor Mises was not only the 20th-century's greatest creative force in economics, he was also its radiant champion of liberty.

When my old friend Scott Stanley of *Conservative Digest*—who is to editing what the Austrian school is to economics—asked me to write this article, he mentioned the Japanese custom of naming great achievers as living national treasures. "Who are our three living national treasures in economics?" he asked.

There are other worthy contenders, but three men stand out as great economists and freedom fighters in the Misesian tradition: Henry Hazlitt, W. H. Hutt, and Murray N. Rothbard.

Henry Hazlitt

Henry Hazlitt's career as economist and journalist spans more than seven decades. An outstanding teacher of the economics of freedom, he did pathbreaking theoretical work, and made the ideas of Austrian, free-market economics accessible to everyone.

One of the most quotable economists of all time, his writing sparkles. And his clear and sprightly style seems—like his commitment to freedom—only to grow stronger with the passing years.

One of his chief accomplishments is the masterful *Economics In One Lesson*. This small volume has converted millions (in eight different languages) to an understanding of the free market and Austrian economics. It destroys the arguments of socialists and interventionists as it explains the truth. Although it was written more than 40 years ago, there is still no better way to start learning good economics.

But it's scorned by establishment economists. And no wonder. If Hazlitt were followed, interventionist politicians and their intellectual bodyguards in the academic world would be unemployed.

If that's not bad enough, his airtight case for the free market is accessible to the layman, and that's anathema to the economic establishment. Thumb through any issue of a top economic journal and you'll know why Hazlitt's book is considered heretical. Not because it doesn't make sense, but because it does; not because it isn't logical, but because it is; not because it isn't true to life, but because it is.

Translate their jargon into English, and we find establishment economists beginning with such axioms as "let's assume everybody knows everything" or "nobody knows anything" or "people never change their minds." Men and women are stripped of their individuality to make them fit into mechanistic computer models, and the economy is seen as static, or at best a series of shifting static states. Deductions from such axioms must, of course, be false.

Hazlitt, like Mises, starts with the assumption that individuals act, that they do so with a purpose, and that as conditions change, their plans change. Do we need to know anything else about mainstream economics than that this is considered "unscientific"?

Most economists are notorious justifiers of special-interest legislation because they ignore what Hazlitt so eloquently charts in *Economics In One Lesson*: the unseen and long-run effects of government policy. To Hazlitt, as an Austrian school economist, "economics consists in looking not merely at the immediate but at the longer effects of any act or policy; it consists in tracing the consequences of that policy not merely for one group but for all groups."

Central bank inflation of the money supply, for example, lowers interest rates initially, but leads to higher interest rates and lower purchasing power in the long run, not to speak of the business cycle of booms and busts. Inflation may benefit the government and those who get the new money first, but it hurts everyone else.

Although a formidable scholar, Hazlitt did not spend his career in a university. He was a working journalist of whom H. L. Mencken once said: "He is one of the few economists in human history who could really write." Born in 1894, Hazlitt went to work in 1913 as a reporter for the *Wall Street Journal*. He was also an editorial writer for the *New York Times* and a columnist for *Newsweek*.

As a very young man, Hazlitt read the Austrian economists Carl Menger, Eugen von Böhm-Bawerk, and Philip Wicksteed. But the main influence on him was Ludwig von Mises. And in 1940 Hazlitt helped—with the late Lawrence Fertig—to raise funds for a job for Mises at New York University.

At a time when every second-rate European Marxist was getting a professorship at Harvard or Princeton, Mises was blackballed by U.S. universities as "too right-wing." Eventually Hazlitt and Fertig were able to persuade NYU—where Fertig was a trustee—to allow Mises to be an unpaid visiting professor.

Mises and Hazlitt became close friends and he later arranged the publication of Mises's *Omnipotent Government, Theory and History, Bureacracy*, and the monumental *Human Action* by Yale University Press, and helped edit the manuscripts as well.

During Hazlitt's years at the *New York Times*, he wrote about the troubles that would flow from the Keynes-designed Bretton Woods monetary agreements. (His eloquent editorials are collected in *From Bretton Woods To World Inflation.*) Bretton Woods, which Supply-Siders wrongly look back on with nostalgia, guaranteed—as Hazlitt predicted—a world of paper money inflation. It also gave us the International Monetary Fund and the World Bank, still major sources of funding for statist regimes.

As Hazlitt has argued, only a true gold standard, with the dollar redeemable in gold domestically as well as internationally, qualifies as sound money. And institutions like the IMF and World Bank only benefit governments and banking interests at the expense of the American taxpayer and the poor in other countries.

Another Hazlitt masterpiece is *The Failure of the "New Economics."* Here Hazlitt did what no one else has ever attempted: a line-by-line refutation of Keynes's *General Theory*. The book is a patient and meticulous shattering of Keynes's fallacies, contradictions, and muddled thinking.

A Renaissance man in the Mises tradition, his output includes 25 books—on economics, philosophy, politics, history, and a wonderful novel, *Time Will Run Back*—plus hundreds of persuasive columns and articles.

The Bretton Woods system did break down, of course, as Hazlitt had predicted. But when, many years before, the publisher of the *New York Times* asked him to reverse his position and endorse Keynes's phony gold standard, he resigned rather than do so. That act of courage and principle exemplifies his whole life.

W. H. Hutt

It's possible for a student of economics to go all the way through graduate school without hearing the name William H. Hutt. Yet his scholarship, bravery, and dogged adherence to economic truth make him a hero.

Hutt, now a visiting professor at the University of Dallas, has labored quietly and with little acclaim for more than 60 years. He is responsible for major breakthroughs in economic theory, a dozen books, and hundreds of articles. Among his most important works are *The Theory of Collective Bargaining* (1930), *Economists and the Public* (1936), *Economists of the Coulour Bar* (1964), *The Strike-Threat System* (1973), and *A Rehabilitation of Say's Law* (1975).

Born in 1899, Hutt graduated from the London School of Economics. He published his first major academic article in 1926, refuting the leftist charge that the Industrial Revolution impoverished workers, when in fact it raised their standard of living dramatically. He went on to become the great defender of working people, and scholarly opponent of their enemy: labor unions.

Many books had been written about labor unions, usually from a leftist perspective, yet no comprehensive theory of collective bargaining had ever been advanced. Hutt did so while teaching at South Africa's University of Cape Town.

In his *The Theory of Collective Bargaining*, which Ludwig von Mises called "brilliant," Hutt exploded the still-common myth that the interests of labor and management naturally clash. That is nothing but a disguised version of Karl Marx's theory of exploitation. On the contrary, Hutt said, the free market brings harmony. Only government intervention—such as laws favoring labor unions against employers and non-union workers—creates conflict.

Hutt also proved that collective bargaining and other union activities depress wages for non-union workers and the poor. He showed how much better off all countries would be if government-sponsored union activities were banned.

Unlike "liberals" and socialists, Hutt recognized that unionization's equal wage structure is destructive. Paying everyone the same, regardless of contribution, destroys the incentive to improve.

He is also an articulate opponent of the force and violence that are endemic to unions, and he has shown that they are necessarily an integral part of their functioning.

These ideas, of course, did not sell well in the 1930s. But that never hindered Hutt. And he took on another leftist idol: Keynes. While Hazlitt was fighting Keynesianism in the U.S., Hutt did the same in the British world.

Economists and the Public was published in the same year as Keynes's *General Theory*, 1936. Hutt's book was already in page proofs when Keynes's book appeared, but he inserted a warning about the dangers of Keynesianism.

In the book, Hutt sought to explain why the obviously superior free market was under attack, and why economists were held in such disrepute. The problem, he said, was that neither economists nor the public understood the nature and effect of competition.

Only unfettered competition protects the general interest against the government and its interests, said Hutt. Far from being a destructive force, competition is the "sole principle of coordination in a complex world" and the greatest liberator of the poor, a class which Marxists and Keynesians claim to love, but succeed only in increasing.

Hutt also unveiled his concept of "consumer sovereignty," which influenced Ludwig von Mises. In the free market, Hutt said, consumers have the right to buy or not to buy, and therefore producers play a subservient role. The only path to success in a free market is for the producer to serve the consumer. In a statist economy, pleasing politicians is the road to riches.

In 1939, Hutt delivered another blow to Keynesianism with *The Theory of Idle Resources*, which exploded Keynes's theory of unemployment. Hutt showed that a resource like labor can be idle only through government intervention that raises its price higher than the community can afford, in light of other demands. This is why minimum wages and unions are so destructive: they inhibit flexibility in the price of labor.

Not satisfied with attacking Keynesianism, in 1964 Hutt wrote the first detailed critique of South Africa's economic apartheid in *The Economists of The Colour Bar*.

Hutt didn't call for "one-man-one-vote" or similar schemes. He criticized the South African government's pro-labor union socialism and interventionism as giving an opening to Communism. Unless the market were freed from state intervention, he showed, there would be bloodshed and a destruction of freedom for everyone. He pleaded for blacks to be given a chance to own their own businesses, and to seek and hold any jobs they were capable of holding, without state discrimination.

Hutt showed that South Africa's economic apartheid was designed largely to protect white labor union members from black competition. The free market, he said, offers the only hope to minorities and the disadvantaged, and for a free society in South Africa. Government controls benefit only loot-seeking special interests.

The Economists of the Colour Bar—which anticipated Walter Williams's analysis of race and government—is a triumph of the union of theory and policy. This is something most economists shun as "unscholarly." But Hutt makes no secret of his desire to influence public opinion toward laissez-faire. For this, he was banned from working in South Africa.

As Ludwig von Mises wrote, W. H. Hutt "rank[s] among the outstanding economists of our age." That he is not ranked as such by the mainstream is a tribute to his achievements and his courage.

Murray N. Rothbard

Ludwig von Mises was the greatest economist and defender of liberty in the 20th century. In scholarship and in passion for freedom, his heir is Murray N. Rothbard.

Rothbard was born in New York City in 1926. His parents, a chemist and a journalist, had met at an anti-big government ball, so from his earliest days he was properly oriented.

He received his Ph.D. from Columbia University, and studied for more than 10 years under Mises at New York University. However, his degree was delayed for years, and he came close to not receiving it at all, because of the unprecedented intervention of a faculty member who was outraged at his topic.

Rothbard's dissertation—*The Panic of 1819*—showed how the Bank of the United States, the Federal Reserve's ancestor, caused the first American depression. This offended Professor Arthur Burns, later chairman of the Federal Reserve under Nixon, who was horrified by Rothbard's anti-central bank and pro-gold standard position.

Ph.D. finally in hand, Rothbard began writing for the libertarian Volker Fund in New York. Like his great teacher Mises,

Rothbard's views prevented him from getting a job at a major university. Finally he was hired by Brooklyn Polytechnic, an engineering school with no economics majors.

He worked there, in a dark and dingy basement office, until last year, when—thanks to free-market businessman S. J. Hall—he was offered a Distinguished Professorship of Economics at the University Of Nevada, Las Vegas.

But his lack of a prestigious academic base did not prevent Rothbard, any more than Hazlitt, Hutt, or Mises, from reaching a wide audience of scholars, students, and the general public. Rothbard is the author of hundreds of pathbreaking scholarly articles and 16 books, including *Man, Economy, and State* (1962), *America's Great Depression* (1963), *Power and Market* (1970), *For a New Liberty* (1973), *Conceived in Liberty* (1976), *The Ethics of Liberty* (1982), and *The Mystery of Banking* (1983).

In *America's Great Depression*, building on Mises's work, Rothbard proved that the Federal Reserve caused that economic calamity, and that other government interventions prolonged and deepened it.

He has also demonstrated that only a gold coin standard, with no central bank and 100% reserves, brings sound money and economic growth. Central banking and its inevitably inflationary monetary policies causes recessions and depressions that are not inherent in a free-market economy. Government, Rothbard shows, is the source of every business cycle in history.

Rothbard was also the first to show that a free market cannot create monopolies, and that government is, as always, the enemy of competition. The real monopolies are open ones like the Post Office, somewhat obscured ones like electric power companies, and worst of all the least-questioned one, the Federal Reserve.

In his great work *Man, Economy, and State*, he provides a logical answer to virtually every argument used against the free market. In the days of real economics, every scholar aspired to write a treatise that covered the whole subject. Since the Keynesian warping of the profession, this has gone out of fashion, and *Man, Economy, and State* is the last such magnum opus. In it, clearly and logically, Rothbard deduces the whole of economics from first principles. It is a tour-de-force unmatched in the modern profession.

In his *Power and Market*, originally part of *Man, Economy, and State*, he develops a comprehensive critique of government coercion. There are two types of government intervention, he shows: triangular, in which the government "compels a pair of people to make an exchange or prohibits them from doing so," and binary, where government directly coerces a citizen for its own benefit, as in taxation. He carefully outlines the bad effects of every possible intervention in the economy, and is especially good on the harmful effects of taxation.

Rothbard also broke new ground in attacking government statistics. As he shows, the government collects statistics to help it plan the economy. (Of course, after millions of pages gathered every year, it still can't get it right!)

Among Rothbard's least favorite statistics is the "trade deficit," which is only considered a problem because government keeps the figures. Thank goodness, he has noted, that trade statistics aren't kept on Manhattan and Brooklyn. "Otherwise we'd hear cries from Brooklyn politicians about the dangerous trade deficit with Manhattan."

Another statistic he dislikes is GNP. This number counts welfare payments and all other government spending as "productivity." His PPR—Private Product Remaining (to producers)—shows a much clearer picture by *subtracting* government spending from the economy. He has also constructed an Austrian "M"—the True Money Supply—which reveals the Federal Reserve's depredations, unlike the constantly changing M1, M2, M3, etc., which are designed to disguise inflation.

Not only is he a brilliant economist, he is also a master of narrative political history, as his four-volume colonial history of the United States, *Conceived in Liberty*, shows; and a great philosopher in the individualist tradition, as demonstrated in *Ethics of Liberty*.

His current project is a massive history of economic thought from an Austrian perspective, commissioned by investment advisor and Austrian economist Dr. Mark Skousen, which covers the ancient Greeks to the present. Judging by the chapters so far, this will be the greatest study of its kind ever written.

The real Great Communicator, Rothbard is a writer of singular style, humor, and power. His words glisten on the page, while statist prose is usually a muddled, hermeneutical mire.

Like Mises, he has inspired millions with his vision of the free society. In the academic world, where devotion to principle is as popular as it is in Washington, he has carried the torch of pure Misesianism.

Three Giants

Like Mises, these three giants exhibit extraordinary ability, courage, personal gentleness, and an unbending adherence to principle.

In an age when selling-out is the norm among politicians—governmental and academic—Hazlitt, Hutt, and Rothbard have held high the banner of truth and freedom. They have faced immense pressure to retreat, but never wavered. Today they are still at work extending the scholarship of freedom.

Despite the barriers they have faced in the past, today their influence is spreading. And it will continue to do so. In their fight for liberty and the free market, these masters have one asset the other side cannot match: the truth.

Murray N. Rothbard: Giant of Liberty

Walter Block and Llewellyn H. Rockwell, Jr.

Murray N. Rothbard is a scholar of unique, indeed, monumental achievements: the founder of the first fully-integrated science of liberty. Consider, first, his accomplishments in economics. His Ph.D. dissertation from Columbia University—*The Panic of 1819*—showed how the Bank of the United States, the Federal Reserve's ancestor, caused the first American depression. It remains the only in-depth historical account of that particular monetary debacle.

In *America's Great Depression*, still the most definitive work on the subject, Rothbard used Austrian trade cycle theory to show that the Federal Reserve caused that economic calamity, and that other government interventions prolonged and even deepened the Depression. In addition, the first two chapters present the most clear and convincing explanation of the Austrian theory of the trade cycle in existence.

Both books utilize tools drawn from the great tradition of Austrian economics—Carl Menger's theory of the development of monetary institutions, Eugen von Böhm-Bawerk's theory of capital and the time-preference theory of interest, and Mises's trade cycle theory and method—perfect each, and weave them together into a systematic praxeological model. He succeeded not only in explaining cyclical fluctuations caused by central bank intervention, but also proved the case for the gold coin standard, no central bank, 100% reserves, and laissez-faire.

After Rothbard's masterful integration, economists can no longer dismiss recessions and depressions as an "inevitable" part of the market process. Instead, he showed, they are caused by central bank inflation and the corresponding distortion of interest rates, malinvestment of capital, theft of savings, and price increases that go with it. Government, of which the central bank is only one arm, is the real source of business cycles.

Rothbard was also the first to explode the fallacy of distinguishing between monopoly prices and competitive prices. This distinction makes sense only in neoclassical pricing models, where businessmen charge higher and higher prices in the inelastic portion of consumers' demand curve. But these static models have nothing to do with the dynamic market process. In the real world, we can only distinguish between free-market prices and those controlled by the government.

This discovery has momentous policy implications: in a free market, where we never see "monopoly (non-competitive) prices," there can be no unjust monopoly profits. This destroys the entire neo-classical justification of anti-trust policy. Monopolies do exist, Rothbard shows, but only when government erects a barrier to entry into the market by granting some firm or industry a special privilege.

Rothbard also revolutionized the entire field of utility and welfare economics—and laid a foundation for other Austrian scholars to build upon—by showing that utility is something that we can know only by observing individual preferences revealed through human action. Utility, a strictly ordinal and subjective concept, cannot be aggregated among individuals, and thus there can be no social utility.

Because of Rothbard's irrefutable theory of utility and demonstrated preference, neo-classical welfare economics can no longer be used to justify state planning. When individuals are free to trade without interference from government, we know that each party expects to benefit from the exchange, i.e. maximize his own subjective utility, or the parties would not exchange in the first place. His conclusion: free markets maximize utility and welfare, whereas government intervention, by the very fact that it forces people to behave in ways in which they otherwise would not, only diminishes utility and welfare. It was this foundation that allowed Rothbard to integrate a rigorous theory of property rights with a scientific theory of economics. Today, others within the profession are trying to do the same, but they will not succeed so long as they cling to theories of efficiency built around faulty utility and welfare concepts.

In his great work *Man, Economy, and State*, Rothbard provides a rigorous defense of economic science and the pure logic of action. In the by-gone days of "real economics," every scholar aspired to write a treatise covering the whole subject. Since the Keynesian and neo-classical warping of the profession, however, this has gone out of fashion, and *Man, Economy, and State* is the last such great work. In it, clearly and logically, Rothbard deduces the whole of economics from its first principles. It is a tour-de-force unmatched in modern economics.

If only his contribution to economics in general were considered, his refutations of neo-classical, socialist, interventionist, and Keynesian fallacies would put him head and shoulders above all other living economists. If only his accomplishments in the field of Austrian economics were taken into account, his place in the firmament would be secure. For it is an understatement to say that he is the most productive of the students and followers of Ludwig von Mises. But his attainments in economics are only the tip of the iceberg. His productivity as a historian is more than sufficient to establish him as a leader in that field as well. In addition to many scholarly articles, his four-volume colonial history of the United States, *Conceived in Liberty*, shows that libertarian ideas have been an American staple since almost the earliest days, and that the American Revolution was very much a libertarian affair. He shows that the received wisdom in history is almost always wrong, since it usually reflects the state's bias.

Permeating all of Rothbard's historical writing is a brillant and original revisionism, a unique and rigorous refusal to accept uncritically the official version. (He is also one of the few historians ever to place his presuppositions, his theory of history itself, on record. He does so properly in the introduction where it belongs, and not all throughout the book in the form of implicit presuppositions.) Whether discussing monetary history, the history of economic thought, the Progressive Era, the New Deal, World War I, or any of his other areas of expertise, Rothbard eruditely and unerringly turns the statist worldview upside down, in search of a commodity unusual among modern historians—truth.

But his exploits in economics and history, extraordinary as they are, are matched by what he has done for the cause of liberty. If he is an eminent historian, and the world's leading Austrian economist, he is no less than the father of libertarianism. He is, as even *National Review* has acknowledged, "Mr. Libertarian." In his *Power and Market*, Rothbard develops a comprehensive critique of government coercion. He vastly expanded the scope of the theory of intervention, and developed three useful categories: autistic, binary, and triangular. Autistic intervention prevents a person from exercising control over his own person or property, as with homicide or infringements on free speech. Binary intervention forces an exchange between two parties, as in highway robbery or income taxes. Finally there is the triangular mode, in which the government "compels a pair of people to make an exchange or prohibits them from doing so," as in rent control or minimum wages. He carefully outlines the deleterious effects of every possible intervention in the economy, and is especially insightful in analyzing the harmful effects of taxation.

In *For a New Liberty*, Rothbard leaves the world of theory and gets down to brass tacks. How would a totally free society actually function? While it is always impossible to predict the future exactly, he shows how the challenges of education, poverty, private roads, courts, police, and pollution might be dealt with under a complete laissez-faire system. In his masterful *The Ethics of Liberty*, Rothbard deals with the hard questions: the criminal system, land redistribution, the vexing problem of children's rights, bribery, boycotts, lifeboat situations; his critiques of other, less-pure advocates of the freedom philosophy such as Hayek, Nozick, and Berlin are alone worth the price of admission. Nor must we lose sight of yet another of Rothbard's particular excellences: his masterful ability to integrate intellectual thought, to see connections where others see only a bewildering complexity, to weave the threads from all of knowledge into a shield which can preserve human rights. He has long called for, and has indeed been the leading exponent of, what he calls the "interdisciplinary study of liberty." From this perspective, the disciplines of economics, history, law, philosophy, sociology, etc., must all be harnessed together to comprise a "seamless web" of liberty. All must be utilized in the glorious struggle to promote the free society, with the teachings of none remaining inconsistent with any other. Were Rothbard's accomplishments limited merely to any one of the many disciplines he has so eloquently mastered, we could be very laudatory. But when we reflect on the fact that he has already made significant contributions to each of them, of the sort that any person would be justly proud to call an entire life's work, we must simply stand in awe.

And when we realize that Rothbard has not only spread himself over practically every social science, but also has integrated them into a moral and intellectual product never before known, that he has, in effect, created an entirely new academic discipline of liberty, then all we can say is that we are delighted, proud, and honored to know him, and to be his students.

—An Excerpt From *Man, Economy, and Liberty*

Henry Hazlitt: Giant of Liberty

Various Authors

For more than seven decades, Henry Hazlitt has taught the economics of freedom. With pathbreaking theoretical work and a unique ability to communicate with the non-economist—shown forth especially in his *Economics in One Lesson*—he has both advanced Austrian economics and made it accessible to everyone.

Henry Hazlitt, a formidable scholar-journalist whom H. L. Mencken called "one of the few economists in human history who could really write," is the author of 25 books and thousands of columns and articles. He also arranged Ludwig von Mises's professorship at New York University and the publication of *Human Action* and three other Mises books by Yale University Press.

Like Mises, Henry Hazlitt combines courage, genius, and gentleness with an unbending adherence to principle. Today, at a very young age 93, he is still at work extending the scholarship of freedom. The Mises Institute has been fortunate indeed to have this great man as a friend and supporter since its earliest days.

On October 17, 1987, in New York City, more than 150 people gathered to pay homage to this extraordinary person at the Institute's Fifth Anniversary Dinner held in his honor. In this special Henry Hazlitt issue of the *Free Market*, we have reproduced the homages and messages delivered at the dinner, and Henry Hazlitt's own captivating talk.

If there were justice in journalism, Henry Hazlitt would have been showered with the Pulitzer and other prizes. But he was not, which matches his treatment by the economics profession.

To help carry on his ideas, we have established the Henry Hazlitt Fund for Economic Journalism to give promising young journalists a chance to study *real* economics.

Media bias against sound money and the free market can't be cured overnight. But the educational programs sponsored by the Hazlitt Fund will have a lasting effect for good.

"The Meaning of Mises"

The Institute's Fifth Anniversary Conference, "The Meaning of Ludwig von Mises," broke new ground in Misesian scholarship on October 16-17 at Pace University in New York City.

Dr. Walter Block of the Fraser Institute compared the Misesian 100% gold standard with other allegedly free-market theories.

Professor Richard Ebeling of the University of Dallas spoke on Mises's demonstration that socialism is an irrational form of social organization, and on the economists who anticipated some of his ideas.

Professor Roger Garrison of Auburn University discussed "Mises and his Method." Mainstream economics believes that mathematics and statistics alone can yield economic theory. But Austrian economics relies on logic and reason for its theory.

Dr. David Gordon of the Mises Institute presented and built upon Mises's critique of false doctrines of history which rely on determinism and relativism, for example Marxism, which teaches a historical "dialectic" instead of a history built on human action.

Professor Hans-Hermann Hoppe of the University of Nevada, Las Vegas, presented a comprehensive apriori deductive approach to Austrian economics, the Misesian theory of knowledge, and a laissez-faire public policy.

Professor Murray N. Rothbard of the University of Nevada, Las Vegas, talked about "Mises as Hero," a ringing tribute to the greatest mind of his time and principled activist for liberty.

Professor Mark Skousen of Rollins College discussed those who predicted the Great Depression, and noted that one of the few who did was Mises.

And Professor Leland Yeager of Auburn University defended Mises's and Hazlitt's theory of ethics, rights, and law.

The papers—which will also include contributions by Professors Roger Arnold of the University of Nevada, Las Vegas, Israel Kirzner of New York University, and Joseph Salerno of Pace University—will be published by Lexington Books under the title "The Meaning of Ludwig von Mises."

Messages and Talks From the Ludwig von Mises Institute's Fifth Anniversary Celebration and Tribute to Henry Hazlitt

Margit von Mises, Chairman Ludwig von Mises Institute

This evening we celebrate the fifth anniversary of the founding of the Ludwig von Mises Institute, and give thanks to a tireless champion of the free market and free society, Henry Hazlitt . . . .

I remember very well the day I met Lew Rockwell, the Institute's president, for the first time. . . . Lew told me he had heard the tape of a speech of mine . . . in which I pleaded for the founding of an institute exclusively working for the Austrian theories of the free market. He asked for my permission to use my husband's name, since he was prepared to found such an institute. At the same time he asked for my help, which I promised to give, if he would promise never to leave the Institute, but to make it his life's work. This he promised, and so this meeting led to the founding of the Ludwig von Mises Institute.

That the Institute has its Fifth Anniversary today is solely the work of Lew Rockwell. Through his effectual administration, his indefatigable diligence, his thorough knowledge of people, and his love for liberty, the Ludwig von Mises Institute has reached its present state.

I have a special wish for the Institute which I want to tell you about. A Ludwig von Mises Institute needs a permanent location in the cultural center of the United States . . . , New York City. I hope that the many friends of Ludwig von Mises and the Institute will take up the idea, and will provide the Institute in the near future with a presentable house.

I myself cannot give it to the Institute, but tonight I promise that when I have to go, it shall receive the Ludwig von Mises bronze head, done so masterfully by Nellie Erickson . . . , which I have now in my apartment. In my thoughts I see the statue standing on a pedestal in the entrance hall of the building in New York City.

This evening is devoted to Henry Hazlitt. Therefore as the widow of Ludwig von Mises, the widow of one of Hazlitt's best friends, I send him greetings and all good wishes.

John V. Denson, Vice Chairman
Ludwig von Mises Institute

It is a distinct privilege for me to join with all of you in honoring Mr. Henry Hazlitt tonight. Ludwig von Mises once remarked:

> The intellectual leaders of the people have produced and propagated the fallacies which are on the point of destroying liberty and Western civilization. What is needed to stop the trend toward socialism and despotism is common sense and moral courage.

Henry Hazlitt, through seven decades, has demonstrated the unflinching moral courage mentioned by Mises. He has also presented the ideas of the free market and individual liberty in concise, common-sense terms, which could be understood by the general reader.

When I studied economics at Auburn University in 1955, I was taught only Keynesian ideas. My intuition told me that what I was being taught was not correct, and that it would lead to the destruction of individual freedom. However, I had no intellectual ammunition with which to reply or rebut. It was not until several years later, when I was in law school, that I discovered Henry Hazlitt's column in *Newsweek*. It was several years after this that I was introduced to the ideas of Ludwig von Mises and read both *Human Action* and *Socialism*. I have often wondered if I would ever have made the commitment to tackle those two large volumes without first having absorbed Henry Hazlitt.

Now we have come 180 degrees at Auburn University. In 1982, two years after I became a trustee, I began to work with Lew Rockwell who had just formed the Mises Institute. We worked together to establish Auburn University as an academic base of the ideas of Ludwig von Mises. The economics department at that time already had a strong contingent of free-market economists and several Misesian scholars. Now the ideas of Mises and Hazlitt are there.

Today on the drawing board at Auburn University are the plans for a new building for the College of Business that will include the Economics Department and a prominent place for the Mises Institute, which will provide it a permanent home for its academic endeavors.

Mr. Hazlitt, those who love liberty will always owe you a debt of gratitude. You have been a prime mover for over 70 years in the sometimes lonely struggle to establish correct economic principles. You have clearly demonstrated the common sense and moral courage that Ludwig von Mises stated would be necessary to change the trends that were on the point of destroying liberty and Western civilization.

There are many hopeful signs that the tide is turning toward the ideas that you and Ludwig von Mises had advocated for many decades.

I am proud to join with all of those present, as well as the many thousands who could not attend, in saying thank you for your courage, for your intellect, for your integrity, and for your love of individual freedom.

Murray N. Rothbard, Vice President
Ludwig von Mises Institute

This is a marvelous occasion, but why haven't there been 20 of these dinners?

In my own case, I was a Hazlittian years before I was a Misesian. In fact, before I had heard of von Mises I knew about Henry Hazlitt. When I was first getting interested in free-market economics, during and just after World War II, Harry was all over the place—in *Newsweek*, on radio and later television—lucid, sound, brilliant, and decisive, carrying the free-market message. And he was the only one.

H. L. Mencken said that Harry Hazlitt was one of the few economists who could write, and that was certainly true. He also got me into a lot of trouble. My first teaching job was at Baruch College, City University of New York, in 1948, before I had heard of von Mises. I was teaching principles of economics—this was before the micro/macro junk came in, so it was in the good old days. We used a fairly decent pre-Keynesian textbook. As a supplement we used Henry Hazlitt's *Economics in One Lesson*, which, of course, was great. But we also had to use a monstrous little left-wing book refuting Harry's book. So on the first day I denounced the left-wing book and told my students not to bother reading it. I was immediately reported to the dean and got in hot water.

Another of my favorites of Harry's is his novel *The Great Idea*. It came out in 1951, and was later reissued as *Time Will*

Run Back. This is *the* great economic novel. The hero falls heir to a world dominated by Soviet dictatorship and starts realizing that things are totally mucked up. Step by step he rediscovers the free market. It is a marvelous lesson in Austrian economics. For example, in what other novel is there a critique of mathematical attempts that try to claim that socialism can calculate? I got an emotional thrill out of this novel, especially when the hero discovers through the market that money is really a gold gram.

In addition to being a writer, a radio/television performer, and a novelist, Harry is also a great scholar. One who is horribly underrated and undervalued. This evening only just begins to rectify the balance.

His great contribution to economics is the *Failure of the "New Economics"*, which came out in 1959. It was a devastating demolition, paragraph by paragraph, of Keynes's *General Theory*. He followed it up with *Critics of Keynesian Economics*.

There are many other contributions to scholarship by Harry. One of them I particularly like is his *Man Vs. the Welfare State*, 1969, the only good critique of Milton Friedman's proposal to replace the welfare state with an even worse welfare proposal called the negative income tax. . . .

This is just a slight sketch of Harry's scholarly and literary accomplishments. . . . He is also a magnificent person. God bless you, Harry.

Ron Paul, Distinguished Counsellor
Ludwig von Mises Institute

I am honored to help praise Henry Hazlitt. But first I want to compliment Lew Rockwell for a great five years with the Mises Institute.

I was one of the first people that Lew came to when he decided to start the Institute and, of course, I did what I could to help. I was a bit skeptical, but Lew, you have proved yourself, and I think it is great.

I, too, Murray, was very much impressed with Henry Hazlitt's *Time Will Run Back*. We all know about *1984* and *Brave New World*. Yet Henry Hazlitt wrote a great novel on how to restore freedom. Toward the end of the book, there is a wonderful statement that I would like to quote:

"If you forbid what is harmful to others, you have a big enough job for any government to take care of. Moreover, you have definite logical boundaries to that job. But if you begin to demand altruism, legally, there are no logical limits until everybody has been forced to give away all he has earned or all he has earned above those who have earned less, and then you are back again to the point where no one has any incentive, whatsoever, to earn or produce anything. . . .

Any society worth living in must of course be infused with a spirit of generosity and benevolence. It can not depend solely on negative virtues, on people's merely respecting one another's liberty or their abstaining from deceit or violence. I concede all of that to be true, but it isn't the function of the government to force people into these positive virtues, it couldn't do it if it tried and the attempt would merely lead to horrible abuses. These positive virtues must come from within the society, itself, and that is merely another way of saying that they must come from within the individual."

In politics today, conservatives want to make individuals better through government, whereas liberals want to make society better by redistributing the wealth. Both approaches lead to the omnipotent state.

In the early 1980s, when I was in Congress fighting the IMF bill appropriations, I called Henry Hazlitt to find out what people said about the IMF when it began. Mr. Hazlitt had been alone in warning the country about the IMF. He mailed me his articles from the 1940s. Possibly I made the suggestion to him, but not too long after, I saw *From Bretton Woods to World Inflation*.

I marvel at individuals who can buck the tide. At the very time of the Bretton Woods meeting, he called it the road to world-wide inflation. Unfortunately, not enough people listened. But fortunately, with our knowledge of Austrian economics today, the spirit of benevolence he talks about in his novel, the spread of Austrian economics, and the leadership of the Mises Institute, I am optimistic in the long run.

And all of us who care about the long run owe a very great debt to Henry Hazlitt.

Mark Skousen
Rollins College

It is really great that we are gathered here to honor Henry Hazlitt, author of the magnificent *Economics in One Lesson*, the book that every economist I know wanted to write. . . .

Several months ago I was talking on the phone to Murray's *favorite* economist, Paul A. Samuelson, about the paradox of thrift. All of you who have been taught from the Samuelson book know about the paradox of thrift: that savings is bad, that it reduces consumption, and that it is bad for the economy. I said, "Henry Hazlitt refutes the paradox of thrift in *Economics in One Lesson*." Paul said, "Ah, but Henry Hazlitt is not an economist."

"Peter Drucker echoes Hazlitt in several of his books." "Well," said Paul, "Drucker is not an economist either."

"What about Irving Fisher, who said one week before the stock market crash that stocks have reached a permanent plateau?" "Oh," Paul said, "he was not a stock market expert." "Yes," I said, "he was an economist!"

Of course, that just shows what the Keynesians know. Henry Hazlitt is a very great economist. But, as the old phrase has it, a man's measure is the work he does and not the title he holds. That is especially true when it comes to Henry Hazlitt, for his accomplishments have been abundant and stunning.

Lord Acton said: "At all times, sincere friends of freedom have been rare and its triumphs have been due to minorities."

Henry Hazlitt has been one of those friends, and one of that minority. However, as Josh Billings noted, "As scarce as truth is, the supply has always been in excess of the demand."

John Fund, Editorial Writer
the *Wall Street Journal*

When Henry Hazlitt went to work for the *Wall Street Journal* the year was 1913 and the income tax and the Federal Reserve System had not yet come into being. Ever since then, as part of a career in journalism that now spans three-quarters of a century, Henry Hazlitt has argued for the restoration of free markets and basic freedoms with a wit and force seldom found in economic journalism. My father used to save Henry Hazlitt's columns from *Newsweek* magazine, and I remember coming across a yellowing file of them when I was thirteen and Richard Nixon was imposing wage and price controls and closing the gold window. Those columns helped my young mind put political events such as those into perspective, and from the audience assembled in this room tonight it is clear I am not alone.

Kenneth Auchincloss
Managing Editor, *Newsweek*

Newsweek sends its warmest greetings and congratulations on this happy occasion. We have always prided ourselves on our columnists as one of the magazine's distinctions, and we take special pride in Henry Hazlitt's 20-year domicile in our pages. Henry always knew what he believed, he stated it clearly, and he never blew with the winds of fashion. What's more—and this is more than can be said for most weekly columnists—his views have stood up very well before the bar of history. He warned against the growth of government deficits. He warned against social programs that hurt the very people they are designed to help. He warned against the expansion of government regulation and intrusiveness that has been, to a great extent, the story of this century. And he was right. Today, his views seem prophetic. At the time he was writing, there were readers—and perhaps even some *Newsweek* editors—who must have considered him old-fashioned, out of touch with the times. But Henry would never have considered trimming his opinions to the patterns of the day. That made him both a very strong journalist and one who was never out of date. Henry, we miss you.

William F. Buckley Jr.
Editor, *National Review*

It is especially mortifying that I should be kept from this celebration by the exigencies of politics. . . . I remember years ago being directed by Harry Hazlitt to the sentence from Mencken to the effect that government is the enemy of all well-disposed, decent, and industrious men. . . .

The last time I lunched with Henry Hazlitt in my home in Stamford, Connecticut, we walked to the car by the garage and he said to me: "How old is this house?" I answered, "It was built in 1907." "Ah," he said, "yes. That is the year I graduated from high school."

I was staggered by this intelligence, but then it occurred to me that Henry Hazlitt was probably about seven years old when he graduated from high school.

His intelligence and his erudition are of the order that makes one wonder if it must not have been a hundred years ago at least that he began his industrious inquiry into the way the world works, or rather should work, if we are to encourage man to be free. I met him first when he was an editor of *The Freeman*. He was flattering enough to offer me a position as an editorial assistant, and I wish I had accepted the offer instead of going with Bill Huie to the *American Mercury*.

Though come to think of it, both men were well equipped to teach me how to run a magazine that year after year runs at a deficit. . . .

We all owe him a great deal. I learned from him early on that no matter how highminded a man's purpose in life, his capacity to laugh is indispensable to the atmosphere he creates. Harry Hazlitt is one of the best laughing companions I have ever known. He and Frances have been a noble couple, interested, interesting, learners and teachers. I am proud to be his friend, I salute him on his enduring accomplishments, and vow to be present five years hence at the next celebration of great gifts.

F. A. Hayek, Nobel Laureate
University of Freiburg

Delighted to learn that Henry Hazlitt is deservedly being celebrated for his long period of beneficial instruction of the public and particularly for having established in the United States the reputation of Ludwig von Mises when totalitarianism drove him out of Europe.

George Bush
Vice President of the United States

Henry, you have been a true giant in the resurgence of conservative thought in the 20th century. . . . I am delighted to join the Ludwig von Mises Institute in saluting you as guest of honor at its fifth anniversary dinner, and send my very best wishes for an enjoyable evening.

Ronald Reagan
President of the United States

Henry, I am pleased and proud to add my congratulations to those of your many colleagues and friends as the Ludwig von Mises Institute honors you at its Fifth Anniversary.

You're being honored for many reasons—your more than seven decades as a scholar and journalist; your many and distinguished contributions to economics; your persistent efforts in behalf of Ludwig von Mises and other scholars; and the wide influence you've had among intellectuals, opinion-makers, and government leaders, including this one.

But, as everyone paying you this truly well-deserved tribute would agree, you're being honored above all for the clarity, the eloquence, the rigorous consistency, and the utterly unflinching courage with which you've studied, explained, and defended economic freedom and individual liberty. In helping those within and without academia to understand the free market and the futility of socialism, you've done all mankind a tremendous and lasting service. I am happy to commend you, and to wish you well always.

Again, congratulations and God bless you.

Llewellyn H. Rockwell, Jr.
Founder and President
Ludwig von Mises Institute

Thank you all for coming to our 5th birthday party, and for helping us to honor a very special and a very great gentleman.

We've heard wonderful talks tonight about Henry Hazlitt's accomplishments in economics, philosophy, and journalism. But, since this is the Mises Institute, I would like to talk for a moment about what he meant to Ludwig von Mises.

When Mises came to this country virtually penniless, Henry Hazlitt took charge. At a time when every second-rate leftist in exile from Western Europe was getting a cushy job at an elite university, Mises was shut out. For he came here with very unfashionable views. Henry set to work to find him an academic post. Together with Lawrence Fertig, he arranged a post at New York University. Consistent with the rest of Mises's life, this was an unpaid professorship. Mises never once had a regular faculty appointment, and the money for his NYU professorship came from free-market individuals, businesses, and foundations. But the entrepreneur of the whole arrangement was Henry Hazlitt.

Henry Hazlitt also arranged the publication by Yale University Press of *Bureaucracy*, *Omnipotent Government*, *Theory and History*, and *Human Action*.

So, on behalf of the Ludwig von Mises Institute, and all of us here tonight, I would like to present you, Harry, with this illuminated scroll, which reads:

The Ludwig von Mises Institute
proudly presents to Henry Hazlitt,
innovative economist, path-breaking philosopher,
and outstanding journalist for liberty,
the Ludwig von Mises Award,
in grateful recognition
of his life-time of achievement
for the free market
in the tradition
of his friend and colleague,
Ludwig von Mises.
Presented in New York City
on the 17th day of October,
in the year 1987.

The scroll is signed by Margit von Mises, Chairman; Burton S. Blumert, Chairman of the Executive Committee; Congressman Ron Paul, Distinguished Counselor; Professor Murray N. Rothbard, Vice President for Academic Affairs; and myself as President. I should add that this beautiful parchment was donated by an admirer of Henry Hazlitt's, calligrapher Alf Ebsen of Willowdale, Ontario.

Ladies and gentlemen, Mr. Henry Hazlitt.

Speech by Henry Hazlitt

If I believed half of this, there would be no living with me. I hope that my wife doesn't notice any deep change when I get back.

My friends, I can't begin to tell you how honored I am by this tribute to me. Such an event in one's life cannot come too late—if the beneficiary is still there.

As I look back on my life it seems on net balance a happy one, though the beginning did not promise well. I was born in Philadelphia. (That is not the bad promise.) My father had diabetes, and died at the age of 28, when I was only two years old. This meant instant poverty for my mother and myself. My father left no life insurance; I do not know whether young men took it out then at such an early age.

My mother had to get a job. She took one at my maternal grandfather's children's hat factory. Children's hats were a big business then. He employed, I believe, over a hundred operators, and my mother became one like his other employees, with no special privileges. This was in spite of the fact that I had been named Henry after him, because he asked for that and promised my parents, if I were so named, that he would give me $10,000 on my twenty-first birthday. But he failed long before then, and I never got the $10,000.

When my mother worked at her job, she parked me at one of my aunts—Tante Mimi, Tante Emmy, or Tante Nellie—(we were originally a German-speaking family from Alsace-Lorraine, and retained these German titles). At her first opportunity, when I was six years old, my mother entered me in Girard College, a home that the Philadelphia philanthropist, Stephen Girard, had set up (and I quote) "for fatherless white boys." (The college was not so long ago compelled by court order to take in fatherless black boys also.) I remained there till the age of nine, when my mother was married again, this time to a man named Frederick Piebes, then her employer, also a manufacturer of children's hats. He took me out of Girard College and adopted me. (I took my original name back at the age of sixteen or so, after my stepfather had died.)

I continued my education at Brooklyn where we lived, at public school, at Boy's High School, then at the College of the City of New York for about one year in the daytime and another year at night. But this college after work eventually proved too much, and I had to give it up.

Meanwhile I had found a job on the *Wall Street Journal*, as secretary to the managing editor, Lockwood Barr, a very kindly man. (I had barely heard of the *Journal* before I took this job, and was merely answering its advertisement in the *New York Times*.) I had not the slightest interest in or knowledge of finance; my head was full of what I thought of as Philosophy. I was taken on because I had given my previous salary as one dollar less a week than the other applicants, and Barr decided I was the "most honest" of the applicants. (The figure I had given was in fact my previous salary.) I was hired at that rate.

I remained on the *Journal* for three years, first as the secretary of the Managing Editor and later as that of the Editor, W. P. Hamilton, an irrascible but brilliant Scotsman. Then I received an offer from the *New York Evening Post* at a higher salary. It came through Palmer Harman, my previous colleague on the *Journal*.

But I had not intended to make this talk an autobiography, or a history of successively better jobs. Rather I should like to use it chiefly to compare some conditions in my early life with those at later times and at the present. The changes in my lifetime—which means in all our lifetimes here—have been enormous, greater than in any previous period. There has been a growth in invention and in accumulated knowledge. The telephone was invented by Alexander Graham Bell in 1876, and began to be installed in significant numbers in homes in 1895. The automobile had no single day of invention, but began to exist in large numbers in the 1890s. Together these two inventions took an outstanding lead in transforming the face of civilization. But did the knowledge and culture of the man in the street make any corresponding advance? Except in knowledge of the inventions themselves, apparently very little.

If I try to make a comparison of public education in the two periods, I am limited by a good deal of forgetfulness about the past and little knowledge of what is going on at present. But I do remember that in languages, for example in public high school, we had native Germans teaching German and native Frenchmen teaching French. If there is anything similar going on today, I do not know about it.

But enough of trivialities.

It has been my privilege to know, and to be the friend of, a great man, the late Ludwig von Mises. He was an economist, the greatest of the present age, fit to rank with Adam Smith and Ricardo. The title of his masterpiece, *Human Action*, enlarged the conception of the realm of economics. I am happy to pay tribute to him here.

Well, when it comes to speeches, old people have the reputation of having no terminal facilities. I want to disprove that. Right now.

The Life and Work of a Dissident Scholar

Jeffrey A. Tucker

Samuel Johnson wrote that the great minds of history are "of large general powers accidentally determined in a particular direction." Ludwig von Mises (1881-1973) had such a mind. We are lucky that he turned to economics—and reconstructed the entire science.

Yet Mises was never given his due. The universities denied him a full-time post. And Mises's stature as a scholar and economist is still largely ignored.

Why is one of the great minds of our time so unrecognized? First, Mises taught reason and logic in an era when the social scientists lauded irrationality and illogic. And second, Mises believed in freedom in an age of omnipotent government.

Yet despite the odds, this dissident scholar was remarkably productive. First, he reconstructed the whole of economic science. And second, he laid a systematic foundation for further rigorous research into the social sciences.

Like other scholars of similar achievement, Mises worked outside the prevailing wisdom, even against the intellectual trends of his time.

Mises's first exposure to Austrian economics came when he read Carl Menger's *Principles of Economics*, and then attended Eugen von Böhm-Bawerk's lectures at the University of Vienna.

Early in Mises's career, government control over money and banking had swept the world. Most economists doubted that money could have its origins or functions in the free market. Mises answered them in his first great work, *The Theory of Money and Credit* (1912).

The book remains the definitive classic on the economics of centralized money and banking. Economists had previously thought that the laws of economics—like the law of marginal utility—did not apply to money. Mises showed that they did. In the same way the free market provides other goods and services, it can also provide money and banking services. With this work, he broke from the past and forged his own school.

The First World War brought with it extensive social and economic control, both in Europe and the United States.

The Warfare State destroyed economies and reversed the progress of liberty. Mises responded with a biting attack on statism and war socialism, *Nation, State, and Economy* (1919). He argued that "modern socialism of necessity must be imperialistic." And that the only way to rebuild after the war, and to prevent future wars, was to expand free markets domestically, to promote free trade internationally, and to strive for political tolerance everywhere.

In the 1920s, the ideologies of socialism, fascism, and communism were overtaking Europe. He responded with a complete refutation of the theory, or non-theory, of socialist economic planning, *Socialism: An Economic and Sociological Analysis* (1922). Not only did he show that socialism was unwise; he showed that it was, in practice, impossible. Without free trade in capital goods, which socialism proposes to abolish, there can be no rational economic calculation. This insight earned him international fame and a group of devoted followers.

It was not enough for Mises to have confronted and destroyed the idea of socialism, including Benito Mussolini's then-proposed *stato corporativo*. Mises also had a vision of society wherein freedom provides the way to social cooperation. His *Liberalism* (1927) is an inspiring defense of political and economic freedom and of the social order of individualism and freedom.

After the 1929 Crash and the publication of John Maynard Keynes's *General Theory* (1936), the interventionists overwhelmed the capitalists in economics departments across Europe and the United States. Mises responded with a sweeping statement reconstructing the whole of the discipline, *Nationaloekonomie* (1940), which later became his English masterpiece *Human Action* (1949). In this, his *magnum opus*, Mises defines and defends economics as the deductive science of individual action, and proposes that all government intervention is not only misguided—it is also counterproductive. This unmatched economic treatise forged an American Misesian movement.

Positivism and empiricism took over as the dominant social science method in the 1950s. Mises responded by directly assaulting their intellectual foundations in *Theory and History* (1957) and *The Ultimate Foundation of Economic Science* (1962), both of which elaborated on earlier essays collected in *Epistemological Problems of Economics* (1933).

For Mises it was not enough to hold correct policy views. How one arrives at those views is also of utmost importance. "It is a complete misunderstanding," Mises said of methodological questions, "to dismiss them as the scholastic quibbling of pedantic professors." On the contrary, method is "the real issue," the one upon which the validity of economics ultimately rests.

Mises's term for the subject matter of economics is praxeology, the logic of action. Praxeological reasoning yields economic principles which are universally valid. No matter when in history or where on the globe one looks, the laws of economics apply. Do the facts fit the economic theory? They do. But empirical facts, and history in general, do not by themselves yield any *economic* knowledge at all.

The conclusions of non-praxeological schools must be as tentative as the historical data from which they derive. They cannot be universal theorems. They must be subjected to continuous empirical "testing" to "prove" their validity.

If this is our standard, free markets could work today but statism may appear to work tomorrow. It's anybody's guess what could work the day after. Not so with praxeology. If one desires prosperity and social cooperation, free markets are the only way.

Mises built a coherent system of economic thought, one which begins with the axiom of human action and deduces the whole of economics—from profits and prices to production and trade cycles. In the Misesian system, economic policy binds to theory that derives from method.

Policy, theory, method—all are part of Misesian economics. For example, Mises had fascinating views on central banking and the business cycle. But they are more powerful when one remembers that they derive logically from universal economic laws, which in turn derive from the fact of human purpose.

That is why Professor Murray Rothbard's new book, *Ludwig von Mises: Scholar, Creator, Hero* (Mises Institute, 1988) is so important. Rothbard includes many hitherto unknown details on Mises's life, and doesn't shy from the harder questions like why most of Mises's best students abandoned him for alien theories and policies.

The Mises who emerges from Rothbard's book is decidedly one of the century's most brilliant intellects. Mises didn't squander his gift for scholarship. He created a system of thought, a science of action, which rescued economics from the depths of nihilism. But what about the "hero" of the title? Samuel Johnson wrote that "the heroes of literary history have been no less remarkable for what they have suffered, than for what they have achieved."

Mises faced incredible challenges: he held no regular academic post, the Nazis ran him out of the country he loved, his brightest students abandoned him late in life, Keynesian doctrine became orthodoxy despite his work, and he watched in horror as statism and war engulfed his century. He once reflected that he "set out to be a reformer, but only became the historian of decline."

Yet Mises remained an uncompromising advocate of economic science and pure laissez-faire until his death. By Johnson's definition of heroism, Mises qualifies. Rothbard sadly notes that Mises never lived to see the Austrian revival which began in 1974 or the growth of the Mises Institute from 1982 to the present.

The Rothbard book does have one failing: it does not mention that Rothbard himself played the major role in keeping the Austrian fires burning during Mises's later years. Where would Austrian economics be without Rothbard's own courage, creativity, and scholarship? Mises's *Human Action* is a masterpiece, but would it have had so much impact without Rothbard's *Man, Economy, and State* (1962), which clarified and refined it? And it was Rothbard who incorporated Misesian economics into a broader science of liberty, which includes law, religion, literature, history, and politics. "Rothbard and the Legacy of Mises" is the missing and unwritten chapter.

In the forward to the German edition of Ludwig von Mises's intellectual biography, *Notes and Recollections* (1977), Nobel Laureate F. A. Hayek wrote that when he looked "for similar figures in the history of thought, I do not find them among the professors, not even in Adam Smith; instead, [Mises] must be compared to thinkers like Voltaire or Montesquieu, Tocqueville and John Stuart Mill."

Rothbard's *Ludwig von Mises: Scholar, Creator, Hero* proves that claim. This detailed accounting and assessment of Mises life and work—the most thorough to date—should be read alongside Mises's books. No one interested in the intellectual history of this century—or in the fight for liberty—can afford to be without it.

5

SOCIALISM

The Politics of Famine

Murray N. Rothbard

The media focuses primarily on the horrifying shots of starving children, and secondarily on the charges and counter-charges about which governments—the Western or the Ethiopian—are responsible for relief not getting to the starving thousands on time. In the midst of the media blitz, the important and basic questions get lost in the shuffle. For example, why does Nature seem to frown only on socialist countries? If the problem is drought, why do the rains only elude countries that are socialist or heavily statist? Why does the United States never suffer from poor climate?

The root of famine lies not in the gods or in our stars but in the actions of man. Climate is not the reason that Russia before Communism was a heavy exporter of grain, while now the Soviet Union is a grain importer. Nature is not responsible for the fact that, of all the countries of East Africa, the Marxist-Leninist nations of Ethiopia and Mozambique are now the major sufferers from mass famine and starvation. Given causes yield given effects, and it is an ineluctable law of nature and of man that if agriculture is systematically crippled and exploited, food production will collapse, and famine will be the result.

The root of the problem is the Third World, where (a) agriculture is overwhelmingly the most important industry, and (b) the people are not affluent enough, in any crisis, to purchase food from abroad. Hence, to Third World people, agriculture is the most precious activity, and it becomes particularly important that it not be hobbled or discouraged in any way. Yet, wherever there is production, there are also parasitic classes living off the producers. The Third World in our century has been the favorite arena for applied Marxism, for revolutions, coups, or domination by Marxist intellectuals. Whenever such new ruling classes have taken over, and have imposed statist or full socialist rule, the class most looted, exploited, and oppressed has been the major productive class: the farmers or peasantry. Literally tens of millions of the most productive farmers were slaughtered by the Russian and Chinese Communist regimes, and the remainder were forced off their private lands and onto cooperative or state farms, where their productivity plummeted, and food production gravely declined.

And even in those countries where land was not directly nationalized, the new burgeoning state apparatus flourished on the backs of the peasantry, by levying heavy taxes and by forcing peasants to sell grain to the state at far below market prices. The artificially cheap food was then used to subsidize foods supplies for the urban population which formed the major base of support for the new bureaucratic class. The standard paradigm in African and in Asian countries has been as follows: British, French, Portuguese, or whatever imperialism carved out artificial boundaries of what they dubbed "colonies," and established capital cities to administer and rule over the mass of peasantry. The new class of higher and lower bureaucrats lived off the peasants by taxing them and forcing them to sell their produce artificially cheaply to the state. When the imperial powers pulled out, they turned over these new nations to the tender mercies of Marxist intellectuals, generally trained in London, Paris, or Lisbon, who imposed socialism or far greater statism, thereby aggravating the problem enormously. Furthermore, a vicious spiral was set up, similar to the one that brought the Roman Empire to its knees. The oppressed and exploited peasantry, tired of being looted for the sake of the urban sector, decided to leave the farm and go sign up in the welfare state provided in the capital city. This makes the farmer's lot still worse, hence more of them leave the farm, despite brutal measures trying to prevent them from leaving. The result of this spiral is famine.

Thus, most African governments force farmers to sell all their crops to the state at only a half or even a third of market value. Ethiopia, as a Marxist-Leninist government, also forced the farmers onto highly inefficient state farms, and tried to keep them working there by brutal oppression.

The answer to famine in Ethiopia or elsewhere is not international food relief. Since relief is invariably under the control of the recipient government, the food generally gets diverted from the farms to line the pockets of government officials to subsidize the already well-fed urban population. The answer to famine is to liberate the peasantry of the Third World from the brutality and exploitation of the state ruling class. The answer to famine is freedom and private property.

Mises and Gorbachev: Why Socialism Still Doesn't Work

Tom Bethell

Last summer, the following headline appeared over a page-one story by Dusko Doder in the *Washington Post*:

> *Gorbachev's Vigor Raises Expectations*
> *New Soviet Leader Focuses on Economy*

Mr. Doder proceeded to inform us that the new Soviet "leader" (what an odd word to use, by the way) had been showing an "almost breathtaking determination to make changes in the Soviet economy."

Two weeks later Serge Schmemann of the *New York Times* wrote of "the depth of excitement and hope that Mr. Gorbachev seems to have tapped across the land in his first 100 days in office."

Since Gorbachev's accession, there have been many similar stories, conveying a ventriloquized media enthusiasm for the new "leader." There can be no doubt that, in the opinion of many U.S. journalists, the socialist economic system of state-controlled resources and central command has not worked well lately in the Soviet Union because the men in charge have been elderly and incompetent. In other words, there is nothing wrong with the system itself—provided it is managed by a skillful, vigorous elite.

Robert Kaiser of the *Washington Post* put it this way in an article headlined "Now Russia Will Change." Gorbachev, he said, is a "new kind of Soviet man." He is "young, well-educated, vital, relaxed and by all outward appearances self-confident." True, Kaiser conceded, there were problems in the economy—"corruption," for example, and "inefficiency."

Also an "entrenched bureaucracy." But all this would no doubt soon change with the vigorous Mr. G. at the helm.

Well, Mr. Kaiser (who was the *Post's* correspondent in Moscow in the early 1970s) is in for a big disappointment. And so are the poor, long-suffering Russian people. Nothing is likely to change, although it is possible that Gorbachev will make things worse.

The great difficulty for Mr. Gorbachev is this: socialist economies all have a serious defect which cannot be resolved by vigor or good intentions. This defect was spelled out by Ludwig von Mises as long ago as 1920—before the evidence of socialist failure was available. His analysis amounted to a prediction that has been verified.

The problem is this: It is one thing for central planners to draw up a plan of production. It is quite another thing to carry it out. Here we encounter the famous "problem of economic calculation" formulated by Mises. How can you (the planners) know what should be produced, before you know what people want? And people cannot know what they want unless they first know the price of things. But prices themselves can only be established when people are permitted to own things and to exchange them among themselves. But people do not have these rights in centrally planned economies.

The planners can, of course, decide beforehand what goods are to be manufactured, whether or not the people really want them. But as Trygve Hoff points out in his book *Economic Calculation in the Socialist Society*, only the most primitive planning can proceed in this way. In real life the planners and their subordinate factory managers bump up against the central fact of economic life—scarcity. There is not enough of everything to go around. One is tempted to say that there is not enough of anything to go around—if it is both desirable and free. (Air seems to be the only exception.)

It is worth noting that when, in the 1920s and 1930s economists tried to rebut Mises, some of them went so far as to challenge the assumption of scarcity, suggesting that it was a chimera stage-managed by nefarious monopolists. But if we assume that scarcity is a reality, as we must, then we are forced to conclude that goods must be priced. And yet the central planners do not know how to price them in the absence of markets.

Prices depend for their formation on the real possibility of personal profit or loss. Try to imagine a serious game of poker played with Monopoly money. All psychological incentive is removed by the knowledge that at the end of the evening, no one playing is really going to lose or gain anything.

In *The Foundations of Morality*, Henry Hazlitt made one of the clearest statements of the problem of socialist pricing:

"If I am a government commissar selling something I don't really own, and you are another government commissar buying it with money that isn't really yours, then neither of us really cares what the price is. When, as in a socialist or communist country, the heads of mines and factories, or stores and collective farms, are mere salaried government bureaucrats, and sell their finished products to still other bureaucrats, the so-called prices at which they buy and sell are mere bookkeeping fictions. Such bureaucrats are merely playing an artificial game called 'free market.' They cannot make a socialist system work like a free-market system merely by imitating prices while ignoring private property."

The Polish economist Oskar Lange tried to save the day for the socialist by claiming that prices could be established by trial and error: set prices at a given level and then move it up or down depending on whether it yields a shortage or a surplus. But here the socialist run into their second great difficulty—the transmission of information to the central planning authority. How do the central planners know where things are in shortage and where they are in surplus? (This problem was first elucidated by F. A. Hayek.) The point is that it is difficult and expensive to move information to a central point.

Alternatively, one could say that only a comparatively small amount of information can be crammed into a central point. Here we may think of another analogy. How do you get a message onto President Reagan's desk? Obviously you can't just call him up, and if you write, your message will compete with the thousands of letters that arrive each day. A lot of money is spent in Washington trying to solve this problem. The same problem exists for Soviet commissars trying to get the attention of the people in Moscow who have decision-making authority.

In response to these various difficulties there are, I believe, three options open to the planning authority (over which Mr. Gorbachev presides). It can turn a blind eye on the various underling officials and managers as they make transactions and exchanges among themselves without getting permission from Moscow. This option—de facto decentralization—is labeled "corruption," however, and it is very unpopular with those who think that socialism should be made to work according to the prescriptions of Lenin. Leonid Brezhnev evidently used the "blind-eye" method. But with Yuri Andropov there was a crackdown. Various officials were shot to discourage the others.

"Crackdown" is in fact the second option, and the one preferred by reformers everywhere, including, of course, American liberals. Gorbachev is Andropov's protégé and he may well try to go this route. Apparently he already tried it in agriculture, over which he earlier presided. Grain production declined from 237 million tons in 1978 to 170 million tons in 1984. (Such declines are normally attributed to "bad weather.") Nonetheless Gorbachev was promoted, and he may well now attempt a more general crackdown. If he does, he would provoke a more general decline in Soviet production.

The third option is for Gorbachev to attempt to decentralize the system—i.e. to legalize many of the actions previously labeled corrupt. This in effect is a movement away from socialism. It would be the best thing Gorbachev could attempt, but here he will run up against the "entrenched bureaucracy" that Robert Kaiser alluded to. Decentralizing the Soviet economy depends on issuing orders that are the functional equivalent of telling captains that they no longer need to obey majors, and corporals that they are on a par with sergeants.

The point is that it is very difficult to get such unpopular orders to pass down the chain of command. Colonels will always find ways of obstructing commands that have the effects of denying their own authority. (In the reverse direction, the Soviet economy suffers from an equally serious problem: just as unpopular orders won't travel downhill, so unpopular information won't travel uphill. Reports of unfulfilled plans and quotas tend to be ameliorated as they move closer to the center.)

Of the various problems associated with the Soviet economy (and all socialist economies) the "entrenched bureaucracy" is the one that U.S. journalists are beginning to appreciate and describe. For example in late May David Ignatius wrote in the *Wall Street Journal*:

> It may prove impossible to both increase the independence of individual Soviet enterprises and retain full central control of the economy. Says Arnold Horelick, the director of the Rand-UCLA Center for the Study of Soviet International Behaviour: "I would describe Gorbachev's reforms as trying to have his cake and eat it, too."

Maybe China will prove me wrong. I hope so. But at present the evident suggests that communism cannot be reformed from within. My guess is that of the three options listed here, the "Brezhnev-blind-eye" is the only one that is remotely workable—not that it produces brilliant results—and Mr. Gorbachev will almost certainly resort to it if he stays in his office for any length of time.

A Trip to Poland

Murray N. Rothbard

This March, I spent a fascinating week at a conference at a hotel in Mrogowo, in the lake country of northern Poland (formerly East Prussia). The conference, a broad-ranging symposium on "Economics and Social Change," was hosted by the Institute of Sociology at the University of Warsaw, and sponsored by a group of English conservative and free-market scholars.

Even though economically, as one of the Western participants noted, Poland is a "giant slum," its countryside, small towns, and cities in evident and grim decay, this gallant nation is intellectually the freest in the Eastern bloc. There is no other country in the Soviet orbit at which a conference of this sort could possibly be held.

The only restriction was that the announced titles of the papers had to be ideologically neutral. But, once the conference ran that particular gauntlet, and the meeting was approved by the authorities, anyone could—and did—say whatever they wished. (In my case, I bowdlerized the title of my paper, "Concepts of the Role of Intellectuals in Social Change Towards Laissez-Faire," by discreetly omitting the last three words, although the actual content of the talk remained the same.)

The first paper of the meeting was delivered by Professor Antony Flew, a distinguished English philosopher, who likes nothing better than to deliver—with intelligence and wit—zingers at the Left. Flew pulled no punches, pointing out the importance and necessity of property rights and the free market. The fascinating thing was that no Polish eyebrow was raised, and no Polish scholar reacted in horror. Quite the contrary. And it was enormously inspiring to see every one of the twenty-odd Polish scholars denouncing the government, even though it was obvious to every one of us that there was a government agent listening intently to the proceedings. (The agent—the travel guide and director of the trip—was obviously highly intelligent, and aware of what was going on.)

The Poles ranged from libertarian to middle-of-the-road to dissident Marxist, but it was markedly evident that not one of them had any use whatsoever for the Communist regime. In addition to being opposed to Communism, none of the Polish scholars at the meeting had much use for *any* government. One told me, "of course, any act of government is done for the power and wealth of the government officials, and not for the 'public interest,' 'common good,' 'general welfare,' or any other reasons offered."

"Yes," I said, "but the government's propaganda always says that they perform these actions for the common good, etc." The Polish professor looked at me quizzically: "Who believes government propaganda?" I replied that, "unfortunately, in the United States, most people believe government propaganda." He was incredulous.

The Polish scholars all knew English very well, a virtue that unfortunately we Westerners couldn't begin to reciprocate. Nevertheless, a real camaraderie developed. One amusing culture gap was the Polish waiters in our hotel (what passes for a "luxury hotel" in Poland is roughly equivalent to a low-end interstate motel in the U.S.) having to deal with the "kids" of the conference, two young English scholars who are insistent vegetarians. Poland is a land with a very high meat consumption per capita (the Communists never collectivised agriculture), but where meat is now rationed, and it was beyond the comprehension of the Polish waiters that two young privileged Westerners would keep calling for "more vegetables" while turning down top-grade beef and pork. Fortunately, there was always a Polish professor nearby who could serve as interpreter for these outlandish requests.

The most moving moment of the meeting came at the banquet on the final night, when the English sociologist who directed the conference, after thanking our Polish hosts, raised a glass and offered a heartfelt toast to "a free, sovereign, and Catholic Poland." Every one of us understood his intent, and everyone in that room, Protestants and unbelievers included, raised a glass and drank with fervor. Including the government agent.

The Misesian Revolution in Poland

Lawrence W. Reed

I've lectured about "The Origin, Nature, and History of Money from an Austrian Perspective" in the United States a couple dozen times. But until it actually happened last November, I never expected to do it in socialist Poland.

I spent a week there, living with and interviewing activists in the Polish underground. I entered and exited the country legally, but my itinerary and escorts were provided by a new opposition group called the Freedom and Peace Movement.

During the trip, the government learned what I was doing and customs agents at the Warsaw airport delayed my departure flight for two hours, strip-searching and interrogating me, and confiscating all my tapes and film. But they could not steal my memories about the Misesian excitement percolating through the vast Polish underground.

The 50 or so students who gathered quietly to hear my first lecture on money listened intently. Then they asked questions which indicated a sophistication far beyond anything I had expected. And their devotion to the free market was intense and scholarly. "How do you know so much about laissez-faire economics?" I asked.

An economics major at Jagiellonian University in Cracow, responded, "Thanks to our underground press, we probably know more than American students." As the week went by, I came to appreciate just how true that was. The burgeoning interest in Austrian economics is, as a professor at the University of Warsaw noted, "the most important recent development" among students of economics. He privately recommends the works of Mises, Hayek, and Rothbard to his students, who then acquire copies on the black (i.e., free) market.

Underground publishing houses in Poland produce hundreds of books and magazines a year, often in editions of more than 10,000. Attending a secret dinner party one evening hosted by several underground printer-entrepreneurs, I was astonished to hear their plans to ultimately publish and distribute every work of Mises's. "Anything Austrian or libertarian immediately becomes a bestseller," said one.

Already, students are reading Mises's *Socialism* and *Theory of Money and Credit*. A professor who attended one of my lectures quoted from Rothbard's *The Mystery of Banking*. The same professor has written a popular underground book advocating that Poles who care about political liberty first work for laissez-faire economics.

The young intellectual activists I met, especially those involved in the Freedom and Peace Movement, explain Polish economic problems from a perspective that would gratify Mises. Everything from toilet-paper shortages to industrial pollution is understood as a direct and inevitable consequence of "central planning" and the absence of a "market-price mechanism." The basket-case Polish economy, said one Cracow student, "is a living laboratory of the silliness of socialism."

Under the surface, Poland is seething with anti-government ferment. And the works of Ludwig von Mises and his students are part of the reason—testimony once again to the potency of truth.

Mises and the Soviet Free Market

Lawrence W. Reed

Not many Soviet citizens have ever read Ludwig von Mises's great *Socialism*. The Soviet government doesn't want the people to know the truth about a command economy. They are supposed to be good, little citizens—pacified and rendered docile by the benevolence of the omnipotent state.

But even if the Soviet public doesn't understand exactly why the official economy doesn't work, they want as little to do with it as possible. In their own actions, they show consistent preference for free markets over government markets, even though demonstrating that preference is risky.

The reason that Soviet socialism has flopped is—as Mises proved in 1922—that all centrally "planned" economies must, by their very nature, fail.

Given the fact of nature that everybody can't have everything they want—that is, that there is economic scarcity—there must be some means of directing resources to their most efficient uses.

One way to do this is to have central planners set prices and production, telling people what to buy, how much to buy, and when to buy. But, as Mises pointed out in *Socialism*:

> In any social order, even under Socialism, it can very easily be decided which kind and what number of consumption goods should be produced. No one has ever denied that. But once this decision has been made, there still remains the problem of ascertaining how the existing means of production can be used most effectively to produce these goods in question. In order to solve this problem it is necessary that there should be economic calculation. And economic calculation can only take place by means of money prices established in the market for production

> goods in a society resting on private property in the means of production. That is to say, there must exist money prices of land, raw materials, semimanufactures; that is to say, there must be money wages and interest rates.

For calculation to occur, says Mises, there must be money prices. Those can only come from free markets, never governments. Socialism is thus always doomed to fail.

The problem of this argument for socialists is it doesn't rely on ethical standards or political ideologies. Neither does it say, like so many arguments in favor of markets, that markets are better because they make people richer. (Although it is, of course, true that socialism is immoral, and that it makes people poor.) It rather says of socialism the most damning thing of all to these alleged scientists: that their "scientific socialism" makes rational economic calculation impossible.

Mises simply argues that all exchange relationships established by the government are necessarily arbitrary. In fact, any government intervention hinders economic calculation, and makes the allocation of resources an irrational process.

We take the miracle of market pricing for granted. But notice what happens when government hampers the pricing mechanism. Think of the times that the U.S. government has put price controls on goods like oil. Pandemonium ensues. The Soviet economy is under constant price controls. How do they know, for example, in clothing production what the proper ratio is between ties and socks? The only way to know is to allow people to freely buy and sell, thus expressing their own subjective valuations and personal preferences, and allow the market to establish the proper ratio.

If there is a problem at the tie-sock level, how could a socialist economy run? It has no pricing system upon which to base judgments about production. How do you make any decisions without market pricing? How are production costs figured? How do you know if you're making profits or losses? There is no way without a market. Prices in the Soviet Union are approximated from their own black market or from other countries.

A spokesman for the Soviet Foreign Ministry, in an unintended tribute to Mises, recently told some visiting Americans that his dream was to have "the entire world Communist. Except New Zealand." Why the exception? "We have to have somebody to tell us the prices."

Mises wrote his critique in 1922. It was the most telling blow socialism ever received, and socialists are still trying to answer it. Mises forced socialists to think about how socialism works in practice. After more than 65 years, he has not been answered.

Socialists of all stripes, from Marx to Galbraith, typically wax eloquent on the alleged evils of capitalism, but never spell out how their version of society would operate. If the economy is to be planned, what's the plan? This is the socialist mystery of the missing blueprints, and Mises was the first to call their bluff.

Whatever kind of economy they want, socialists inevitably claim that the Soviet economy isn't it. That's not real socialism, they say. But no matter what socialists want, when the means of production are put in the hands of the state, the Soviet economy is what they're going to get: rich politicians, impoverished masses, and irrational use of resources. The Soviet Union is socialism in action.

I have visited the Soviet Union three times since March 1985, and I have always been impressed by the size and vitality of the underground economy, the vast and murky world of the "black" market—the free network of illegal production and trade that enables millions of dissatisfied comrades to meet their needs.

Ordinary Russians have taught themselves to dodge and weave around the state with surprising skill and daring, as Hedrick Smith notes in his bestseller, *The Russians*:

> This counter-economy has become an integral part of the Soviet system, a built-in permanent feature of Soviet society. It encompasses everything from petty bribing, black

> marketing, wholesale thieving from the state, and underground private manufacturing, all the way up to a full-fledged *godfather* operation which was exposed and led to the downfall of a high Communist Party figure. . . . It operates on an almost oriental scale and with a brazen normality that would undoubtedly incense the original Bolshevik revolutionaries.

On more than one occasion, I have been propositioned for my blue jeans or tennis shoes (once even in Red Square) by young Russians who seem to appear out of nowhere, quickly arrange a time and place to consummate the transaction, then disappear into the crowd.

A vast market in American dollars bubbles beneath the surface of official life in Russia, despite harsh penalties. A short walk down the street from one's hotel usually brings one or two currency traders to your side, whispering "rubles for dollars" at three and four times the legal rate.

One young man in Leningrad told me he earns about 400 rubles a month, but less than a quarter of it is legal. The rest he earns by marketing contraband books and other items smuggled in from the West. Last year he bought a car—rarely a private possession in the workers' paradise—for about 8,000 rubles. He registered it in his father's name, so the state wouldn't question where he got the money.

Russian dentists, he told me, do not use Novocain, even when pulling teeth, thanks to state misallocation. But he pays his dentist a little extra under the table. Many dentists have their own illegal private practices—complete with pain-killers—during off-hours, and that's when the quality of care goes up.

American movies are popular in the Soviet underground. People duplicate copies and sell dozens all over Leningrad. If you're caught, you get years in the slammer.

Practically everybody in the Soviet Union is trading and exchanging on the free market. Still, empty official slogans are plastered on buildings or mounted on rooftops all over the place proclaiming "The Plan of the 27th Party Congress Will Be Fulfilled" or, even more laughable, "The Party and the People Are One!"

The Soviet state has been successful so far in keeping articles and books by Ludwig von Mises and other free-market thinkers extremely rare. Still people grumble about the state, then go about their private and profitable affairs. But I'd like to change that. If the insights of *Socialism* became widely known, Gorbachev would be staring a real revolution in the face.

Freedom vs. Planning

Richard Ebeling

As the 20th century began, the most widely held vision of the future was socialist: capitalism would be replaced by central planning and the state would own all the means of production.

The 20th century is ending with the socialist ideal in complete disarray. The heads of socialist governments everywhere declare that economic progress requires individual initiative and private enterprise. They admit that only competition and a market price system can bring economic coordination to a complex system of division of labor.

All of this was anticipated by Ludwig von Mises almost 70 years ago in his famous 1920 article, "Economic Calculation in the Socialist Commonwealth" and in his monumental treatise, *Socialism: An Economic and Sociological Analysis* (1922).

Mises conclusively demonstrated that without market-generated prices, expressed in terms of a common medium of exchange, it is impossible to use society's scarce resources in a rational manner. A central planner might know the technological potentials of the resources at his disposal, but he has no way to know what economic values to assign to those resources. He cannot know how to allocate resources among alternative lines of production, and thus cannot rationally service consumers' demands. This insight means that our choice of economic systems can only be between free-market capitalism and "planned chaos." "There is no third solution, no middle way," says Mises.

It is clear that socialism has lost the war on the battlefield of ideas. But free-market capitalism has not yet won. Both in the United States and around the world, policy-makers promote the "mixed economy," a hodgepodge of competition and state control. Intellectuals on both the collectivist left and the conservative right have enshrined the idea of state intervention.

Capitalism delivers the goods, they say, but the distribution of these goods is "unfair." The profit motive is a powerful engine for individual initiative and creativity, but too often the commodities produced are "socially undesirable" and exist only at the expense of the good society. And while competition is desirable to keep producers on their toes, too much of a good thing can be bad. Thus government needs to protect competitors from "unfair" competition, domestic and foreign.

Free market replies to every one of these arguments for state intervention can be found in the writings of Ludwig von Mises: in *Liberalism*(1927), *Critique of Interventionism* (1929), *Human Action* (1949), *Planning for Freedom* (1952), *The Anti-capitalist Mentality* (1956), and *Economic Policy* (1979).

What about the argument that capitalism "unfairly" distributes the goods produced by it? Mises demonstrates that the argument is based on a false conception of the free-market process. Production and distribution are two sides of the same coin. Production requires the combined use of various factors of production, and labor is one of those resources.

Each resource is offered a price, through entrepreneurial judgments, for its service equal to its relative value as a contribution to the production of commodities. Each factor of production contracts for the services it will render before there is a product available for sale.

The entrepreneur develops expectations about what consumers would be willing to pay in the future for the product being considered, and offers wages to laborers and payment for services of other resources.

But who are the consumers? Ultimately, they are the very same laborers and resource owners whom the entrepreneur is considering hiring. It is thus the laborers and resource owners, in their roles as consumers, who determine what their own relative income shares will be. They do so through their decisions about what they wish to buy and what prices they are willing to pay for them.

Thus, if some groups of workers believe they are "unfairly" paid, they have no one to accuse but themselves and the other laborers. They have failed to spend a greater percentage of their income on the particular products that the workers produce.

"Producers" and "consumers" are really the same people. And because this is always true in the free market, the second charge against free-market capitalism, that it produces "socially undesirable" products, also fails.

First, as Mises forcefully argued, there is no dichotomy between "society" and the individuals comprising it. Nothing happens to or for "society" that doesn't originate with the individuals whose actions create societal relationships.

Second, in the free market, competition makes the entrepreneur the servant and not the master of the economic process. The entrepreneur must ultimately supply what individuals in their role as consumers demand. An entrepreneur who fails to do this will be driven from business and other entrepreneurs more sensitive to consumer wishes will replace him.

Finally, when people say that some product is "socially undesirable," they really mean that people in society are demanding things of which they disapprove. But rather than attempt to use reason to persuade others to change their buying preferences, they want to use government to coerce them into abstinence. To answer this, Mises argued that freedom is indivisible. Once it is admitted that government has the right to infringe on the peaceful and personal preferences of individuals in one area, state interference cannot logically be excluded from other spheres. At the end of this road is the totalitarian state (see *Liberalism*, pp. 52-57).

In *Human Action*, Mises showed that free markets mean social cooperation, not social conflict. It is through this process of competition that we know who, among the various suppliers, can most successfully satisfy consumers' demands at the least cost and, therefore, at the lowest price. And through this process each individual finds his most efficient and profitable place in the social system of the division of labor.

He who asks for state protection from the rigors of competition, Mises explains, is asking for special privilege at the expense of the other members of society. He is demanding special regulations, tariffs, or subsidies in order to receive a higher relative income than what others in the free-market economy are willing to pay him for his products or services.

If the government grants the special privilege, the results are disruptive of the peaceful free market process of economic change and progress. When other members of society begin to obtain government privileges and protections, the cumulative effect is declining production, less innovation, higher prices, and a lower standard of living for the members of the whole society.

Mises's most important contribution to understanding the fallacies of state intervention is his demonstration that "the Middle-of-the-Road Leads to Socialism." All government interventions and regulations are inherently destabilizing and disruptive. And the logical consequences of one set of interventions is that the government will extend its controls to more and more sectors of the economy to "repair" the damage created by the first set of controls.

If, for example, the government imposes price controls in one part of the economy, the controls will distort the existing free-market relationships between prices and the costs of production. If the controlled price is set below the costs of production, sellers in that part of the economy will no longer be able to produce the same amount of the product as before. If the government wants high production levels, it must extend the price controls to the prices of the factors that go into making that product. But those factors of production have, in turn, been produced with other resources whose prices will also have to be controlled.

The interdependency of all prices and all markets in a system of division of labor means that if the government decides to control one part of the economy, it must end up controlling all of it. Finally, when the controls and regulations pervade every portion of the economy, the free market is completely supplanted by the state, and socialism replaces capitalism through piecemeal interventionism. In short, as Mises says, "the middle-of-the-road policy is not an economic system that can last. It is a method for the realization of socialism by installments."

But what would *logically* happen if government remains on the interventionist road is different from what must happen.

Mises repeatedly observed that the Western world was moving toward collectivism. But he also emphasized that "the trend can be reversed as was the case with many other trends in history." In the realm of human action no choices are "inevitable." History is made by men, and men are ultimately guided by ideas.

A victory for free-market capitalism is possible. Just as theory and experience refuted the case for socialism, the same can happen to state intervention and the "mixed economy."

In fact, in terms of practical results, state intervention is already defunct. But people must be shown how to read the signs left behind by a controlled, taxed, and welfarist "mixed economy." People must understand why it happened and what it demonstrates, that if we want peace, prosperity, and liberty, there is no alternative to free-market capitalism.

Thanks to Ludwig von Mises, we have the arguments and insights to lead us in the battle of ideas.

Why Socialism Must Fail

Hans-Hermann Hoppe

Socialism and capitalism offer radically different solutions to the problem posed by scarcity: everybody can't have everything they want when they want it, so how can we effectively decide who will own and control the resources we have? The chosen solution has profound implications. It can mean the difference between prosperity and impoverishment, voluntary exchange and political coercion, even totalitarianism and liberty.

The capitalist system solves the problem of scarcity by recognizing the right of private property. The first one to use a good is its owner. Others can acquire it only through trade and voluntary contracts. But until the owner of the property decides to make a contract to trade his property, he can do whatever he wants with it, so long as he does not interfere with or physically damage the property owned by others.

The socialist system attempts to solve the problem of ownership in a completely different way. Just as in capitalism, people can own consumer products. But in socialism, property which serves as the means of production are collectively owned. No person can own the machines and other resources which go into producing consumption goods. Mankind, so to speak, owns them. If people use the means of production, they can do so only as caretakers for the entire community.

Economic law guarantees that harmful economic and sociological effects will always follow the socialization of the means of production. The socialist experiment will always end in failure.

First, socialism results in less investment, less saving, and lower standards of living. When socialism is initially imposed, property must be redistributed. The means of production are taken away from current users and producers and given to the community of caretakers. Even though the owners and users of the means of production acquired them through mutual consent from previous users, they are transferred to people who, at best, become users and producers of things they didn't own previously.

Under this system, previous owners are penalized in favor of new owners. The non-users, non-producers, and non-contractors of the means of production are favored by being promoted to the rank of caretaker over property which they had not previously used, produced, or contracted to use. Thus the income for the non-user, non-producer, and non-contractor rises. It is the same for the non-saver who benefits at the expense of the saver from whom the saved property is confiscated.

Clearly, then, if socialism favors the non-user, non-producer, non-contractor, and non-saver, it raises the costs that have to be born by users, producers, contractors, and savers. It is easy to see why there will be fewer people in these latter roles. There will be less original appropriation of natural resources, less production of new factors of production, and less contracting. There will be less preparation for the future because everyone's investment outlets dry up. There will be less saving and more consuming, less work and more leisure.

This adds up to fewer consumption goods being available for exchange, which reduces everyone's standard of living. If people are willing to take the risk, they will have to go underground to compensate for these losses.

Second, socialism results in inefficiencies, shortages, and prodigious waste. This is the insight of Ludwig von Mises who discovered that rational economic calculation is impossible under socialism. He showed that capital goods under socialism are at best used in the production of second-rate needs, and at worst, in production that satisfies no needs whatsoever.

Mises's insight is simple but extremely important: because the means of production under socialism cannot be sold, there are no market prices for them. The socialist caretaker cannot establish the monetary costs involved in using the resources or in making changes in the length of production processes. Nor can he compare these costs with the monetary income from sales. He is not allowed to take offers from others who want to use his means of production, so he cannot know what his foregone opportunities are. Without knowing foregone opportunities, he cannot know his costs. He cannot even know if the way he produces is efficient or inefficient, desired or undesired, rational or irrational. He cannot know whether he is satisfying less or more urgent needs of consumers.

In capitalism, money prices and free markets provide this information to the producer. But in socialism, there are no prices for capital goods and no opportunities for exchange. The caretaker is left in the dark. And because he can't know the status of his current production strategy, he can't know how to improve it. The less producers are able to calculate and engage in improvement, the more likely wastes and shortages become. In an economy where the consumer market for his products is very large, the producer's dilemma is even worse. It hardly needs to be pointed out: when there is no rational economic calculation, society will sink into progressively worsening impoverishment.

Third, socialism results in over-utilization of the factors of production until they fall into disrepair and become vandalized. A private owner in capitalism has the right to sell his factor of production at any time and keep the revenues derived from the sale. So it is to his advantage to avoid lowering its capital value. Because he owns it, his objective is to maximize the value of the factor responsible for producing the goods and services he sells.

The status of the socialist caretaker is entirely different. He cannot sell his factor of production, so he has little or no incentive to insure that it retains its value. His incentive will instead be to increase the output of his factor of production without regard to its dwindling value. There is also the chance that if the caretaker perceives opportunities of employing the means of production for private purposes—like making goods for the black market—he will be encouraged to increase the output at the expense of capital values. No matter which way you look at it, under socialism without private ownership and free markets, producers will be inclined to consume capital values by over-using them. Capital consumption leads to impoverishment.

Fourth, socialism leads to a reduction in the quality of goods and services available for the consumer. Under capitalism, an individual businessman can maintain and expand his firm only if he recovers his costs of production. And since the demand for the firm's products depends on consumer evaluations of price and quality (price being one criterion of quality), product quality must be a constant concern of producers. This is only possible with private ownership and market exchange.

Things are entirely different under socialism. Not only are the means of production collectively owned, but so too is the income derived from the sale of the output. This is another way of saying that the producer's income has little or no connection with consumer evaluation of the producer's work. This fact, of course, is known by every producer.

The producer has no reason to make a special effort to improve the quality of his product. He will instead devote relatively less time and effort to producing what consumers want and spend more time doing what *he* wants. Socialism is a system that incites the producer to be lazy.

Fifth, socialism leads to the politicization of society. Hardly anything can be worse for the production of wealth.

Socialism, at least its Marxist version, says its goal is complete equality. The Marxists observe that once you allow private property in the means of production, you allow differences. If I own resource A, then you do not own it and our relationship toward resource A becomes different and unequal. By abolishing private property in the means of production with one stroke, say the Marxists, everyone becomes co-owner of everything. This reflects everyone's equal standing as a human being.

The reality is much different. Declaring everyone a co-owner of everything only nominally solves differences in ownership. It does not solve the real underlying problem: there remain differences in the power to control what is done with resources.

In capitalism, the person who owns a resource can also control what is done with it. In a socialized economy, this isn't true because there is no longer any owner. Nonetheless the problem of control remains. Who is going to decide what is to be done with what? Under socialism, there is only one way: people settle their disagreements over the control of property by superimposing one will upon another. As long as there are differences, people will settle them through political means.

If people want to improve their income under socialism they have to move toward a more highly valued position in the hierarchy of caretakers. That takes political talent.

Under such a system, people will have to spend less time and effort developing their productive skills and more time and effort improving their political talents.

As people shift out of their roles as producers and users of resources, we find that their personalities change. They no longer cultivate the ability to anticipate situations of scarcity, to take up productive opportunities, to be aware of technological possibilities, to anticipate changes in consumer demand, and to develop strategies of marketing. They no longer have to be able to initiate, to work, and to respond to the needs of others.

Instead, people develop the ability to assemble public support for their own position and opinion through means of persuasion, demagoguery, and intrigue, through promises, bribes, and threats. Different people rise to the top under socialism than under capitalism. The higher on the socialist hierarchy you look, the more you will find people who are too incompetent to do the job they are supposed to do. It is no hindrance in a caretaker-politician's career to be dumb, indolent, inefficient, and uncaring. He only needs superior political skills. This too contributes to the impoverishment of society.

The United States is not fully socialized, but already we see the disastrous effects of a politicized society as our own politicians continue to encroach on the rights of private property owners. All the impoverishing effects of socialism are with us in the U.S.: reduced levels of investment and saving, the misallocation of resources, the overutilization and vandalization of factors of production, and the inferior quality of products and services. And these are only tastes of life under total socialism.

Massachusetts and the Mussolinization of America

Llewellyn H. Rockwell, Jr.

Official socialism has probably never been a threat in America, but the corporate state has. And is.

It all began in 1919 when ex-Marxist Benito Mussolini wrote the Fascist Party platform, calling for central planning through a "partnership" of government, business, and labor. By 1925 he was in total power.

Not all of Mussolini's admirers were in Italy. The cover story of the *New York Times Magazine* for October 24, 1926, gushed:

> The most approachable as well as the most interesting statesman in Europe. He is a voracious learner who never makes the same mistake twice. . . . The whole country is keyed up by his energy. . . .
>
> The whole economic structure of the nation has been charted out in a graph that shows it as a huge corporation with the Government as the directorate. He explains it clearly and patiently, reminding you that he started his career as a teacher.

An earlier *New York Times* editorial (October 31, 1922) had explained:

> In Italy as everywhere the great complaint against democracy today is its inefficiency. . . . Neither the failures nor the successes of (Russia's) Bolshevist Government offer much of an example to the Western world. Dr. Mussolini's experiment will perhaps tell us something more about the possibilities of oligarchic administration.

Although Herbert Hoover in many ways prefigured him, it was Franklin D. Roosevelt who first tried to create an explicit corporate state in America with his National Recovery Administration (NRA). With its fascist-style Blue Eagle emblem, the NRA coordinated big business and labor in a central plan, and outlawed competition. The NRA even employed vigilante groups to spy on smaller businesses and report if they violated the plan.

Just as in Mussolini's Italy, the beneficiaries of the U.S. corporate state were—in addition to the government itself—established economic interest groups. NRA cheerleaders included the National Association of Manufacturers, the U.S. Chamber of Commerce, the American Bar Association, the United Mine Workers, the Amalgamated Clothing Workers, and—above all—Gerard Swope of General Electric, who helped draft the NRA act.

Only the courage of the Supreme Court, which ruled that the NRA was unconstitutional, prevented the establishment of a fascist economy in our country. FDR denounced the "nine old men" and tried to pack the court with NRA proponents. But the American people, including most of his supporters, opposed the power grab, and he lost. That did not end the battle, however.

Today, there are many elements of a corporate state in Washington. But in Massachusetts, Michael Dukakis has come closest to actually establishing one. Wrote the *Washington Post* recently:

> Corporate Massachusetts is in a *de facto* alliance with the state and a host of potentially conflicting interests, including . . . organized labor . . . , all of whom serve on agency boards and are also recipients of agency grants. . . .
>
> Not only has Dukakis drawn these business leaders into what amounts to limited partnerships with state government, with the governor as the dominant general partner, but also these quasi-public agencies have formed a web of

> financial arrangements with at least 3,000 corporations across the state. The state government effectively has been entrenched in almost every nook and cranny of the private sector.

The tools Dukakis used to create this alliance for central planning included a larger bureaucracy; subsidized loans, bailouts, and outright grants for big businesses; and guaranteed high wages for unions.

Those on the Massachusetts gravy line include the insurance industry, especially John Hancock Mutual Life; high-tech corporations like our old friend GE, Digital Equipment Corp., and Raytheon; and banks like the Bank of Boston. Each is represented on the boards of the Massachusetts Capital Resources Corp., the Massachusetts Industrial Finance Agency, and similar corporate-statist entities. And all march in profitable lock-step with the state. The only losers are taxpayers, consumers, and businesses without political connections.

The *Post* notes that Dukakis's policies "diverge sharply from the more traditional type of partisan politics emphasizing ideological splits between business and labor."

With guaranteed profits, corporations are partially liberated from consumer control. In return, they agree to pay the above-market wages that labor unions demand, and otherwise cooperate with the state. But what will be the economic result?

In 1920, Ludwig von Mises showed in "Economic Calculation in the Socialist Commonwealth" that there can be no rational central planning.

In a free market, consumers' spending decisions tell producers what and how much to produce. If consumers prefer Fords to Chevrolets, they tell Ford Motor Company to make more cars by buying more of them, thereby driving up the price of Fords relative to Chevrolets and attracting more investment to Ford. Because of the free market in capital goods, Ford is able to devote more resources to production than Chevrolet.

This process enables firms to rationally calculate the "structure of production" from the beginning to the end, to use scarce resources to satisfy the most highly valued goals of consumers.

Mises showed that under socialism, economic calculation is impossible. Since capital goods are owned collectively, they cannot be bought or sold and therefore can have no money prices. Therefore, the desires of consumers cannot be served, *no matter what the intentions of the producers*. This is why the Soviet shoe factory is incapable of making the styles, colors, or numbers of shoes that consumers want, no matter how hard the managers try.

But Mises's argument must also apply to the corporate state. To the extent that some corporations enjoy state-privileged positions, they are partially protected from competition. Their capital goods have money prices, unlike under socialism, but they are not *freely* set prices. Thanks to state favoritism, competitors have less opportunity to bid those resources away, so consumers' desires cannot be fully served.

We saw an example of this with the Chrysler bailout. Consumers sought to divert resources from the Chrysler Corp. to other car manufacturers, which produced better products at better prices. So in response to the pressure group composed of Chrysler executives, union workers, large shareholders, and big bank creditors, politicians gave the company massive federal financing. Consumers wanted rational economic calculation, but the government prevented it, thereby making the rest of us poorer.

The bigger the corporate state becomes, the less consumers' desires will be satisfied. As Misesian analysis shows, the corporate state must be an economic failure, no matter what miracles are claimed. Tragically, fascism is all too often a political success.

The Collapse of Socialism

Murray N. Rothbard

We are now living thorough the most significant and exciting event of the 20th century: nothing less than the collapse of socialism.

Before the rise of the new idea of socialism in the mid and late 19th century, the great struggle of social and political philosophy was crystal-clear. On one side was the exciting and liberating idea of classical liberalism, emerging since the 17th century: of free trade and free markets, individual liberty, separation of Church and State, minimal government, and international peace. This was the movement that ushered in and championed the Industrial Revolution, which, for the first time in human history, created an economy geared to the desires of and abundance for the great mass of consumers.

On the other side were the forces of Tory statism, of the Old Order of Throne and Altar, of feudalism, absolutism, and mercantilism, of special privileges and cartels granted by Big Government, of war, and impoverishment for the mass of their subjects.

In the field of ideas, and in action and in institutions, the classical liberals were rapidly on the way to winning this battle. The world had come to realize that freedom, and the growth of industry and standards of living for all, must go hand in hand.

Then, in the 19th century, the onward march of freedom and classical liberalism was derailed by the growth of a new idea: socialism. Rather than rejecting industrialism and the welfare of the masses of people as the Tories had done, socialists professed that they could and would do far better by the masses and bring about "genuine freedom" by creating a state more coercive and totalitarian than the Tories had ever contemplated. Through "scientific" central planning, socialism could and would usher in a world of freedom and superabundance for all.

The 20th century put the triumphant idealism of the 19th into practice, and so our century became the Age of Socialism. Half the world became fully and consistently socialist, and the other half came fairly close to that ideal. And now, after decades of calling themselves the wave of the future, and deriding all their opponents as hopelessly "reactionary" (i.e. not in tune with modern thinking), "paleolithic," and "Neanderthal," socialism, throughout the world, has been rapidly packing it in. For that is what *glasnost* and *perestroika* amount to.

Ludwig von Mises, at the dawn of the Socialist Century, warned, in a famous article, that socialism simply could not work: that it could not run an industrial economy, and could not even satisfy the goals of the central planners themselves, much less of the mass of consumers in whose name they speak. For decades Mises was derided, and discredited, and various mathematical models were worked out in alleged "refutation" of his lucid and elegant demonstration.

And now, in the leading socialist countries throughout the world: in Soviet Russia, in Hungary, in China, in Yugoslavia, governments are rushing to abandon socialism. Decentralization, markets, profit and loss tests, allowing inefficient firms to go bankrupt, all are being adopted. And why are the socialist countries willing to go through this enormous and truly revolutionary upheaval? Because they are really saying that Mises was right, after all, that socialism doesn't work, and that only desocialized free markets can run a modern economy.

Some are even willing to give up some political power, allow greater criticism, secret ballots and elections, and even, as in Soviet Estonia, to allow a one-and-one half party system, because they are implicitly conceding that Mises was right: that you can't have economic freedom and private property without intellectual and political freedom, that you can't have *perestroika* without *glasnost*.

It is truly inspiring to see how freedom exerts its own "domino effect." Country after socialist country has been trying to top each other to see how far and how fast each one can go down the road of freedom and desocialization.

But much of this gripping drama has been concealed from the American public because, for the last 40 years, our opinion-molders have told us that the *only* enemy is Communism. Our leaders have shifted the focus away from socialism itself to a variant that is different only because it is more militant and consistent.

This has enabled modern liberals, who share many of the same statist ideas, to separate *competing* groups of socialists from the horrors of socialism in action. Thus, Trotskyists, Social Democrats, democratic socialists, or whatever, are able to pass themselves off as anti-Communist good guys, while the blame for the Gulag or Cambodian genocide is removed from socialism itself.

Now it is clear that none of this will wash. The enemy of freedom, of prosperity, of truly rational economics is socialism period, and not just one specific group of socialists.

As even the "socialist bloc" begins to throw in the towel, there are virtually no Russians or Chinese or Hungarians or Yugoslavs left who have any use for socialism. The only genuine socialists these days are intellectuals in the West who are enjoying a comfortable and even luxurious living within the supposed bastions of capitalism.

6

Privatization vs. Government Ownership

Airport Congestion—A Case of Market Failure?

Murray N. Rothbard

The press touted it as yet another chapter in the unending success story of "government-business cooperation." The traditional tale is that a glaring problem arises, caused by the unchecked and selfish actions of capitalist greed. And that then a wise and far-sighted government agency, seeing deeply and having only the public interest at heart, steps in and corrects the failure, its sage regulations gently but firmly bending private actions to the common good.

The latest chapter began in the summer of 1984 when it came to light that the public was suffering under a 73% increase in the number of delayed flights compared to the previous year. To the Federal Aviation Agency (FAA) and other agencies of government, the villain of the piece was clear. Its own imposed quotas on the number of flights at the nation's airports had been lifted at the beginning of the year, and, in response to this deregulation, the short-sighted airlines, each pursuing its own profits, over-scheduled their flights in the highly remunerative peak hours of the day. The congestion and delays occurred at these hours, largely at the biggest and most used airports. The FAA soon made it clear that it was prepared to impose detailed, minute-by-minute maximum limits on takeoffs and landings at each airport, and threatened to do so if the airlines themselves did not come up with an acceptable plan. Under this bludgeoning, the airlines came up with a "voluntary" plan that was duly approved at the end of October, a plan that imposed maximum quotas of flights at the peak hours. Government-business cooperation had supposedly triumphed once more.

The real saga, however, is considerably less cheering. From the beginning of the airline industry until 1978, the Civil Aeronautics Board (CAB) imposed a coerced cartelization on the industry, parcelling out routes to favored airlines, thus severely limiting competition, and keeping fares far over the free-market price. Largely due to the efforts of CAB chairman and economist Alfred E. Kahn, the Airline Deregulation Act was passed in 1978, deregulating routes, flights, and prices, and abolishing the CAB at the end of 1984.

What has really happened is that the FAA, previously limited to safety regulation and the nationalization of air traffic control services, has since then moved in to take up the torch of cartelization lost by the CAB. When President Reagan fired the air-controllers during the PATCO strike in 1981, a little-heralded consequence was that the FAA stepped in to impose coerced maxima of flights at the various airports, all in the name of rationing scarce air-control services. An end of the air-controller crisis led the FAA to remove the controls in early 1984, but now here they are, more than back again, as a result of the congestion.

Furthermore, the quotas are now in force at the six top airports. Leading the parade in calling for the controls was Eastern Airlines, whose services using Kennedy and LaGuardia airports have, in recent years, been outcompeted by scrappy new People's Express, whose operations have vaulted Newark Airport from a virtual ghost airport to one of the top six (along with LaGuardia, Kennedy, Denver, Atlanta, and O'Hare at Chicago). In imposing the "voluntary" quotas, it does not seem accidental that the peak hour flights at Newark Airport were drastically reduced (from 100 to 68), while the LaGuardia and Kennedy peak hour flights were actually increased.

But, in any case, was the peak hour congestion a case of market failure? Whenever economists see a shortage, they are trained to look immediately for the maximum price control below the free-market. And sure enough, this is what has happened. We must realize that all commercial airports in this country are government-owned and operated—all by local governments except Dulles and National, owned by the federal government. And governments are not interested, as is private enterprise, in rational pricing, that is, in a pricing that achieves the greatest profits. Other political considerations invariably take over. And so every airport charges fees for its "slots" (landing and takeoff spots on its runways) far below the market-clearing price that would be achieved under private ownership. Hence congestion occurs at valuable peak hours, with private corporate jets taking up space from which they would obviously be out-competed by the large commercial airliners. The only genuine solution to airport congestion is to impose market-clearing pricing, with far higher slot fees at peak than at non-peak hours. And this would accomplish the task while encouraging rather than crippling competition by the compulsory rating of underpriced slots imposed by the FAA. But such rational pricing will only be achieved when airports are privatized—taken out of the inefficient and political control of government.

There is also another important area to be privatized. Air control services are a compulsory monopoly of the federal government, under the aegis of the FAA. Even though the FAA promised to be back to pre-strike air control capacity by 1983, it still employs 19% fewer air controllers than before the strike, all trying to handle 6% greater traffic.

Once again, the genuine solution is to privatize air-traffic control. There is no real reason why pilots, aircraft companies, and all other aspects of the airline industry can be private, but that somehow air control must always remain a nationalized service. Upon the privatization of air control, it will be possible to send the FAA to join the CAB in the forgotten scrap heap of history.

Privatization

Murray N. Rothbard

Privatization" is a new in-term, on local, state, and federal levels of government. Even functions that our civic textbooks tell us can only be performed by government, such as prisons, are being accomplished successfully, and far more efficiently, by private enterprise. For once, a fashionable concept contains a great deal of sense.

Privatization is a great and important good in itself. Another name for it is "desocialization." Privatization is the reversal of the deadly socialist process that had been proceeding unchecked for almost a century. It has the great virtue of taking resources from the coercive sector, the sector of politicians and bureaucrats—in short, the non-producers—and turning them over to the voluntary sector of creators and producers. The more resources remain in the private, productive sector, the less a deadweight of parasitism will burden the producers and cripple the standard of living of consumers.

In a narrower sense, the private sector will always be more efficient than the governmental because income in the private sector is only a function of efficient service to the consumers. The more efficient that service, the higher the income and profits. In the government sector, in contrast, income is unrelated to efficiency or service to the consumer. Income is extracted coercively from the taxpayers (or, by inflation, from the pockets of consumers). In the government sector, the consumer is not someone to be served and courted; he or she is an unwelcome "waster" of scarce resources owned or controlled by the bureaucracy.

Anything and everything is fair game for privatization. Socialists used to argue that all they wish to do is to convert the entire economy to function like one huge Post Office. No socialist would dare argue that today, so much of a disgrace is the monopolized governmental Postal Service. One standard argument is that the government "should only do what private firms or citizens cannot do." But *what* can't they do? Every good or service now supplied by government has, at one time or another, been successfully supplied by private enterprise. Another argument is that some activities are "too large" to be performed well by private enterprise. But the capital market is enormous, and has successfully financed far more expensive undertakings than most governmental activities. Besides the government has no capital of its own; everything it has, it has taxed away from private producers.

Privatization is becoming politically popular now as a means of financing the huge federal deficit. It is certainly true that a deficit may be reduced not only by cutting expenditures and raising taxes, but also by selling assets to the private sector. Those economists who have tried to justify deficits by pointing to the growth of government assets backing those deficits can now be requested to put up or shut up: in other words, to start selling those assets as a way of bringing the deficits down.

Fine. There is a huge amount of assets that have been hoarded, for decades, by the federal government. Most of the land of the Western states has been locked up by the federal government and held permanently out of use. In effect, the federal government has acted like a giant monopolist: permanently keeping out of use an enormous amount of valuable and productive assets: land, water, minerals, and forests. By locking up assets, the federal government has been reducing the productivity and the standard of living of every one of us. It has also been acting as a giant land and natural resource cartelist—artificially keeping up the prices of those resources by withholding their supply. Productivity would rise, and prices would fall, and the real income of all of us would greatly increase, if government assets were privatized and thereby allowed to enter the productive system.

Reduce the deficit by selling assets? Sure, let's go full steam. But let's not insist on too high a price for these assets. Sell, sell, at whatever the assets will bring. If the revenue is not enough to end the deficit, sell yet again.

A few years ago, at an international gathering of free-market economists, Sir Keith Joseph, Minister of Industry and alleged free-market advocate in the Thatcher government, was asked why the government, despite lip-service to privatization, had taken no steps to privatize the steel industry, which had been nationalized by the Labor government. Sir Keith explained that the steel industry was losing money in government hands, and "therefore" could not command a price if put up for sale. At which point, one prominent free-market American economist leaped to his feet, and shouted, waving a dollar bill in the air, "I hereby bid one dollar for the British steel industry!"

Indeed. There is no such thing as no price. Even a bankrupt industry would sell, readily, for its plant and equipment to be used by productive private firms.

And so even a low price should not stop the federal government in its quest to balance the budget by privatization. Those dollars will mount up. Just give freedom and private enterprise a chance.

Government vs. Natural Resources

Murray N. Rothbard

It is a common myth that the near-disappearance of the whale and of various species of fish was caused by "capitalist greed," which, in a short-sighted grab for profits, despoiled the natural resources—the geese that laid the golden eggs—from which those profits used to flow. Hence, the call for government to step in and either seize the ownership of these resources, or at least to regulate strictly their use and development.

It is private enterprise, however, not government, that we can rely on to take the long and not the short view. For example, if a private investor or business firm owns a natural resource, say, a forest, it knows that every tree cut down and sold for short-run profits will have to be balanced by a decline in the capital value of the forest remaining. Every firm, then, must balance short-run returns as against the loss of capital assets. Therefore, private owners have every economic incentive to be far-sighted, to replant trees for every tree cut down, to increase the productivity and to maintain the resource, etc. It is precisely *government*—or firms allowed to rent but not own government—whose every incentive is to be short-run. Since government bureaucrats control but do not own the resource "owned" by government, they have no incentive to maximize or even consider the long-run value of the resource. Their every incentive is to loot the resource as quickly as possible.

And so it should not be surprising that every instance of "overuse" and destruction of a natural resource has been caused, not by private property rights in natural resources, but by government intervention or crippling of such a market. Destruction of the grass cover in the West in the late 19th-century was caused by the Federal government's failure to recognize homesteading of land in large-enough technological units to be feasible. The 160-acre legal maximum for private homesteading imposed during the Civil War made sense for the wet agriculture of the East; but it made no sense in the dry area of the West, where no farm of less than one or two thousand acres was feasible. As a result, grassland and cattle ranches became land owned by the federal government but used by or leased to private firms. The private firms had no incentive to develop the land resource, since it could be invaded by other firms or could revert to the government. In fact, their incentive was to use up the land resource quickly to destroy the grass cover, because they were prevented from owning it.

Water, rivers, parts of oceans, have been in far worse shape than land, since private individuals and firms have been almost universally prevented from owning parts of that water, from owning schools of fish, etc. In short, since homesteading private property rights has generally not been permitted in parts of the ocean, the oceans and other water resources have remained in a primitive state, much as land had been in the days before private property in land was permitted and recognized. Then, land was only in a hunting-and-gathering stage, where people were permitted to own or transform the land itself. Only private ownership in the land itself can permit the emergence of *agriculture*—the transformation and cultivation of the land itself—bringing about an enormous growth in productivity and increase in everyone's standard of living.

The world has accepted agriculture, and the marvelous fruits of such ownership and cultivation. It is high time to expand the dominion of man to one of the last frontiers on earth: *aquaculture*. Already, private property rights are being developed in water and ocean resources, and we are just beginning to glimpse the wonders in store. More and more, in oceans and rivers, fish are being "farmed" instead of relying on random supply by nature. Whereas only three percent of all seafood produced in the United States in 1975 came from fish-farms, this proportion tripled to twelve percent by 1984.

In Buhl, Idaho, the Clear Springs Trout Company, a fish-farm, has become the single largest trout producer in the world, expanding its trout production from 10 million pounds per year in 1981 to 14 million pounds this year. Furthermore, Clear Springs is not content to follow nature blindly; as all farmers try to do, it improves on nature by breeding better and more productive trout. Thus, two years ago Clear Springs trout converted two pounds of food into one pound of edible flesh; now Clear Springs scientists have developed trout that will convert only 1.3 pounds of food into one pound of flesh. And Clear Springs researchers are in the process of developing that long-desired paradise for consumers: a boneless trout.

At this point, indeed, all rainbow trout sold commercially in the United States are produced in farms, as well as 40% of the nation's oysters, and 95% of commercial catfish.

Aquaculture, the wave of the future, is already here to stay, not only in fishery but also in such activities as off-shore oil drilling and the mining of manganese nodules on the ocean floor. What aquaculture needs above all is the expansion of private property rights and ownership to all useful parts of the oceans and other water resources. Fortunately, the Reagan Administration rejected the Law of the Sea Treaty, which would have permanently subjected the world's ocean resources to ownership and control by a world-government body under the aegis of the United Nations. With that threat over, it is high time to seize the opportunity to allow the expansion of private property in one of its last frontiers.

Privatize the Roads

Walter Block

If the government demanded the sacrifice of 50,000 citizens each year, an outraged public would revolt. If a religious sect planned to immolate 523,335 in the next decade, it would be toppled. If a Manson-type cult murdered 790 people to celebrate Memorial Day, the press would demand the greatest manhunt in this country's history.

If we learned of a disease that killed 2,077 children under the age of five each year, or a nursing home that allowed 7,346 elderly people to die each year, no stone would be left unturned to combat the enemy.

If private enterprise were responsible for this butchery, a cataclysmic reaction would ensue: Congressmen would appoint investigative panels, the Justice Department would seek out antitrust violations, corporate executives would be jailed, and there would be growing cries for nationalization.

In fact, the government is indeed responsible for a real-life slaughter of these exact proportions: the toll taken on our nation's roadways. Whether at the local, state, regional, or national level, it is government that builds, runs, manages, administers, repairs, and plans the road network.

While many blame alcohol and excessive speed as causes of highway accidents, they ignore the more fundamental reason of government ownership and control. Ignoring this is like blaming a snafu in a restaurant on the fact that a poorly maintained oven went out, or that the waiter fell on a greasy floor with a loaded tray. Of course the proximate causes of customer dissatisfaction are uncooked meat or food in their laps. Yet how can these factors be blamed by themselves, while the role of the restaurant's management is ignored?

It is the restaurant manager's job to insure that the ovens are performing satisfactorily, and that the floors are properly maintained. If he fails, the blame rests on his shoulders, not on the ovens or floors. We hold responsible for the murder, the finger on the trigger, not the bullet. If unsafe conditions prevail in a private, multi-story parking lot, or in a shopping mall, the entrepreneur in question is held accountable.

Why then is there apathy to the continuing atrocity of government roads? Why is there no public outcry? Probably because most people do not see any alternative to government ownership. Just as no one "opposes" or "protests" a volcano, which is believed to be beyond the control of man, there are few who oppose governmental roadway control. But it is my contention that to virtually eliminate highway deaths we need to put ownership and control of roads into private hands, and let the entire service be guided by the free market.

The notion of a fully private market in roads, streets, and highways is likely to be rejected out of hand because people feel that government road management is inevitable. Governments have always owned roads, so any other system is unthinkable.

But there is nothing unique about transportation: the economic principles we accept as a matter of course in practically every other arena of human experience apply here too. As always, the advantage enjoyed by the market is the automatic reward and penalty system imposed by profits and losses. When customers are pleased, they continue patronizing those merchants who have served them well. Businesses that succeed in satisfying consumers earn a profit, while entrepreneurs who fail to satisfy them are soon driven to bankruptcy.

The market process governs the production of the bulk of our consumer goods and capital equipment. This same process that brings us fountain pens, frisbees, and fishsticks can also bring us roads.

Why would a company or individual want to build a road or buy an already existing one? For the same reason as in any other business: to earn a profit. The necessary funds would be raised in a similar manner: by floating and issuance of stock, by borrowing, or from past savings of the owner. The risks would be the same: attracting customers and prospering, or failing to do so and going bankrupt. Just as private enterprise rarely gives burgers away for free, use of road space would require payment. A road enterprise would face virtually all of the same problems shared by other businesses: attracting a labor force, subcontracting, keeping customers satisfied, meeting the price of competitors, innovating, borrowing money, expanding, etc.

The road entrepreneur would have to try to contain congestion, reduce traffic accidents, and plan and design new facilities in coordination with already existing highways, as well as in conjunction with the plans of others for new expansion. He would also take over the jobs the government does now like (sometimes) filling potholes, installing road signs and guard rails, maintaining lane markings, repairing traffic signals, and so on for the myriad of "road furniture" that keeps traffic moving.

Under the present system, a road manager has nothing to lose if an accident happens and several people are killed on a government turnpike. A civil servant draws his annual salary regardless of the accident toll piled up on his domain. But if he were a private owner and he had to compete with other road owners, sovereign consumers who care about safety would not patronize his road, and thus the owner would lose money and go bankrupt.

A common objection to private roads is the specter of having to halt every few feet and toss a coin into a tollbox. This simply would not occur on the market. Imagine acommercial golf course operating on a similar procedure: forcing the golfers to wait in line at every hole, or demanding payment every time they took a swipe at the ball. Such an enterprise would very rapidly lose customers and go broke. Private roads would create economies of scale, where it would pay entrepreneurs to buy the toll collections rights from the millions of holders, in order to rationalize the system into one in which fewer toll gates blocked the roads.

One scenario would follow the shopping center model: a single owner or builder would buy a section of territory and build roads and houses. Just as many shopping center builders maintain control over parking lots, malls, and other common areas, the entrepreneur would continue the operation of common areas such as the roads, sidewalks, etc. Tolls for residents, guests, and deliveries might be pegged at low levels, or be entirely lacking, as in modern shopping centers.

Consider a road on which traffic must continuously be moving. If it's owned by one person or company, who either built it or bought the rights of passage from the previous owners, it would be foolish for him to install dozens of tollgates per mile. There now exists inexpensive electrical devices which can register the car or truck passing by any fixed point on the road. As the vehicle passes the check point, an electrical impulse can be transmitted to a computer that can produce one monthly bill for all roads use, and even mail it out automatically. Road payments could be facilitated in as unobtrusive a manner as utility bills are now.

It is impossible to predict the exact shape of an industry that does not exist. I am in no position to set up the blueprint for a future private market in transport. I cannot tell how many road owners there will be, what kind of rules of the road they will set up, how much it will cost per mile, etc. I can say that a competitive market process would lead highway entrepreneurs to seek newer and better ways of providing services to their customers.

Now we come back to the question of safety. Government road managers are doing a terrible job. Consider what transpires when safety is questioned in other forms of transportation to see a corollary. When an airline experiences an accident, passengers think twice before flying that airline and typically it loses customers. Airlines with excellent safety records have discovered that the public is aware of safety and make choices based upon it. An "exploding Pinto" wouldn't stay on a private road long, nor would reckless drivers and potholes.

I don't know all the details of how a future free-market road system might work. But I do know that "there has to be a better way." And it is the free market.

The Case for a Free Market in Body Parts

Walter Block

In days of yore, there was no "crisis" in spare body parts. Organ transplants were an utter impossibility, the stuff of science fiction. But nowadays, thanks to the magnificent discoveries and new techniques of modern medicine, it is possible to transplant hearts, livers, kidneys, corneas, and other organs. People who would have been consigned to death, or tenuous and painful lives only a few years ago, can today avail themselves of these medical miracles and lead healthy, productive lives.

However, instead of being the occasion for unrelieved rejoicing, these new breakthroughs have given us a whole host of new problems.

Most important, there is a shortage of body organs suitable for transplant, which has strained medical ethics to the breaking point. For, given the limited supply of donor-organs, our doctors have had to choose which of the many needy recipients shall have this life-giving aid and which shall not. And the doctors have no criteria upon which to base the choice other than their own arbitrary decision.

The difficulty is that our legal-economic system has not kept up with medical technology. The law prohibits people from using the property rights we each have in our own persons. Specifically, it has banned trade, or a marketplace, in live spare body parts.

What? Allow the profit incentive to work in this field? The very idea brings to mind images of grave robbers, Frankenstein monsters, and gangs of "organ thieves" stealing people's hearts, livers, and kidneys, as in Robin Cook's novels.

But let's consider this idea on its own merits. Will a free market increase the number of donors, save lives, and free doctors from the need to pick which people shall be saved and which consigned to a lingering and painful death?

As any first year student in economics can tell us, whenever a good is in short supply, its price is too low. And the case of spare body parts is no exception. In fact, the laws that prohibit a marketplace in human organs have effectively imposed a zero price on these items. At a zero price, we cannot be surprised that the demand for human organs has vastly outstripped the supply.

If the price of human organs were allowed to rise to its market level, barring new technological breakthroughs in artificial organs, there would still be a high demand from people needing an organ transplant to sustain their lives. Thus the immediate effect of a free market would be mainly on the amount supplied.

While it is never possible to fully know how an industry now prohibited by government edict would function, we can anticipate that the major sources would be young healthy people killed in car and other accidents and people who die from diseases such as heart attacks, which leave their other organs undamaged.

If the organ industry were legalized, new firms would spring up, or perhaps insurance companies and hospitals would do the work. These companies or hospitals would offer thousands of dollars to people who met the appropriate medical criteria if they agreed that upon their death their organs would be owned by the firm in question. Then these firms would in turn sell these organs, for a profit, to people in need of a transplant.

In addition these new firms would, as at present, try to obtain consent from the relatives of newly deceased persons for use of their organs. But only under a free market could these firms offer cash incentives for donors, not to mention the chance to save another life.

The effect of programs would be to vastly increase the supply of donor organs. No longer would potential recipients have to make do without transplants. And because the system is based on freedom, those who objected on religious or other grounds would not have to take part.

Nor need we fear that those who engaged in this business would earn "exorbitant" profits. For any such tendency would call forth new entrants into the market, increasing supply even further, and reducing profits to levels which could be earned elsewhere.

Liberty is the answer. If we want to save the American people pain, sorrow, suffering, and tragedy, we will work to institute a free market in body parts.

Abolish the SEC

Graeme B. Littler

Official academics call the Securities and Exchange Commission (SEC) a savior of capitalism. In fact, it is an enemy of the free market.

The SEC was set up in 1934 by Franklin D. Roosevelt to regulate securities markets. There was almost no public opposition. Official opinion of all sorts agreed with the first New Dealer, Herbert Hoover, that falling stock prices were caused by "sinister, systematic bear raids . . . , vicious pools . . . pounding down" stock prices so traders could "profit from the losses of other people."

Similar sentiments prevail today among the politicians who advocate more power for the SEC. But rather than giving the SEC more money and power, Congress should abolish it. Here are just some of the reasons why.

One: The SEC Erects Barriers to Competition.

Thanks to the SEC, raising capital through the issuance of new stock is an extremely time-consuming, highly technical, and costly process. It requires a mountain of paperwork, the filing and refiling of documents, and very expensive CPAs and lawyers. Many small companies—which don't have the resources and knowledge to negotiate this bureaucratic maze—can't raise new money and grow. Large, established firms do just fine, however, and they like the lessened competition.

Two: The SEC is Anti-Shareholder.

The SEC defends the interests of entrenched, old-line corporate management over the true owners of companies, the shareholders, by hampering corporate "raiders." Raiders seek to make a profit by buying out a firm's owners, firing top-heavy and inefficient management, and installing people who will make the company more profitable.

The SEC requires "raiders" to file public reports after they acquire five percent or more of a company's stock, in accordance with the Williams Act, which was devised by the SEC and corporate lobbyists. These filings are designed to tip off management about possible tender offers, thus giving them plenty of time to scheme a takeover defense to secure their jobs at shareholder expense.

Three: The SEC Turns Innocent People into Criminals.

Last year's biggest scapegoat was the insider trader, who committed the "crime" of buying or selling stock on the basis of non-public information. But it is the SEC's own complicated and time-consuming takeover rules that make inside information valuable in the first place. Without the filing requirements, "raiders" would quietly acquire shares voluntarily in the market from people who want to sell. Without SEC-mandated delays, there would be no "inside information" to capitalize on.

There is nothing wrong with using inside information. In fact, insider trading is economically beneficial in the sense that it causes security prices to adjust faster to critical new information. Insider trading is a victimless crime. There is no moral requirement to tell the owner of the property you're buying that you know how to make a profit out of it. No stockholder was ever forced to sell shares against his will.

Four: The SEC Protects the Brokerage Industry Cartel.

Since the SEC restricts entry into the brokerage industry, it is the enforcer of a highly profitable cartel. With brokerage houses as its constituents, it's not surprising to see the SEC campaigning against the recent efforts to repeal the Glass-Steagall Act, which restricts competition.

Five: The SEC Profits From Its Blunders.

As Ludwig von Mises observed, government regulation generates unforeseen problems, which excuses more regulation, which causes still more unforeseen problems. The SEC has a history of growing and profiting from crises. It has, for example, capitalized on the 1986 insider-trading scandal by getting a bigger budget and more staff, the dream of every D.C. bureaucrat. In fact, its budget is 62% higher today than in 1982. And today, it's busy using the Crash of 1987 to justify more regulation, especially of the competitors of Wall Street in the futures and options markets.

Six: The SEC Favors Price Controls.

The SEC is pushing for the power to shut down the financial markets in times of "emergency." SEC chairman David Ruder also endorses the idea of daily trading limits on stocks, which would halt trading once a stock price hits its SEC-set maximum daily limit. It is very damaging—even in government-caused emergencies—to prevent willing sellers and buyers from making a trade.

Seven: The SEC Invades Privacy.

Acting on behalf of the SEC, the U.S. government pressured Switzerland, England, Japan, and others, to swap information on the stock market dealings of private citizens.

For all these reasons the SEC should be abolished and the laws backing it repealed. This would dramatically simplify selling new stock and thus be a boost for new businesses, competition, and the free market. And industry self-regulation and normal police agencies will protect against fraud.

The securities industry is not problem-free, of course, and never will be. But it will function better without the Big Problem, Washington, D.C., in charge of it.

Cancel the Postal Monopoly

Llewellyn H. Rockwell, Jr.

In the 18th century, as he had for millennia, the urban peddler went from door to door with a sack on his back. When we see this antique method of economic organization, not in a museum setting at Colonial Williamsburg but daily on the streets of every city and town in America, we know the government is in charge.

The Post Office has been a federal agency since 1775. And since 1872 it has been illegal for anyone but government employees to deliver a letter. In that year, at Post Office behest, Congress outlawed the low-priced, fast delivery of the Pony Express. It was to be the last express service available to regular mail customers.

A few years ago, a Rochester, New York, teenager offered his neighbors same-day bicycle delivery at 10¢ each for Christmas cards in his subdivision. Soon Postal Inspectors—who seem to be the only fastmoving part of the "service"—arrived at his house and threatened to arrest and jail him unless he stopped.

Somehow, even from just a common-sense viewpoint, this doesn't look like something that should be illegal. But indeed he was violating two parts of the postal laws. He was delivering first class mail—which is a federal monopoly—and he was leaving his mail in mailboxes.

By law, all "mail receiving devices" belong to the Postal Service and can be used only by it. That is, the mailbox which you buy and install on your property belongs to the U.S. government. (Note: it belongs to the government in the sense that your silverware belongs to the burglar who just took it at the point of a gun. Property can be owned only by those who acquire it honestly and voluntarily though production or trade.)

The penalty this teenager faced was a $500 fine and six months in jail for each count of the potential indictment, i.e. for each letter delivered. This is from the same government that thinks nothing of freeing murderers and rapists after "rehabilitating" them for a year or two. But then the government has always taken "crimes" against itself far more seriously than actual crimes against the people.

With the government in charge, the bureaucratized service keeps getting worse. It takes longer and longer for mail to arrive. And the Post Office long ago abolished twice-a-day delivery and is working on ending door-to-door delivery as well. Most big offices have the mail dumped in a pile at their front door; postal workers used to sort and distribute it. Then there's the "cluster box" system for residential areas, where rows of boxes are placed far away from homes in a place convenient for the postal workers.

Typical of government, as the service declines, the price of stamps keeps going up, from 22¢ to 25¢ most recently. That makes a total increase of 675% since 1958, more than twice as fast as the general price level, which has gone up 300% (thanks to another government monopoly, the Federal Reserve). In addition, the Post Office gets billions a year in direct subsidies.

Where does all this money go? Mostly to the bureaucrats themselves. The postal system spends 84% of its budget on its 746,000 employees, 100,000 of them added during the austere years of the Reagan administration.

The average postal employee—who is an unskilled worker by private sector standards—earns $30,000 a year in wages and perks. And a GAO study found that this same average worker takes 50 days of paid leave a year (vacation, "sick" time, holidays, etc.). That's 10 weeks of repose, although considering the pace of work in the Post Office, it may be hard to tell the difference.

There's an old story about a UPS delivery man meeting a friend who worked for the Post Office during Christmas time. "How are you doing?" asked the government employee. "Just great!" said his UPS friend. "Business has never been better. Volume is way up. How about you?"

"Terrible," said the postal employee. "There's too much mail!"

In a government enterprise, customers are at best a nuisance. If the Post Office could get away with it, it would prefer no mail and no customers. That's why, during lunch hour, only one window is open, and why the P.O. takes every opportunity to cut service. The recent abolition of Saturday window hours is only the latest example.

There is only one answer to the Post Office problem, and UPS and Federal Express show us the way: privatization, i.e. repealing the laws which give the Post Office a monopoly. However, real privatization means letting the free market decide, not contracting out to politically connected businesses as advocated by the President's Commission on Privatization. Such a process leaves the bureaucrats in charge and is an invitation to political corruption.

We cannot know what kinds of communications services free-market entrepreneurs would provide for us. We can only know that they would be far more efficient than the present apparatus, that they would make use of new electronic and computer technology, and that they would be pro-consumer.

The Post Office charges that this would not work. It claims, for example, that rates would go up. Coming from the biggest champion of higher rates, I find this unconvincing. But certainly the rate structure would change. There would be a whole array of alternatives available, varying in price according to distance, speed, handling, etc.

The Post Office says that we would no longer be able to mail a letter from Washington, D.C., to Hawaii for 25¢. But why should it cost the same amount to send a letter across town as across the continent? This is typical government pricing: one high price for everything, which a bureaucracy can administer much more easily than a rational rate schedule. It rightly costs more to ship freight or make a phone call over long distances, and postal service should be no different.

The Post Office also says that rural delivery would stop. That's nonsense, of course, but people in sparsely populated areas might have to pay more for some services, just as city dwellers have to pay more for fresh vegetables and firewood. The free market would reduce the difference to transportation costs, however, thanks to arbitrage and entrepreneurship, and there would be constant competition to make transportation cheaper. And UPS delivers 25% of its packages to rural routes and makes a profit at it.

The Post Office also claims that only the U.S. government can secure our privacy and guarantee access to the mails. But this is Newspeak. Government is the great *invader* of our privacy, mail and otherwise. In the 1970s, the CIA routinely opened mail. And the same thing is happening now to opponents of the administration's foreign policy. And the Post Office claims the right to search the mails for "contraband," a practice that would never occur to UPS or Federal Express.

As to freedom of access to the mail service, the Post Office frequently claims the right to decide what can be mailed. It's banned novels, refused to deliver National Health Federation booklets because they conflicted with the "weight of scientific opinion," and censored advertising.

Mail, says the Post Office, is a "natural monopoly." But there is no such thing, only the natural tendency of people who want to live off the taxpayers through monopoly to claim there is. If any monopoly were actually natural, it wouldn't need a government gun to enforce it.

The Post Office is a socialist organization. It is inconsistent with the American vision of liberty. It's time to end socialized mail delivery and allow free-market competition.

Lies, Damned Lies, and Social Security

Patrick W. Watson

The feds may call "Social Security" a retirement program, but it's actually an unsound, unfair, unworkable, and immoral system of wealth redistribution. It's bankrupting America and destroying rather than creating financial security.

Franklin D. Roosevelt introduced Social Security in 1936. Congress, which as usual was only too happy to go along with executive violations of the Constitution, promised that Social Security would "provide safeguards against all of the hazards leading to destitution and dependency." Instead of safeguarding against dependency, Social Security has increased it.

Like earthquakes which announce themselves with small tremors, the burden of Social Security was at first almost unnoticeable. In 1937, the tax rate was 1% on the first $3,000 in earnings; the maximum was thus $30 a year, to be matched by the employer.

In the post-war years Social Security grew as Congress and presidents added more benefits until the program became an Omnibus Vote-Buying Act. Congress passed across-the-board benefit increases of 7% (1965), 13% (1967), 15% (1969), and then in 1972 tied benefits to the Consumer Price Index, yielding an annual "cost-of-living adjustment."

The SS taxes also grew larger, of course. In 1937 the maximum was $30 annually. By 1970 it was $374.40, an increase of over 1,000%. In 1971 Abraham Ellis—author of the prescient *Social Security Fraud* was called a right-wing alarmist for predicting that by 1987 the tax would rise to 5.9% of the first $15,000, or $885. He was wrong; actual 1987 rates were 7.15% of the first $43,800, or $3,131. Even this pessimist was 300% too optimistic.

When the program began, there were 100 workers paying into the system for every three people drawing benefits. By 1985 those 100 workers supported 32 retirees. Barring drastic changes in the birthrate, by 2030 there will be 52 retirees drawing benefits for every 100 workers paying in. Over time, then, the ratio of workers to retirees has shifted from 33-1 to 3-1, with worse to come.

In July 1987 the median age was 32.1 years in the United States, the highest ever. The fastest-growing group was that between 35-44 years: the baby boomers. By 2010 the first of these will be retiring. Will there be any benefits to collect? Maybe, but only at tremendous cost to the rest of us.

Then there is the Social Security "trust fund." It works like this: your employer, acting as an unpaid tax collector, deducts 7.5% of your wages up to $45,000 a year, matches this amount, and sends it all to Washington. The Social Security Administration deposits it into the Treasury, and in return receives IOUs (Treasury Bonds) payable sometime in the future. Congress and the president then spend the cash on endive research and other incumbency enhancement schemes.

What happens in 20 or 30 years when the IOUs are due? The U.S. government has no money of its own, of course. It can pay back the Social Security trust fund only through more taxes, more borrowing, or more inflating. All three come out of the people's pocketbook.

The first person to retire under Social Security was Miss Ida Fuller. When she retired in 1939, she had paid in only $22. On January 31, 1940, she got her first check: $22.54. Ida Fuller lived to be 100 years old, and the checks kept coming, just as FDR promised. In 34 years of retirement they totaled over $20,000.

Once long-lived people like Ida Fuller were the exception. Now they are the rule. Yet while more and more people live into their 80s and even 90s, the official retirement age remains 65. Why? Because in the 1880s the authoritarian German Chancellor Otto von Bismarck set 65 as the retirement age for his Social Security program. But the average life expectancy in Germany was then 45.

A child born in America in 1776 would, on average, die at 35. Even in 1950, people 65 and over made up only 7.7% of the population. Now that figure stands at 12%, and by 2020 should be 17.3%.

Neil Howe writing in the *American Spectator* says there are no believable projections for public health-care spending in the next century. Even conservative estimates are off the charts. However, he thinks we could easily see 20 or 30% payroll taxes 40 years from now, just to pay for Medicare and Medicaid! Add in the cash benefits and you could lose half your paycheck even before income tax is deducted. No one seriously believes we will see such taxes. More likely we will either change the system drastically or go through an economic collapse.

Social Security is built on lies, thievery, and coercion. Notice that Social Security check stubs refer to FICA (Federal Insurance Contributions Act). In truth Social Security is a tax. You are required by law to pay; if you refuse the government puts you in jail. But they call it a "contribution" as if we were giving to the United Way. Nor is there any "insurance." If a private insurance policy were as unsound as Social Security, its sellers would go to jail.

Private con games like the classic "Ponzi scheme" are illegal. But when the government runs them, they become social and secure. Charles Ponzi was a 1920s swindler whose trick was to sell people an investment that promised a big return, then take their money, pay off earlier customers, and move on. The supply of such investors is finite, so while those who got in early did well, sooner or later it had to come to a screeching halt.

Social Security works the same way, except that the "investors" have no choice. Even Ponzi didn't force people to invest at the point of a gun. The government does. The law makes a distinction between fraud and robbery based on coercion. Since the state has a monopoly on legal coercion, and can ultimately bring deadly force to bear on those who resist it, can we call the required "investment" in Social Security anything less than robbery?

The semantical games don't end there. The government says that employees pay the FICA tax and employers match it. But this is an accounting trick. The economic reality is that the worker pays it all because the matching payment is just another cost of labor.

Social Security injures the nation's economy and therefore hurts everyone. If the billions drained away by Social Security every year were put to productive use, our economy would be much less troubled than it is today. Instead, capital is wasted on nonproductive government projects.

Keynesians tell us that government spending creates jobs and stimulates the economy. But they forget to look at how the money would have been used otherwise. Taxation destroys jobs, and by taxing employment, Social Security creates unemployment and hurts small business.

What should we do about this dinosaur in our midst? Several plans have been offered. Unfortunately they range from the patch-up Lee Smith outlined in *Fortune* last year to the gradualist scheme offered by Peter Ferrara which calls for government to force people to invest in a "Financial Security Account" or stay in the Social Security system. Free marketeers must oppose both in principle. Only a principled stand has any chance of surviving the lobbying of the American Association of Retired Persons.

In the meantime, we should take care of ourselves and not rely on Social Security, support those who want to change it for the better, warn of the present system's dangers and immorality, and oppose inflationary fix-it schemes and every other intervention in the economy. Advancing lasting solutions based on liberty is the only chance we have of abolishing rip-offs like Social Security.

The Conservative Sanctification of Big Government

Llewellyn H. Rockwell, Jr.

The most disheartening aspect of the Reagan years has been the Inside-the-Beltway conservative love affair with big government.

Education Secretary William Bennett has been nagging Stanford University for changing its core curriculum. As a cultural conservative, I agree with much of what he says. But am I the only person on the Right who thinks federal bureaucrats have no business telling universities what to teach?

Where are all my conservative friends, who used to denounce federal interference in education, now that Washington is dictating a national curriculum? Or did their denunciations apply only when they weren't doing the interfering?

In December 1980, Ed Meese called the Department of Education "a ridiculous bureaucratic joke." And he was right. From the day Jimmy Carter established it—as a payoff to the leftist NEA teachers union—it has been an expensive, intrusive, unconstitutional, and centralizing instrument of state power.

The 1980 Republican platform promised to abolish the Education Department, and Ronald Reagan campaigned on the pledge. But—like so much else—both were forgotten when the cash and jobs could be directed to "our" side.

Instead of abolition, we've seen distension, with the administration and Congress increasing the Department's budget from $10 billion in Carter's last year to $22 billion in 1988. The head cheerleader for more spending on "education" (actually, *anti*-education, of course) has been Bennett. At the direction of his ideological control, Irving Kristol, Bennett has lobbied furiously for more spending, and criticized those with a "budget-driven agenda" (i.e. benighted folks who think government already spends too much).

The giant Department of Education runs a complicated array of programs, each with its own budget, its own interest groups, its own bureaucrats, and its own regulatory mandates and prohibitions, which have to be interpreted, explained, and enforced. It is an immense burden on schools and teachers, not to speak of taxpayers.

Bennett—with conservatives rooting him on—has centralized control over teaching methods, teacher selection, pay, promotion, textbooks, and a host of other areas that are none of the federal government's business. And he has increased the federal bias against private education. It is all reminiscent of the neoconservative Napoleonic "reforms" of French education, designed to support an authoritarian state and force all children into a politically approved mold.

Since liberals have always favored federal control of education, we now have no organized opposition in Washington to school centralization. Federal control of education has been sanctified, so long as it is used to promote "conservative values" (which presumably don't include parental control of childrens' education).

And this is no isolated incident. The same thing has happened with the National Endowments for the Humanities and Arts, the Department of Energy, the Federal Trade Commission, OSHA, EPA, and a host of other agencies. Conservatives denounced them when Carter was in office, but now that they offer jobs and grants for the boys, there isn't a peep.

Washington conservatives defended Ed Meese until he fired his movement-conservative press secretary. Then they attacked the Attorney General too. How dare he, top conservatives sputtered: that press aide was "one of us."

Lord Bolingbroke, writing more than 200 years ago, said that politics consists of rewarding one's friends, punishing one's enemies, and lining one's pockets. Nothing much has changed, of course. But there were those who thought the conservatives might be different.

The Case Against Government Child Care

Kathleen M. Spotts

American families need more affordable child care. But the answer is not more government involvement. When child care is run, funded, and regulated by the government, it can only make the existing problem worse. And it's bad for our liberty as well.

Promoters of more government intervention claim it will make "quality child care" more available to poor and middle-income families. But such programs decrease the legal options that working families have, and the high costs of compliance with regulations drive informal child care underground. Most important, government interference in child care threatens the independence of the family and the long-term interests of children.

Young couples with children may think they want government child care. But they don't realize that Americans like themselves will be the biggest losers in this Faustian bargain with the State. They risk losing their right to raise their children as they—and not bureaucrats—see fit.

It is not difficult to see why calls for action on child care have grown to a deafening level. Half the married mothers with children under five are working, twice the number who did in 1970. By 1995 two-thirds of all preschool children are expected to have working mothers.

Licensed, regulated child care costs an average of $3,000 per child per year. Most families can't afford that, especially single-parent families whose annual incomes are less than $10,000. Many of these families now make unofficial arrangements in the black (i.e. free) market, which includes relatives, neighbors, and other unlicensed child-care providers.

It's already illegal in most states to provide more than 20 hours a week of child care in your home without government permission. Yet legislators are proposing to federalize these laws and make them harsher. Their prime vehicle is the "ABC bill," the Act for Better Child Care Services, sponsored by Senator Christopher Dodd (D-CT) and Representative Dale Kildee (D-MI).

The ABC bill would create a brand-new, full-blown federal "entitlement" program, complete with subsidies, grants, licenses, loans, regulations, certificates, and inspections. The program would be administered by the states but overseen by a federal child-care administrator backed by an army of bureaucrats.

ABC would authorize $2.5 billion in the first year and "such sums as may be necessary" thereafter. If licensed child care costs $3,000 per child per year and 16 million children are eligible, simple multiplication tells us that the program will cost at least $48 billion annually. And knowing how government programs work, after that, the sky is the limit.

The ABC bill would only be the first step. We can expect pressure groups to launch a full-time effort to make sure there's no turning back. That's why Senator Orrin Hatch's (R-UT) bill isn't much better. He proposes a "conservative" alternative (i.e. more regulation, some tax credits, and vouchers), but with its direct tax subsidies in the form of vouchers—not to speak of its regulations—it too would encourage powerful lobbying groups to make sure it leads to total federal control.

Advocates of more regulation cite the case of Jessica McClure, the 18-month-old Texas girl who fell down a well last year. According to the misnamed Children's Defense Fund, Jessica fell because she attended an "unregulated Texas family day-care program." Stamp out unregulated family day care, CDF says, and such accidents would end. This is nonsense, of course. Regulated industries are much less responsive to consumer demands than unregulated ones. And actual government agencies are even worse. Private child-care centers, on the other hand, are accountable to parents and subject to market competition. They are therefore far more likely to look after the safety of their client's children.

Advocates of government child care claim they want child care to be more available, yet at the same time they want rigid and federalized regulations. Regulations can only *lessen* the number of child-care centers because fewer providers will have the time, resources, labor, and facilities to qualify under Washington's official rules.

Regulations will not improve the quality of child care. They will restrict competition and establish a cartel of the largest firms, which are the only ones that can afford the costs of dealing with the government. It's no coincidence that the big businesses in the industry are actively lobbying for regulations which will crush small firms.

Another bad idea would force businesses to provide child care for employees' children. Such programs would be very costly for private firms, which would cover their losses by laying off workers. Moreover, they would avoid hiring young women with children. The very people that such programs are allegedly designed to help—young working mothers—would be the ones most hurt.

Some activists would even nationalize child-care centers. But government-run child-care centers will be no different from other government agencies. Would we want our children to be cared for by post office workers or bureaucrats at the department of motor vehicles? The workers could get special training in child care, but that's not what really matters. More important are the rewards and penalties a job offers.

Once a profit-making enterprise is turned over to the government, its entire character changes. It is no longer concerned about profit and loss. Like all bureaucracies, it's run for the benefit of the bureaucrats. Employees can't be fired, they waste money, and customers become an interference rather than a blessing. Such a system would have to work against the best interests of children.

In a private child-care center, the customer is king, employees have reason to work hard, and resources are used efficiently. Profits can only come through providing quality child care at an affordable price.

As a social worker, I work daily with poor mothers who use the underground market to secure child care. And I heartily approve. These mothers know far better than the D.C. government what's best for their children. In one case, a poor working mother had a loving neighbor take care of her child for three years. It was illegal (no license, no minimum wage, no inspections, etc.), but everyone benefited from the arrangement. Then in July, an informer turned her in, and the government shut down the neighbor's business. The result: this mother now has to spend *half* her paycheck on inferior government-approved child care. Everyone is worse off but the government itself, which has increased its power over family life.

Since government can only make things worse, I have a three-point plan guaranteed to increase the availability of quality, affordable child care. First, repeal all regulations and licenses, which would make much more care available. Second, grant unlimited tax credits to families who use child-care services, making them more affordable. And third, repeal the minimum wage law, which would dramatically increase the number of officially employable child-care workers.

I grant that my proposal would have little chance of passing, given the pressure groups stampeding to Washington. But the alternative will be an ominous and bipartisan increase in bureaucratic power over families and children.

7

BUDGETS, TAXES, BUREAUCRACY, AND INTERVENTIONISM

Love in the Bureaucracy

Bradley Miller

As long as bureaucrat-bashing remains sport royal, there is hope. But how much? Even now, confronting bureaucracy's relentless encroachments and entanglements, who ya gonna call?

The Reagan administration phoned Ollie North, a "man of action," a "take-charge guy" who can "cut through red tape" and "get things done." But most of us must call a faceless functionary at the Reports and Publications Division of the Environmental Protection Agency's Water and Waste Management Administration's Emergency Service's Department's Request and Complaint Office's Bureau of Trash,

Metal Bulk, and Dead Animal Removal, and get put on hold. In other words, we must call Bureaucratic Man.

As of this writing it seems unlikely that North will go to jail, but powerful evidence indicates that what he tried to do was neither popular nor legal, and could even doom the very group his efforts were designed to help: the Nicaraguan contras. Yet to many, including the president who fired him from the National Security Council, North is a national hero. Even his detractors grant he's a forceful and attractive personality.

Surveys have found that most Americans don't know which side is which in Nicaragua, but tell pollsters they're against sending their tax money down there. So it's clear that North's popularity either has nothing to do with the goals he was pursuing, or emerged despite them.

In fact, the root of Americans' love of him is their hatred of the bureaucracy he defied, just as the 1980 and 1984 elections reflected more hatred of Carter and Mondale than love of Reagan.

North comes across as a forthright, patriotic, God-fearing, family-loving, ruggedly handsome, bemedaled man of action. But America is not lacking in such chaps, and North is far from unflawed. What stirred America was the sight of him thrown before those perceived as niggling, blood-sucking representatives of the world's biggest and most overpaid bureaucracy. The bureaucracy manufactures the red tape North tried to cut through (never mind toward what ends or in violation of what laws). It stands between the rest of us and the freedom to do what we want, and its spider web of regulations is woven and enforced by gray little men who can't be fired short of behavior so outrageous it would make most of us candidates for the funny farm.

In *Harper's*, Leonard Reed has reported that only one-tenth of one percent of federal bureaucrats are fired for incompetence. At the higher bureaucratic levels such unbearable bungling lands you not in the funny farm but—

no joke—in a "turkey farm," where unbearable bunglers are put through training sessions to turn them into bearable bunglers, i.e., bureaucrats competent enough not to inspire excessive public outrage, and sensible enough to realize that if they do their jobs too well they'll lose them.

In his great book *Bureaucracy*, written in 1944, Professor Ludwig von Mises says the distinguishing mark of the bureaucrat is that he is driven not by the profit motive but by the necessity to follow and enforce rules. Mises points out that a bureaucracy, so understood, isn't intended to be profitable, so its worth can't be assessed by profit-and-loss statements. Businesses also have bureaucratic aspects, but the free market imposes limits on them. An overload of bureaucrats diminishes profits by diminishing efficiency, innovation, and morale. That's why schemes to bring business methods to government come to grief. As Mises says, business and government are fundamentally different, and the methods appropriate to one are alien to the other.

The picture is even far bleaker than this. Not only is Bureaucratic Man uninterested in doing good work by business standards; doing such work would cost him his job. An anti-poverty warrior so good he eradicated poverty would have nothing to do, so such wars aren't intended to be won, but endlessly expanded. This thins the ranks of those who work for a living, and swells the ranks of those who vote for a living. In sum, it makes a joke of representative government.

How bad is it? Guess who said the following:

> If we do not halt this steady process of building commissions and regulatory bodies and special legislation like huge inverted pyramids over every one of the simple constitutional provisions, we shall soon be spending many billions of dollars more.

So said Franklin Roosevelt, father of today's welfare state. By today's standards FDR was doubtless an efficiency expert.

But by now the deathly effects of bureaucracy on the commonwealth are too well known to need elaboration. Bureaucracy is at once a monstrous evil and banality, and, as its consummation in totalitarianism has shown, it makes the most monstrous evils banal. Banality, indeed, is its highest virtue. Bureaucratic Man wants merely to rust out in ease, security, and respectability, not to wear himself out pursuing greatness. He doesn't love, in any deep sense, his work or spouse, for love entails risk and demands energy. BM asks only for comfort.

It's as hard to picture Nietzsche's superman or Aristotle's large-souled man in this kingdom of clerks as it is to imagine Pascal at a PTL picnic. The ultimate triumph of the bureaucratic state, which has long been realized in such Periclean lands as Bulgaria, Albania, and North Korea, is to obliterate all traces of even Mick Jagger's street-fighting man.

Bureaucratic Man is far lower than Winston Smith in Orwell's *1984*, who in the end loved Big Brother. Deep love and deep hate are both inconceivable to BM, so no goon squads are needed to keep him in line. Intellectually and emotionally, after all, his whole life amounts to an endless standing in line to get the necessities for more standing in line.

As technology progresses, it becomes clear that BM is far lower than a machine. Anything BM can do, machines can do better at a fraction of the cost and irritation.

Unfortunately, BM, freed from drudgery by automation, doesn't devote himself to the art of love or even the love of art, two reasons to live. Instead, automation has exposed—not created—a world in which, as Mises says, "the man who is aware of his inability to stand competition scorns 'this mad competitive system.' He who is unfit to serve his fellow citizens wants to rule them."

BM created this world. If he knows nothing else, BM is at least aware of his limitless inability, which fills him with envy of his superiors, whom he tries, with depressing success, to suffocate through government. Government work is tedious, so it's hard to get superior men to do it, but in today's hi-tech age, government by actual robots would be much more efficient and humane than government by BM.

Rotation in Office

Llewellyn H. Rockwell, Jr.

The Articles of Confederation of 1777, our first "Constitution," was superior in a number of ways to the document adopted 200 years ago. (It's easy to forget, amidst all the celebrations, that the Constitution as originally drafted had few limits on government power; it was saved only by the Bill of Rights that the Jeffersonians demanded.)

One of the great clauses of the Articles mandated annual election of Congressmen (by the various state legislatures), and said that no Congressman "may serve for more than three years in any term of six years."

But politicians hate to be out of office, and this great idea—originated by Thomas Jefferson—was stricken from the Constitution. It was resurrected, however, by that great modern Jeffersonian (and Mises Institute Distinguished Counsellor) Ron Paul who introduced legislation while serving in Congress to limit Congressmen to four two-year terms; Senators to two four-year terms; and Supreme Court and other federal judges to one eight-year term.

It was Dr. Paul's view, and Jefferson's, that continuation in office helped create big government. Both these men also applied what Jefferson called "rotation in office" to all government employees.

For more than the first half of our country's history, when a new administration came into office, it installed its own people in all civilian government jobs. This healthy and purgative process prevented the build-up of bureaucracy. Not surprisingly, it was despised and denigrated by statists as the "spoils system."

About a century ago, big government advocates, in the first flush of the statist "progressive" era, instituted the idea of civil service—the monstrous idea that civilian bureaucrats should have lifetime tenure in office.

When we have our first 20th century Jeffersonian administration, its agenda will include not only the gold standard, the free market, and a constitutional foreign policy, but the restitution of rotation in office for all government employees, elected and appointed.

The Balanced-Budget Amendment Hoax

Murray N. Rothbard

It is a hallmark of the triumph of image over substance in modern society that an administration which has submitted to Congress budgets with the biggest deficits in American history should propose as a cure-all a constitutional amendment mandating a balanced budget. Apart from the high irony of such a proposal from such a source, the amendment-mongers don't seem to realize that the same pressures of the democratic process that have led to permanent and growing deficits will also be at work on the courts that have acquired the exclusive power to interpret the Constitution. The federal courts are appointed by the executive and confirmed by the legislature, and are therefore part and parcel of the government structure.

Apart from these general strictures on rewriting the Constitution as a panacea for our ills, the various proposed balanced-budget amendments suffer from many deep flaws in themselves. The major defect is that they only require a balance of the future *estimated* budget, and not of the actual budget at the end of a given fiscal year. As we all should know by this time, economists and politicians are expert at submitting glittering projected future budgets that have only the foggiest relation to the actual reality of the future year. It will be duck soup for Congress to estimate a future balance; not so easy, however, to actually balance it. At the very least, any amendment should require the actual balancing of the budget at the end of each particular year.

Secondly, balancing the budget by increasing taxes is like curing influenza by shooting the patient; the cure is worse than the disease. Dimly recognizing this fact, most of the amendment proposals include a clause to limit federal taxation. But unfortunately, they do so by imposing a limit on revenues as a percentage of the national income or gross national product. It is absurd to include such a concept as "national income" in the fundamental law of the land; there is no such real entity, but only a statistical artifact, and an artifact that can and does wobble according to the political breeze. It is all too easy to include or exclude an enormous amount from this concept.

A third flaw highlights again the problem of treating "the budget" as a constitutional entity. As a means of making the deficit look less bleak, there has been an increasing tendency for the government to spend money on "off-budget" items that simply don't get included in official expenses, and therefore don't get added to the deficit. Any balanced-budget amendment would provide a field day for this kind of mass trickery on the American public.

We must here note a disturbing current tendency for "born again" pro-deficit economists in conservative ranks to propose that "capital" items be excluded from the federal budget altogether. This theory is based on an analogy with private firms and their "capital" versus "operating" budgets. One would think that allegedly free-market economists would not have the affrontery to apply this to government. Get this adopted, and the government could happily throw away money on any boondoggle, no matter how absurd, so long as they could call it an "investment in the future." Here is a loophole in the balanced-budget amendment that would make any politician's day!

A fourth problem is that the various proposals make it all too easy for Congress to override the amendment. Suppose Congress and/or the president violate the amendment. What then? Would the Supreme Court have the power to call the federal marshals and lock up the whole crew? To ask that question is to answer it. (Of course, by making the budget balance *prospective* instead of real, this problem would not even arise, since it would be almost impossible to violate the amendment at all.)

But isn't half a loaf better than none? Isn't it better to have an imperfect amendment than none at all? Half a loaf is indeed better than none, but *even worse* than no loaf is an elaborate camouflage system that fools the public into thinking that a loaf exists where there is really none at all. Or, to mix our metaphors, that the naked Emperor is really wearing clothes.

We now see the role of the balanced budget amendment in the minds of many if not most of its supporters. The purpose is not actually to balance the budget, for that would involve massive spending cuts that the Establishment, "conservative" or liberal, is not willing to contemplate.

The purpose is to continue deficits while deluding the public into thinking that the budget is, or will soon be, balanced. In that way, the public's slipping confidence in the dollar will be shored up. Thus, the balanced-budget amendment turns out to be the fiscal counterpart of the supply-siders' notorious proposal for a phony gold standard. In that scheme, the public would not be able to redeem its dollars in gold coin, the Fed would continue to manipulate and inflate, but all the while this inflationist policy would now be cloaked in the confidence-building mantle of gold.

In both plans, we would be dazzled by the shadow, the rhetoric of sound policy, while the same old program of cheap money and huge deficits would proceed unchecked. In both cases, the dominant ideology seems to be that of P. T. Barnum: "There's a sucker born every minute."

How Government Intervention Plagued Our 19th-Century Economy

Lawrence W. Reed

The recessions and depressions of the 19th century are often cited as proof of the "inherent instability" of the free market. (Indeed, the promoters of the Federal Reserve System in 1913 argued for a central bank as a way of preventing future downturns!) This is, of course, a bum rap.

The 1800s were freer than today, but there was more than enough government intervention to cause serious setbacks in the economy. And Austrian trade cycle theory explains exactly how.

The source of the business cycle, Mises discovered, is government-engineered expansion of money and credit. Such a policy artificially depresses interest rates at first, deranges the structure of production by generating unsustainable malinvestments, and inevitably leads to contraction and painful readjustments.

The first economic calamity of the century occurred in 1808 when a federal embargo on overseas shipping produced widespread bankruptcies and unemployment. After that, five major cyclical depressions struck the American economy: in 1819, 1837, 1857, and 1893. The typical economic history text lists among the "causes" things like railroad speculation, stock crashes, trade imbalances, commodity price booms and busts, etc.

These are not, of course, causes at all, but merely symptoms. Only Austrian trade cycle theory as propounded by Ludwig von Mises, Murray N. Rothbard, and others, makes sense of the mess and provides a coherent explanation of these five depressions.

The 1819 collapse followed a flagrant credit expansion by the Second Bank of the United States, created by the feds in 1816. The definitive work on the experience is still Rothbard's PhD thesis, *The Panic of 1819*.

Rothbard documented the extensive culpability of the Second Bank. In its very first year, it issued $23 million on a specie reserve of about $2.5 million. The expansion of credit, which eventually involved state banks as well, was actively encouraged by the U.S. Treasury. The government even made it legal for inflating banks to fraudulently suspend payment of specie, ripping off hapless depositors in the process.

Then, in a series of deliberate deflationary moves, the Second Bank pulled the rug out from under the very house of cards it had built. It forced a drastic reduction in the money supply starting as early as the middle of 1818. The depression, which came a few months later, was the unavoidable outcome of gross manipulation of money and credit.

Those who blame the gold standard for this debacle are wrong. In fact, the country was not even on a gold standard at the time. In 1792, the official policy was "bimetallism," according to which silver and gold were to circulate side by side at a governmentally fixed ratio. (The ratio between the prices of any two commodities, including gold and silver, is always changing on the market, and an attempt to fix the ratio by government fiat always leads to trouble. In this instance, it forced the country onto a de facto silver standard from the start. The same sort of intervention proved to be a major factor in the later crisis of 1893.)

The Second Bank's shenanigans created the depression of 1837. Anticipating a political battle to renew the Bank when its charter ran out in 1836, Bank authorities early in the decade embarked upon a rapid expansion of the money supply. Reserve ratios were pushed to their lowest levels of the entire antebellum period. Orchestrating "good times" through easy money was the Bank's way of fighting hard-money, anti-central bank President Andrew Jackson.

Jackson, however, flattened the inflation by requiring specie in payment for federal lands and by vetoing the Bank's charter. In the quick contraction that followed, the inflationary malinvestments promoted by the bank were liquidated. But Washington persisted with its policy of bimetallism. In addition, state and local governments responded to the 1837 collapse with a wave of anti-banking laws, outlawing banks altogether in some places and exacerbating the depression. This is hardly laissez-faire or gold standard behavior.

By the early 1850s, state governments got into the inflation act. Exerting control over their extensive network of state-chartered banks, they pressured the banks to monetize state debt. The result was another round of credit expansion, dangerous reduction of specie reserves, and a temporary, artificial boom in the economy, followed by panic and depression in 1857. Because the pressure on banks to monetize debt occurred principally in the Northern states, the subsequent collapse was considerably less pronounced in the South.

The general depression of 1873 also provides a clear example of government as the guilty party. In the prior decade, both Northern and Southern regimes abandoned a specie standard altogether and printed massive quantities of irredeemable, legal tender paper.

In the Confederacy, high taxes, a paper hyperinflation, and Northern scorched-earth military policies plunged the region into depression in 1865.

In the North, despite crippling tax hikes, revenues fell far short of the funds necessary to prosecute the war. No less than $5.2 billion in "greenbacks" were printed. At the war's conclusion, a greenback dollar was worth only 35 cents in gold. The Northern economy struggled for a few more years, but with the complete cessation of paper inflation in the 1870s, collapse and readjustment began by 1873.

Recovery had barely commenced when the central government began a new form of monetary intervention, this one tied to silver. In 1878, Congress passed (over President Hayes's veto) the Bland-Allison Act, which mandated the Treasury's purchase of $2-$4 million in silver bullion per month. The metal was to be minted into silver dollars, each containing 371.25 grains of silver. Since the gold dollar was defined as 23.22 grains of gold, this established a ratio between the two metals of 16 to 1.

But the free-market value of silver in terms of gold was at least 18 to 1 in 1878. By overvaluing silver and undervaluing gold, Bland-Allison set Gresham's Law into motion. "Bad" money (officially overvalued silver) began to drive "good" money (officially undervalued gold) out of circulation, deranging the nation's finances and engendering a steady loss of confidence in the currency. On top of it all, Bland-Allison authorized the Treasury to issue paper silver certificates along with the depreciating silver dollars.

The inflationists of the period—who pushed for this intervention in the belief that "more money" would aid the economy in general and debtors in particular—were not satisfied. Throughout the 1880s, they pushed for even more inflation under the guise of "doing something for silver."

Their crowning folly was enacted into law in 1890—the Sherman Silver Purchase Act. It required the Treasury to buy virtually the entire output of American silver mines—4.5 million ounces per month; mint it at 16 to 1 at a time when the gold/silver ratio in the free market was actually greater than 30 to 1; and issue new paper "Treasury Notes" simultaneously.

Drugged by easy money, the economy took on the classic symptoms of a boom. Unemployment and interest rates in 1891 and 1892 fell dramatically. Capital goods industries worked feverishly. Foreigners, however, were the first to sense danger and began withdrawing their capital from America as early as 1891.

The economic reversal started in 1893, and led to the worst depression in 50 years. It also produced one of the more scholarly addresses ever delivered before the House of Representatives. Congressman Bourke Cochran of New York, a first-rate historian, traced the history of coinage in England and explained how debasing the currency led to recurrent depressions. Applying that principle to his day, he declared:

> I think it safe to assert that every commercial crisis can be traced to an unnecessary inflation of the currency, or to an improvident expansion of credit. The operation of the Sherman Law has been to flood this country with paper money without providing any method whatever for its redemption. The circulating medium has become so redundant that the channels of commerce have overflowed and gold has been expelled.

Viewing the crisis of 1893, contemporary historian Ernest Ludlow Bogart said:

> It must be said that the net results of this experiment of "managed currency," that is, one in which the government undertakes to provide the necessary money for the people, were disastrous. For the maintenance of a suitable supply, the operation of normal economic forces is more reliable than the judgment of a legislative body.

The economy of 19th-century America was punctuated by serious economic setbacks. They were caused not by the free market, but by the destructive manipulations and interventions of government authorities. This was not a century of government as innocent bystander, but of government as the incessant bungler, running roughshod over the principle of sound and honest money. (Although, without a Fed and other government interventions, the recoveries from these panics were quick.)

We can learn much from the experiences sketched here. Monetary reform, if it is to be genuine and successful, must sever money and banking from politics. That's why a modern gold standard must have: no central bank; no fixed rations between gold and silver; no bail-outs; no suspension of gold payments or other bank frauds; no monetization of debt; and no inflation of the money supply, all of which have proved so disastrous in the past.

Anything short of the discipline and honesty of a true gold coin standard will inevitably self-destruct, consuming our wealth and liberties, and nurturing the omnipotent state.

Send Out the Clowns

Llewellyn H. Rockwell, Jr.

Only in the cloud cuckoo-land that is Washington, D.C., could the budget summit held by the Congress and the Reagan administration be taken seriously.

After the Crash, the politicians panicked. Not because of any harm to the American people, but because such events can hurt all incumbents. The result was a sideshow that—not unsurprisingly—has *not* calmed the markets.

Federal deficits and spending do not cause the business cycle, but if we are to prevent the coming inflationary recession from becoming something worse, we have to curb not only the Fed but the spendthrifts in elected office.

True to form, both party establishments are adopting exactly the wrong sort of policies. Instead of—at the very least—cutting federal spending across the board to immediately balance the budget, they are minutely shaving *projected* spending by one third of one percent.

Instead of—at the very least—cutting incentive-destroying, business-obliterating taxation, they are increasing it, and spending $1.5 billion more on "tax compliance and enforcement."

Instead of repealing the trade barriers raised by the most protectionist administration and Congress since Herbert Hoover, they are increasing them, overtly through quotas and tariffs and covertly by devaluing the dollar.

Given the specter of the Federal Reserve pumping in more "liquidity" to solve the problems its previous inflation caused, we face either an immediate recession or a postponed (and worse) one. That is inevitable. What is not inevitable is the duration and intensity of the bust and the political results that will flow from it.

We can work to influence the politicians. But their reaction to the coming economic debacle shows once again that we cannot count on them to act correctly until we have changed the climate of ideas.

Twenty years ago, politicians talked and acted like statists. Today, they still act the same, but they use our rhetoric. And that's because the people want a change. Thanks to our movement, we have made tremendous intellectual progress.

It is our job to continue that progress, and not to allow the government again to use a crisis to increase its power over us. The example of Ludwig von Mises, in combining scholarship and activism, shows us how to proceed. And the mood of the American people gives us the opportunity.

How our Economic Constitution Has Deteriorated

Robert Higgs

Many people think of the Constitution as essentially unchanged, yet today's document bears little resemblance to the original of 1787 in its relation to the economy. The original words remain, but they have been formally amended in critical ways; and reinterpreted by the Supreme Court so that their practical effect has become almost the opposite of the intent.

The original Constitution promoted economic development in many ways. For example, it resolved the disputes over the West by providing for the admission of new states on equal terms with the old, thereby fostering settlement of the vast interior. Provision for duty-free interstate trade increased productivity. The Constitution made state governments less intrusive by prohibiting their issuance of paper money and their passage of laws impairing the obligation of contracts.

By the mid-19th century, rapid economic growth had become the normal condition of the economy. But under the surface, an irresolvable contradiction was growing. The lump that would not digest was slavery.

In view of its importance in the southern economy and the deep disagreements between northerners and southerners about it, slavery received scant mention in the original Constitution. (The words "slave" and "slavery" do not appear at all.) Congress could not interfere with the international slave trade for 20 years; slaves escaping into free states had to be returned; and three-fifths of the slaves were counted in determining representation in Congress. Otherwise the Constitution left slavery to the states.

For seven decades, a succession of political compromises kept the conflict between North and South from boiling over, but finally either the will or the ability to fashion acceptable compromises ran out, and the Civil War ensued.

In the war's aftermath the old Constitution was fundamentally altered. The Thirteenth Amendment abolished slavery. The Fourteenth guaranteed to all citizens, including the freed slaves, protection from state actions that would abridge the privileges and immunities of citizenship, deprive them of life, liberty, or property without due process, or deny them equal protection of the laws. The Fifteenth Amendment guaranteed the right of the freedmen to vote. The amendments of the 1860s transferred power from the states to the national government. Though disputes over states' rights persisted, claims of dual sovereignty lost most of their force.

During the post-civil War era, Americans enjoyed unprecedented economic growth, an achievement favored by the Supreme Court's insistence that due process of law included protection of economic liberties—rights of private property and freedom of contract. Then, government actions caused the economy to plunge into deep depression in the early 1930s. Governments at all levels responded by expanding their powers over economic affairs. At first the Supreme Court resisted many of these measures. Starting in 1937, though, the Court reversed so many important decisions on economic matters that its turnabout must be considered a constitutional revolution. The heart of the Court's new position was a broad reading of the Commerce Clause. Practically everything, no matter how manifestly local, was seen as part of interstate commerce and therefore subject to regulation by Congress and its agencies.

During the past 50 years, the United States has developed a welfare state not much different from those of Western Europe. Economic affairs, once overwhelmingly private, have become pervasively politicized. Taxes now equal 40% of the national income—up from 13% as recently as 1929. The free-market economy has come to be regulated in minute and expensive detail, with the costs born largely by consumers. Citizens have lost much of the economic liberty their ancestors esteemed.

American traditions and political pressures have kept the government from totally destroying all private property rights. But the Constitution, which formerly served to guarantee economic liberties, no longer provides much if any substantial protection. One may well doubt whether the economic dynamism that made the average American rich by world standards will prove permanently compatible with a constitutional regime so permissive of governmental intrusion into economic affairs.

But the Constitution can be changed, as it has been changed before. In 1865 the Constitution gave the slaves freedom from their masters. We can hope that someday the Constitution will be changed again to give all Americans economic freedom from our masters in Washington.

Nine Myths About the Crash

Murray N. Rothbard

Ever since Black, or Meltdown, Monday October 19th, the public has been deluged with irrelevant and contradictory explanations and advice from politicians, economists, financiers, and assorted pundits. Let's try to sort out and rebut some of the nonsense about the nature, causes, and remedies for the crash.

Myth One: It was not a crash, but a "correction."

Rubbish. The market was in a virtual crash state since it started turning down sharply from its all-time peak at the end of August. Meltdown Monday simply put the seal on a contraction process that had gone on since early September.

Myth Two: The crash occurred because stock prices had been "overvalued," and now the overvaluation has been cured.

This adds a philosophical fallacy to Myth #1. To say that stock prices fell because they had been overvalued is equivalent to the age-old fallacy of "explaining" why opium puts people to sleep by saying that it "has dormitive power." A definition has been magically transmuted into a "cause." By definition, if stock prices fall, this means that they had been previously overvalued. So what? This "explanation" tells you nothing about why they were overvalued or whether or not they are "over" or "under" valued now, or what in the world is going to happen next.

Myth Three: The crash came about because of computer trading, which in association with stock index futures, has made the stock market more volatile. Therefore computer trading and/or stock index futures, should be restricted/outlawed.

This is a variant of the scapegoat term "computer error" employed to get "people errors" off the hook. It is also a variant of the old Luddite fallacy of blaming modern technology for human error and taking a crowbar to wreck the new machines. People trade, and people program computers. Empirically, moreover, the "tape" was hours behind the action on Black Monday, and so computers played a minimal role. Stock index futures are an excellent new way for investors to hedge against stock price changes, and should be welcomed instead of fastened on—by its competitors in the old-line exchanges—to be tagged as the fall guy for the crash. Blaming futures or computer trading is like shooting the messenger—the markets—that brings bad financial news. The acme of this reaction was the threat—and sometimes the reality—of forcibly shutting down the exchanges in a pitiful and futile attempt to hold back the news by destroying it. The Hong Kong exchange closed down for a week to try to stem the crash and, when it reopened, found that the ensuing crash was far worse as a result.

Myth Four: A major cause of the crash was the big trade deficit in the U.S.

Nonsense. There is nothing wrong with a trade deficit. In fact, there is no payment deficit at all. If U.S. imports are greater than exports, they must be paid for somehow, and the way they are paid is that foreigners invest in dollars, so that there is a capital inflow into the U.S. In that way, a big trade deficit results in a zero payment deficit.

Foreigners have been investing heavily in dollars—in Treasury deficits, in real estate, factories, etc.—for several years, and that's a good thing, since it enables Americans to enjoy a higher-valued dollar (and consequently cheaper imports) than would otherwise be the case.

But, say the advocates of Myth #4, the terrible thing is that the U.S. has, in recent years, become a debtor instead of a creditor nation. So what's wrong with that? The United States was in the same way a debtor nation from the beginning of the republic until World War I, and this was accompanied by the largest rate of economic and industrial growth and of rising living standards, in the history of mankind.

Myth Five: The budget deficit is a major cause of the crash, and we must work hard to reduce that deficit, either by cutting government spending, and/or by raising taxes.

The budget deficit is most unfortunate, and causes economic problems, but the stock market crash was not one of them. Just because something is bad policy doesn't mean that all economic ills are caused by it. Basically, the budget deficit is as irrelevant to the crash, as the even larger deficit was irrelevant to the pre-September 1987 stock market boom. Raising taxes is now the favorite crash remedy of both liberal and conservative Keynesians. Here, one of the few good points in the original, or "classical," Keynesian view has been curiously forgotten. How in the world can one cure a crash (or the coming recession), by raising taxes?

Raising taxes will clearly level a damaging blow to an economy already reeling from the crash. Increasing taxes to cure a crash was one of the major policies of the unlamented program of Herbert Hoover. Are we longing for a replay? The idea that a tax increase would "reassure" the market is straight out of Cloud Cuckoo-land.

Myth Six: The budget should be cut, but not by much, because much lower government spending would precipitate a recession.

Unfortunately, the way things are, we don't have to worry about a big cut in government spending. Such a cut would be marvelous, not only for its own sake, but because a slash in the budget would reduce the unproductive boondoggles of government spending, and therefore tip the social proportion of saving/consumption toward more saving and investment.

More saving/investment in relation to consumption is an Austrian remedy for easing a recession, and reducing the amount of corrective liquidation that the recession has to perform, in order to correct the malinvestments of the boom caused by the inflationary expansion of bank credit.

Myth Seven: What we need to offset the crash and stave off a recession is lots of monetary inflation (called by the euphemistic term "liquidity") and lower interest rates. Fed chairman Alan Greenspan did exactly the right thing by pumping in reserves right after the crash, and announcing that the Fed would assure plenty of liquidity for banks and for the entire market and the whole economy. (A position taken by every single variant of the conventional economic wisdom, from Keynesians to "free marketeers.")

In this way, Greenspan and the federal government have proposed to cure the disease—the crash and future recession—by pouring into the economy more of the very virus (inflationary credit expansion) that caused the disease in the first place. Only in Cloud Cuckoo-land, to repeat, is the cure for inflation, more inflation. To put it simply: the reason for the crash was the credit boom generated by the double-digit monetary expansion engineered by the Fed in the last several years. For a few years, as always happens in Phase I of an inflation, prices went up less than the monetary inflation. This, the typical euphoric phase of inflation, was the "Reagan miracle" of cheap and abundant money, accompanied by moderate price increases.

By 1986, the main factors that had offset the monetary inflation and kept prices relatively low (the unusually high dollar and the OPEC collapse) had worked their way through the price system and disappeared. The next inevitable step was the return and acceleration of price inflation; inflation rose from about 1% in 1986 to about 5% in 1987. As a result, with the market sensitive to and expecting eventual reacceleration of inflation, interest rates began to rise sharply in 1987. Once interest rates rose (which had little or nothing to do with the budget deficit), a stock market crash was inevitable. The previous stock market boom had been built on the shaky foundation of the low interest rates from 1982 on.

Myth Eight: The crash was precipitated by the Fed's unwise tight money policy from April 1987 onward, after which the money supply was flat until the crash.

There is a point here, but a totally distorted one. A flat money supply for six months probably made a coming recession inevitable, and added to the stock market crash. But that tight money was a good thing nevertheless. No other school of economic thought but the Austrian understands that once an inflationary bank credit boom has been launched, a corrective recession is inevitable, and that the sooner it comes, the better.

The sooner a recession comes, the fewer the unsound investments that the recession has to liquidate, and the sooner the recession will be over. The important point about a recession is for the government not to interfere, not to inflate, not to regulate, and to allow the recession to work its curative way as quickly as possible. Interfering with the recession, either by inflating or regulating, can only prolong the recession and make it worse, as in the 1930s. And yet the pundits, the economists of all schools, the politicians of both parties, rush heedless into the agreed-upon policies of: Inflate, and Regulate.

Myth Nine: Before the crash, the main danger was inflation, and the Fed was right to tighten credit. But since the crash, we have to shift gears, because recession is the major enemy, and therefore the Fed has to inflate, at least until price inflation accelerates rapidly.

This entire analysis, permeating the media and the Establishment, assumes that the great fact and the great lesson of the 1970s, and of the last two big recessions, never happened: i.e., inflationary recession. The 1970s have gone down the Orwellian memory hole, and the Establishment is back, once again, spouting the Keynesian Phillips Curve, perhaps the greatest single and most absurd error in modern economics.

The Phillips Curve assumes that the choice is always either more recession and unemployment, or more inflation.

In reality, the Phillips Curve, if one wishes to speak in those terms, is in reverse: the choice is either more inflation and bigger recession, or none of either. The looming danger is another inflationary recession, and the Greenspan reaction indicates that it will be a whopper.

The Crash Commission Report

Ron Paul

The crash of 1929, and the depression of the 1930s, entrenched the welfare-warfare state. Intellectuals, taking their cue from government propagandists, wrongly blamed the free market and the gold standard for the disaster. In a variation on the same theme, they are blaming the October 19 crash on insufficient government regulations.

Most prominent among the various stock market study commissions is the president's. But its recommendations are disappointing for anyone who values free markets. The stock market wasn't too impressed either. When the commission released its 340-page report, the Dow promptly fell 140 points.

The president's commission missed the true lessons of the crash—that Federal Reserve inflation causes the business cycle of booms and busts—and its recommendation for more regulation will only make matters worse.

The president had appointed Nicholas Brady, chairman of Dillon Read and an especially well-connected member of the Eastern Establishment, to head the commission. Also on it was John Opel, chairman of the New York Federal Reserve Bank, where the report was actually written.

"To help prevent a repetition of the events of mid-October and to provide an effective and coordinated response in the face of market disorder," said the report, "we recommend: one agency should coordinate the few, but critical, regulatory issues which have an impact across the related market segments and throughout the financial system; clearing systems should be unified across marketplaces to reduce financial risk; margins should be made consistent across marketplaces to control speculation and financial leverage; circuit breaker mechanisms (such as price limits and coordinated trading halts) should be formulated and implemented to protect the market system." Finally, "the Federal Reserve is well qualified to fill that role."

All markets *are* linked as never before, but the rules they want to impose will only "coordinate" the various sectors of American finance. This is a world market, as October 19th showed. Their own logic should compel the commission to call for unified world regulation of markets—an idea that delights world government advocates and that has already been suggested by people in the Securities and Exchange Commission.

Every one of the proposed regulations is, of course bad, but one of the worst is the vague call for a "circuit breaker mechanisms," namely "price limits and coordinated trading halts." This means the government would stop trading when things get "out of hand."

Raising barriers between willing buyers and sellers just makes markets less efficient, not to speak of violating the individual rights of would-be market participants. Plus price swings will inevitably be exaggerated once the market is opened again, as the case of the Hong Kong stock market showed, when it closed down for an entire week after the crash, and dropped even more precipitously later.

When government manipulates trading, it helps only the insiders (like Dillon Read investment bankers).

What was the fundamental cause of the October crash according to the Brady Commission? They don't know. And it's obvious that nobody on the Commission understands the business cycle. They illustrate their ignorance in appendix VIII of the report where they admit—20 years after Murray Rothbard's *America's Great Depression*—they don't know what caused the 1929 Crash and the Great Depression. Of course, it was Federal Reserve intervention that caused it and the Brady Commission wants more of the same.

Like Br'er Rabbit begging not be thrown into the briar patch, the Fed responded to the Brady report by saying it wasn't sure it wanted more power. That's nonsense. They're salivating at the prospect.

If the new regulations are imposed, they won't, as the report claims, "ensure that our securities market will maintain its global preeminence." They will only ensure that the old financial Establishment will keep its influence in Washington.

Commissions like Brady's serve to reinforce the myth that the crash was caused by a mere technical maladjustment. Thus they conclude that we need a mere technical change. But the problem is more fundamental than that. The Federal Reserve—the dollars they create and the government they fuel—is the source of our problems.

The Regulatory-Industrial Complex

Sam Wells

The free market is great for consumers and producers, but some businessmen find government regulation an easier road to profits. That's why they try to use government to protect them from the rivalry of the market.

There is nothing wrong with wanting to be on top, of course, so long as it is done peacefully. But when businessmen use the government to gain a monopoly, they cease being market competitors and become a political pressure group.

Some businesses advocate "fair trade" laws against "unfair competition," government price floors, licenses, taxes on competitors, and other political measures.

Taxi monopolies are powerful on the city level. They lobby government to make new drivers go through lengthy procedures or acquire expensive licenses to own a taxi. These laws don't exist to protect the public; they protect a privileged industry from competition and work against the public interest.

Dairy monopolies and utility companies are powerful on the state level. In New York, the dairy industry lobbies for protection from its New Jersey competitors who sell milk at a cheaper price. Utility companies get special privileges to be the sole provider of water, electricity, and natural gas. In all these cases, the consumer loses his freedom to choose.

At the national level, to take just two examples, the Post Office has a monopoly on mail and the Federal Reserve has a monopoly on money and banking.

Socialism is the final monopoly. Here the government allows no competition and only limited trade. Nationalizing an industry puts monopolists in power by merging their competitors under their control. Nationalizing an entire economy gives those on top the biggest boon of all. It's no coincidence that statist U.S. industrialists like Dwayne Andreas of Archer-Daniels-Midland and Armand Hammer of Occidental Petroleum get along so well with the elites that run the Soviet economy.

In each case—local, state, and federal monopolies and under socialism—monopolists find that they gain more through special privileges from the government than they do from the free market. And they do so at our expense.

This isn't something new. At the turn of the century, as historian Gabriel Kolko explains in the *Triumph of Conservatism* (1963):

> Competition was unacceptable to many key business and financial interests. . . . As new competitors sprang up, and as economic power was diffused throughout an expanding nation, it became apparent to many important businessmen that only the national government could "rationalize" the economy. Although specific conditions varied from industry to industry, internal problems that could be solved only by political means were the common denominator in those industries whose leaders advocated greater federal regulation. Ironically, contrary to the consensus of historians, it was not the existence of monopoly that caused the federal government to intervene in the economy, but the lack of it.

One classic example is the Interstate Commerce Commission, a federal agency set up at the behest of the railroad industry in 1887, which has been a menace to consumers ever since. The ICC was this nation's first "independent" regulatory agency, charged with preventing "cut-throat" competition in the transportation industry. The railroad industry sold it as a boon to consumers.

During the hearings on the Interstate Commerce Act of 1887, the leaders of the railroad industry lobbied hard for the ICC. Why? They wanted the government to outlaw price competition, which threatened established, old-line railroads. The ICC's first action was to do exactly that. Over the years, the ICC brought less competition, higher prices, and lousy train service. Like a pact with Satan, the ICC eventually helped ossify and then destroy the railroad industry, but by that time, the original owners and managers had long since gone to their reward far richer than they would have been in a world of free competition.

The ICC—and other similar Progressive Era agencies like the FTC—set the stage for more cartelization under FDR's

National Industrial Recovery Act, which was drafted by Gerard Swope of General Electric, the Chamber of Commerce, the American Bar Association, and dozens of other business groups and leaders. As E. W. Hawley shows in his classic study, *The New Deal and the Problem of Monopoly* (1966), big business lobbied for the NIRA because they had a "vision of a business commonwealth, of a rational, cartelized business order in which the industrialists would plan and direct the economy, profits would be insured, and the government would take care of recalcitrant 'chiselers.'"

In America, special interests are the minority. They are greatly outnumbered by taxpayers, voters, and competitors. But the interests get what they want in politics because they are well-organized, have well-defined goals, and can reward those in government who do their bidding. Consumers and taxpayers are spread out, disorganized, and pay a small marginal cost per intervention. Unfortunately, an interventionist economy tends to grant favors to well-organized minorities at the expense of the majority, even in a democracy where the will of the majority supposedly triumphs.

The special interests created the Interstate Commerce Commission, the Federal Reserve System, the Food and Drug Administration, the Federal Trade Commission, the Export-Import Bank, the Commodity Credit Corporation, the Securities and Exchange Commission, the Environmental Protection Agency, the Consumer Product Safety Commission, and a host of other agencies. In case after case, the agency served the special interests by promoting oligopoly and monopoly and retarding competition to the detriment of consumers.

The way to avoid such abuses is not by giving even more power to the political regulators who, after all, are already comfortably in bed with the vested interests.

The way to quash the regulatory-industrial complex is through a separation of Market and state, a strict adherence to the policy of laissez-faire. Only a purely free market will stop privilege-seeking businessmen from clustering around Washington like flies around a garbage can. Under a free market, the only road to profits will be to please the consumer.

Who Really Benefits From Foreign Aid?

Sam Wells

A coalition of Third World regimes, businessmen, and bureaucrats is scheming for your wallet.

What they want is more: more tax dollars extracted from Americans to redistribute under the name of "foreign aid," allegedly to lend a helping hand to "developing" countries so they can climb out of poverty.

Opponents of such policies are said to be selfish and uncaring, or perhaps they have some other more fundamental character flaw. American taxpayers are told to sacrifice their paychecks for the greater good of the poor around the world. How it is that the United States, Britain, Switzerland, Canada, Australia, Sweden, etc. were able to develop *without* foreign aid is never explained.

Assertions, emotion, and power drive these aid programs; not facts or reason. Peter T. Bauer and others have demonstrated that the hundreds of billions flowing from developed nations to the Less Developed Countries (LDCs) actually *retard* progress in those countries while bleeding the donor nations of precious capital.

U.S. government foreign aid, in all its various forms, is *not* assistance to poor people. It is aid to foreign *governments*, political regimes almost always of an authoritarian or totalitarian nature. Very little of this money ever gets to the poor people in those foreign lands.

Foreign aid is not charity from rich people to poor people. It is money extracted by government coercion (taxes) from working-class Americans and sent to the ruling cliques in foreign regimes. Politicians and civil servants in those countries dish it out to favored special interests, regardless of any "need."

That's why U.S. foreign aid dollars have helped buy, among many other things, modern TV stations in places where there is no electricity; dress suits for Greek undertakers; extra wives for Kenyan government officials; stretch limousines for African dictators; wasteful "national pride" boondoggles such as the construction of expensive capitals (Brasilia, Islamabad, and Dodoma in Tanzania); and filled the Swiss bank accounts of corrupt politicians. And since foreign aid goes to ruling elites, it helps entrench them in power.

Much of the largesse is pumped into state-run industries and collectivist programs run by socialist bureaucrats. By shoring up socialist systems, our foreign aid money virtually assures economic stagnation, political oppression, and therefore even fewer opportunities for poor people to climb out of their misery.

Julius Nyerere, Tanzania's Marxist dictator, has received hundreds of millions in U.S. foreign aid, even while he brutalizes peasants, pulverizes whole villages, and murders political prisoners who dares to question his forced collectivization.

In Ethiopia, the socialist government uses food to control the population and as a weapon against dissenters. Its collectivist agricultural policies have—not surprisingly—caused famine. But foreign aid has only strengthened the grip of the dictatorial regime over its abject subjects.

Moreover, U.S. foreign aid has often been granted to both sides in the endless parade of wars between feuding nation-states: India and Pakistan, Ethiopia and Somalia, Israel and Egypt, Algeria and Morocco, etc. Of course, the munitions manufacturers don't mind; they receive more orders for their wares from sovereign belligerents whose bank accounts are replenished by American citizens.

The foreign-aid scam also benefits politically privileged U.S. corporations. The recipient national regime must spend some of the aid money to purchase goods from U.S. exporters, with taxpayer-subsidized loans through the Export-Import Bank, the Commodity Credit Corporation, or the Overseas Private Investment Corporation. The corporation, the recipient government, U.S. bureaucrats—everybody wins in such a transaction. Except the U.S. taxpayer and the poor citizens of the foreign land.

From 1946 to the present, the U.S. government has given over $400 billion in foreign aid to other governments. Figuring the lost interest on that amount, the real total comes to a staggering $2.6 trillion. And foreign aid has zoomed during the Reagan years. In 1979, the U.S. government doled out $9.5 billion; this year it will waste over $21 billion on foreign aid. Few other budget items have increased as fast. The Reagan administration has spent more than $114 billion dollars on foreign aid—more than the total of foreign aid spending of the Nixon, Ford, and Carter administrations put together. The president once even threatened a veto because Congress had appropriated *too little* for foreign aid.

The U.S. Constitution nowhere permits the taxing of American citizens for the benefit of foreign governments, U.S. corporations, or U.S. bureaucrats. For the sake of morality, efficiency, and fairness, let's leave foreign aid to those private organizations that actually help, and get the government out.

A Plague From Both Their Houses: the Economic Advisors to Bush and Dukakis

Lew Rockwell

In primitive societies, witchdoctors legitimized government tyranny by naming it the mandate of heaven. In return, they got a cut of the earthly loot.

In the United States, some economists serve the same function. For promoting government intervention as scientific, and advising on the most efficient forms, they receive power, prestige, and money from Washington.

Although these "political economists" differ over candidates and parties, and quibble over small theoretical questions, they are inevitably followers of John Maynard Keynes, the 20th century's most influential justifier of state economic planning.

In the Keynesian tradition, the economic advisors to George Bush and Michael Dukakis share the same intellectual premises, and advocate government power over individuals and businesses, and extensive government intervention in the economy.

Bush's Economists

Michael Boskin

The top economic advisor to the Bush campaign is Professor Michael Boskin of Stanford University. The *Wall Street Journal* (5/23/88) calls him a "mainstream conservative," but that's only within the Keynesian spectrum. As the *New York Times* (6/5/88) notes, Boskin "makes a bow to the late John Maynard Keynes." But it is more than a bow. It is a genuflection.

Keynes believed that at the first sign of a recession, the government should dramatically increase spending . . . on anything: public works, social welfare, corporate subsidies, the military, etc. It is only important that the spending create a budget deficit, which can then be inflated away through fiat paper money.

But it is government intervention and credit creation that create unemployment and the business cycle in the first place. As the chaos of the 1970s showed—thanks to the policies of Richard "We-are-all-Keynesians-now" Nixon—Keynesian "countercyclical" policies produce unemployment *and* inflation at the same time.

Nevertheless, in *Reagan and the Economy* (Institute for Contemporary Studies, 1987), Boskin still advocates these failed policies:

> Most economists, including myself, oppose an annually balanced budget. . . . A preferable scheme would be a budget balanced over the business cycle, running deficits in recessions and surpluses in expansionary periods (p. 136).

This is what Franklin D. Roosevelt did in the 1930s when he increased taxes and spending in the midst of a depression. But once the economy recovered, *despite* the New Deal, his successors somehow forgot about running surpluses. And now, with the U.S. economy allegedly in recovery since 1983, Keynesians say deficits don't matter.

The people still worry about it, however, so Boskin proposes to define most of the deficit out of existence with a "capital budget." All the spending that politicians could call "investment" would be counted as increased assets and not as regular spending. Today, for example, when the government spends $100 million on a new office building for welfare bureaucrats, it's considered spending. Boskin would call the building an investment and subtract the $100 million from the deficit.

There is probably no government spending—aside from transfer payments—that some politician couldn't label an investment. So with Boskin's capital budget in place, the government could always run a surplus, no matter how much spending exceeded revenue.

Government spending can never be an investment in the private-sector sense. In fact, government spending is anti-investment. Every penny must be seized from individuals in the private sector who otherwise would have put it to productive use. We can know there is a loss, but not how much, because, as Henry Hazlitt has noted, we can't know what profitable investments *were not made* by entrepreneurs, and what social benefits therefore never resulted.

As Ludwig von Mises showed, bureaucrats—because they operate outside of the price system—have neither the information nor the incentive to invest. Their activities must always lead to a net social loss.

On spending, Boskin calls for a "flexible freeze." Why not an actual freeze? Because, says Boskin, the government should spend *more* in such areas as "education, drug enforcement, and AIDS research." So, while a "flexible freeze" sounds real, it actually means nothing. And if any spending were frozen, Boskin says it should promptly be unfrozen during a downturn "as in 1974-75 or 1981-82" (*New York Times*, 6/5/88). As Keynes said, in downturns "the government must and can replace private demand by public spending" (*The General Theory*, p. 322).

Actually, a recession or a depression is—despite Keynes and Boskin—the very time to *cut* government spending and get Washington out of the way of the market's natural recovery from the Federal Reserve-caused bust.

Boskin's first love, however, is taxes, which he studied at the University of California at Berkeley during its most left-wing period. His PhD dissertation won first prize from the National Tax Association, an organization of federal, state, and local tax collectors dedicated to promoting "revenue enhancement."

All told, Boskin has published two books and 25 articles on taxation and right now, he advocates "a broad new federal consumption tax" (*Wall Street Journal*, 5/23/88), which would have a "neutral" effect on the economy (*Reagan*, p. 162).

But taxes can never be neutral. Taxation transfers resources from producers to non-producers through coercion, which must necessarily disturb market exchange and the structure of production.

Boskin has also written extensively on social security. After two more books and five articles, he concludes that privatization is not the answer. Instead he favors raising benefits and supports the higher taxes engineered by Fed chairman Alan Greenspan when he headed the Reagan social security commission.

Privatization would mean voluntarism, but Boskin advocates "compulsory coverage" because "some individuals . . . may not save at all or may fail to anticipate or allow for unfavorable contingencies" (*Too Many Promises*, 1986, p. 102). So responsible government must take care of irresponsible individuals.

It's no wonder that liberal Keynesian Lawrence Summers praises Boskin as a "smart, solid guy. He's from the Rockefeller-Feldstein wing of the Republican party" (*Wall Street Journal*, 5/23/88). Nor that on Boskin's resume, his first character reference is Secretary of State George Schultz, one of America's top corporate statists (and another successful political economist).

"Boskin has hurtled along the fast track of academia that brought other economists to the upper reaches of government, including Arthur Burns," says the *New York Times* (6/5/88). The comparison is apt. Burns, another Republican Keynesian, chaired both Nixon's council of economic advisors and the Federal Reserve, where he helped design and implement Nixon's high inflation and price and wage controls, while claiming to be for sound money and free markets.

Burns also delighted in slamming shut the "gold window"—which severed the final tie between the dollar and gold.

Says Boskin: "Public service is important and noble. . . . I hope to go to Washington for a few years" (*NYT*).

Martin Feldstein

The other senior Bush economist is Professor Martin Feldstein of Harvard, also a Republican Keynesian. Feldstein is also president of the National Bureau of Economic Research, set up more than 70 years ago to encourage statist economic research, and a member of the Trilateral Commission. Founded by David Rockefeller, the commission—to which Bush also belongs—seeks, in its own words, to end the "separation between the political and economic realm" (*Toward a Renovated International System*, 1977). That is, it advocates cartelization of the world economy.

As chairman of the council of economic advisors in the first Reagan administration, Feldstein was the major advocate of higher taxes, and he helped design and push the four Reagan tax increases of those years. Since leaving the administration, he has consistently called for more inflation, higher taxes, and international devaluation of the dollar.

Feldstein, who like Boskin is on the conservative end of Keynesianism, says that sometimes government can make mistakes, but only as "the unintended and unexpected byproducts of well-meaning policies" (*The American Economy in Transition*, p. 3).

But government policies—despite their rhetoric of compassion and humanitarianism—are rarely well-intended. In the name of helping the poor, labor unions and their kept politicians impose minimum wage laws, which then throw people out of work. But this is not an unexpected or unintended consequence; it is precisely what the unions want: to create a labor cartel by reducing job opportunities for marginal workers and therefore competition for their overpaid members.

Federal regulation of business imposes very high costs, often causing small enterprises to shut their doors, or not to open at all. But that is precisely why it is championed by many large firms. Regulation imposes a higher relative burden on the small company than on the corporate giant, and thus also reduces competition.

As another example, the Federal Reserve inflates the money supply precisely because this benefits big banks and the government, no matter what the cost to the rest of us. It claims to be a stabilizing force, when it is just the opposite.

Government intervention is almost never undertaken with good intentions. It is imposed because tax eaters—pressure groups or politicians and bureaucrats—have succeeded in using the government to live off the taxpayers.

But Feldstein insists that government intervention is well-meaning because this lets the government and its interests off the hook for all the disasters. It also excuses Feldstein, since he has built his career on providing an intellectual justification for these policies.

On May 31, Feldstein and Boskin met with Bush at his summer mansion on the Maine coast. At their urging, Bush called for more Federal Reserve inflation. Not speeding up the printing presses, said the vice president, could "shut down economic growth in this country" (*Washington Post*, 6/1/88). But in the long-run, it is inflation that will do exactly that.

Politicians and their economists never seem to care about the long run. Like Keynes—who was a nihilist at heart—they have very short time horizons. As Keynes quipped, the long run was unimportant; "in the long run we are all dead."

Dukakis's Economists

Robert Reich

George Bush's advisors are conservative Keynesians; Michael Dukakis's are liberal Keynesians. Professor Robert Reich of Harvard's Kennedy School of Government, for example, advocates an "industrial policy" of "active government" in "partnership" with large corporations (*Minding America's Business*, 1982, p. 331-2).

In this book, Reich calls for centralized direction of business, massive subsidies to favored corporations, more regulation, legal barriers to new entrepreneurs, "a whole range of special tariffs, quotas, loans, and guarantees," and a "knowledgeable" team of government bureaucrats running everything.

All this is in keeping with Keynes, who wrote in 1936 that he wanted "to see the State . . . taking an ever greater responsibility for directly organizing investment" (*The General Theory*, p. 164).

Reich claims that his plan will "curb market power" and check the size of business. But his policies would deliberately create one huge government-approved cartel, and make it impossible for small businesses to compete, all at high cost to consumers and taxpayers.

Reich wants "government's role in industry . . . much more open, more explicit, and more strategic" (*The Next American Frontier*, 1983, p. 14), as during World War I, the New Deal, and World War II, when:

> [S]ocial planning . . . dominated national discourse. . . . Indeed, large government agencies and large corporations were almost indistinguishable, both to the people who worked within them and to outsiders who dealt with them . . . (p. 58).

The free market responds to consumers, whereas Reich cares only about big government and big business. It doesn't matter that consumers want home computers, gasoline, or diet sodas. He would take resources away from these areas and devote them to "semi-conductors and fiber optics" (p. 338).

Statists always seem enamored of the latest market-supplied technology (that their policies would have prevented from coming into being). Lenin, for example, loved electrification. So, in the Soviet Union today, there is electricity even in the meanest, farthest outposts of the empire. People may not have decent clothes, food, housing, medical care, or education—let alone appliances that run on electricity—but they have electric current. (Of course, the reliability and quality of the current in the Third World's largest economy is another question.)

Reich wants to subsidize research and development, but the government's sole choice is to stifle them or get out of their way. It is individuals in the market who create new technology. The government, cut off from prices, consumers, and entrepreneurs, cannot know what is best—fiber optics, semiconductors, diet soda, or anything else.

Only entrepreneurs can forecast the desires of tomorrow's consumers and make sure they are fulfilled efficiently. Reich wants government in charge, siphoning funds to favored big business as in the "Massachusetts miracle," with the entrepreneur's and consumer's only role to obey. Dukakis calls these ideas "thoughtful and well worth thinking about" (*Wall Street Journal*, 5/23/88).

Lawrence H. Summers

Dukakis claims he will balance the budget by increasing the size and power of the Internal Revenue Service. The idea comes from a student of Michael Boskin's, Keynesian Professor Lawrence H. Summers of Harvard, the other top advisor to Dukakis.

Summers comes by his views almost genetically. Both of his parents are Keynesian economists at the University of

Pennsylvania, and his uncles include two of the top Keynesians in America, Paul A. Samuelson of MIT and Kenneth J. Arrow of Stanford. Like Boskin, Summers received an award from the National Tax Association for his work. And in addition to studying under Boskin, Summers was also a student and protégé of Martin Feldstein, and worked for Feldstein in the Reagan administration.

An enthusiastic taxer, Summers recently edited a two-volume series co-published by the NBER (which Feldstein heads and where Boskin is a senior academic) on *Tax Policy and the Economy* (1987 and 1988), chock-full of essays on how and why to raise taxes.

Along with favoring higher taxes and more "vigorous" collection methods, Summers—like Boskin—wants to impose broad consumption taxes. And he says that economists and policy makers are too concerned about inflation. They should focus on the other side of the Phillips Curve: unemployment.

The Phillips Curve sums up the Keynesian notion that we must have either unemployment or inflation, but cannot have both. The doctrine died after high levels of inflation and unemployment in the 1970s, but Summers still believes in it.

In fact, the Phillips Curve is the reverse of the truth. More inflation brings more unemployment, and sounder money means more jobs. There is no trade-off between the two government-created plagues of monetary debauchment and joblessness. They are visited upon us hand-in-hand.

Summers also calls—with Boskin—for a major government effort to collect more economic statistics, an ominous idea.

Consumers get their information from personal experience, friends, and advertising. Business people need only know about their own markets. But government gathers data about the entire economy to control us.

Unlike consumers and business people, politicians and bureaucrats stand *outside* the market. But to try to run it, they need information about what is going on inside it. Collecting economic statistics imposes huge costs on business, but the government is willing to spare no cost to us, for, as Professor Murray N. Rothbard has noted, "statistics are the eyes and ears of the bureaucrat, the politician, the socialistic reformer."

Brothers Under the Skin

Republican or Democrat, all four of these Keynesians differ only in degree. For example, liberal Keynesians think saving is ridiculous, and want government to discourage it, whereas Boskin thinks that *some* saving is OK.

There are as many varieties of Keynesian economics as there are economists in Washington, D.C. Its doctrines are muddy and open to different interpretations, which is one reason it's so popular: it can be used to justify any interventionist policy, Republican or Democrat.

The Keynesian answer to every economic ill is government stimulation of total demand to increase consumption, investment, and prices. How is this "aggregate demand" to be stimulated? Through government spending and deficits, funded by taxation during booms and inflation during busts.

Before Keynes, most non-socialist economists held to some sort of sound economics. There were no models pretending that the whole of the economy, with millions of individuals and billions of decisions, could be crammed into a group of equations. Economic laws and the logic of human action governed economists' thinking, so most economists advocated a free market.

That ended with the "Keynesian revolution," which gave the first intellectual justification to what politicians wanted to do anyway. All of a sudden, economists—who used to criticize inflation, deficits, and high spending—were applauding these policies.

Not surprisingly, Keynesians of one stripe or another have filled prominent posts in every administration since Herbert Hoover (and his advisors were proto-Keynesians). FDR took all of Keynes's propositions seriously, and sought to centralize investment decisions in Washington and drive prices up through the destruction of wealth (burning crops, killing animals, inflating the money supply, and raising taxes). He also hired the unemployed for unwanted and unnecessary tasks, and cartelized business and banking in the name of promoting a higher level of coordination.

FDR-style Keynesianism is rare today. But the basic themes of Keynesian economics still constitute the mainstream: that countercyclical fiscal policy is necessary to compensate for the free market; that investment and consumption are in lock-step, and when one is primed, the other booms; that there is a necessary trade-off between inflation and unemployment; that interest rates are properly manipulated by the central bank, as is the supply of money; that this monetary manipulation can successfully redirect investment; that inflation promotes growth; that consumption is economically superior to savings; and that the free market cannot properly allocate resources. All are exactly wrong, but no one—aside from the Austrian school—has ever challenged the fundamental Keynesian assumptions.

Today, most prominent economists reflect the theory's bad policy implications to one degree or another. And that is true of these four economists, who although they may be competitors, are Keynesian brothers under the skin. They also share an ambition to use their undoubted intellectual powers to serve big government and thus advance their careers. As Joseph A. Pechman of the liberal Brookings Institution says: All are "made from the same cloth" (*NYT*, 6/5/88).

Ludwig von Mises discussed such men in *Human Action* (1966 [1949], p. 869):

> The early economists devoted themselves to the study of the problems of economics. . . . They never conceived of economics as a profession. The development of a profession of economists is an offshoot of interventionism [with] the specialist who is instrumental in designing various measures of government interference. . . . He is an expert . . . at hindering the operation of the market economy.
>
> There are thousands and thousands of such professional experts busy in the bureaus of the governments and of the various political parties and pressure groups . . . and pressure-group periodicals. . . . The eminent role they play is one of the most characteristic features of our age of interventionism.
>
> There can be no doubt that [this] class of men . . . includes extremely talented individuals. . . . But the philosophy that guides their activities narrows their horizon. By virtue of their connection with definite parties and pressure groups, eager to acquire special privileges, they become one-sided. They shut their eyes to the remoter consequences of the policies they are advocating. With them nothing counts but the short-run concerns of the group they are serving. The ultimate aim of their efforts is to make their clients prosper at the expense of other people.

From examining these four men, we can know that big government and its associated special interests cannot lose in 1988. Yes, the subsidies may go to one interest group rather than another, but both sides agree on political control of our economic lives, and on higher taxes and more state planning. No matter who is elected, Keynesianism will be in control.

Not that Boskin and Feldstein, or Reich and Summers, will exercise any real influence. Rather, like the witchdoctor, their function is to give a pseudo-scientific cover to the interventionist policies of their candidate and his backers. Thus these economists are worth studying for their predictive value, if not for worth of their ideas.

For that, we need economists who share the vision of Ludwig von Mises, and instead of promoting the interests of big government, oppose any interference with the peaceful prosperity of the free market.

The Coming World Central Bank

Ron Paul

International statists have long dreamed of a world currency and a world central bank. Now it looks as if their dream may come true.

European governments have targeted 1992 for abolishing individual European currencies and replacing them with the European Currency Unit, the Ecu. Next they plan to set up a European central bank. The next step is the merger of the Federal Reserve, the European central bank, and the Bank of Japan into one world central bank.

The Ecu is a basket of ten European currencies weighted according to their respective country's economic strength. The German mark gets the highest weight while the Irish pound, the Danish krone, and the Greek drachma get lower. The Ecu doesn't qualify as a working currency yet, but it is already being used by international banks and multinational corporations. And traveler's checks denominated in Ecus are also popular in Europe.

The Ecu first appeared in 1979. Its creators quickly found that its usefulness was limited without a clearing system, so Credit Lyonnais of Paris and Morgan Guaranty Bank of New York formed the Ecu Banking Association, made up of top central bankers and government officials. In March 1986 they set up the European Investment Bank and SWIFT (the

Society for Worldwide Interbank Financial Telecommunications) to process Ecu transactions. Within a few months, all major central banks had signed on, and today, Ecu transactions represent the fifth largest trading volume in international currency markets.

The big push for the European central bank began after the October 1987 stock market crash as politicians seized the moment of crisis to advance their agenda. "The logic of developments . . . demand that the European currency takes over from the national ones," argued socialist French President Francois Mitterrand.

In November 1987, European politicians, businessmen, and bankers formed the Action Committee for Europe to promote the European central bank, arguing that Europe needs one currency and "a common authority to manage it."

The European central bank (ECB) will be modeled after the Federal Reserve. Like the Fed in 1913, it will have the institutional appearance of decentralization, but also like the Fed it will be run by a cartel of big bankers in collusion with politicians at the expense of the public.

Margaret Thatcher is the only influential holdout in Europe. And she objects because she thinks the influence of Germany's central bank will allow less inflation than she wants! But like all central banks, the ECB is designed to inflate. And it will have a particularly free hand. With twelve separate currencies, exchange rate fluctuations allow people to sell more inflationary currencies for the stronger ones, providing some constraint on inflation. That will no longer be the case with the Ecu.

The head of the European Monetary System, former French President Valery Giscard d'Estaing, says Thatcher will join when the Ecu becomes "a real currency." However, no government or group of governments can create a currency out of thin air. They must pay attention to the economic laws that Ludwig von Mises proved with his "regression theorem," namely, that currencies must originate in the free market. But unlike the International Monetary Funds Special Drawing Rights (SDRs), European governments did not create the Ecu out of nothing. It is composed of existing currencies which in turn had their origins in gold and silver.

The plan for the transition has central banks fixing the trading range of the Ecu relative to other currencies while allowing them to freely circulate side by side. Then governments will overvalue the Ecu relative to other European currencies, and people will sell their pounds, lira, and marks for the Ecu, putting into effect a kind of backwards Gresham's Law.

"There is one hitch," says *Forbes* magazine. "Although currencies that make up the Ecu maintain a balance relative to one another, the entire currency basket fluctuates against the dollar, so cashing in Ecus for dollars could result in a gain or a loss."

One of the few constraints now operating on the Fed is that if it inflates too much, people will dump the dollar for a more stable currency. That's why there is a push to achieve international monetary "stability" (that is, equal rates of inflation) by cartelizing what will then be three remaining central banks of the industrialized world into one world central bank charged with manipulating one world currency.

The Economist of London says that "Thirty years from now, Americans, Japanese, Europeans, and people in many other rich countries" will be "paying for their shopping with the same currency. Prices will be quoted not in dollars, yen, or D-marks" but in terms of a new world currency.

Central banking is a horrendous idea to begin with. Merging central banks will be even worse. The resulting institution would become, as Dr. Edwin Vieira has remarked, "the biggest agent of economic and political irresponsibility the world has ever seen." Today, if the U.S. Congress has a sudden fit of economic sanity, it could restrict the Fed's power. The mere threat of that serves as a limit. But the world central bank would be subject to no authority.

The world central bank might be based on the International Monetary Fund or the World Bank, says the *Economist*. But I think the more likely candidate is the Bank for International Settlements (BIS), the "central banker's bank" in Basle, Switzerland. World central bankers have been holding "consultative meetings" there once a month for over a year. Recently, the meetings have concentrated on giving the BIS "lender of last resort functions and responsibilities." That means the power to create money and credit out of thin air.

They all want, as *Banker* magazine noted, "a world in which national policy authority is greatly reduced, and replaced by more powerful international policy-making bodies."

Finance Minister Edouard Balladur of France writes in the *Wall Street Journal* that we should "entrust a small group of distinguished people of unquestionable moral authority" with the job of designing "a world order" that is "binding on all." But such an elitist idea would only produce a monster. That is why those of us who believe in individual liberty and free markets must actively oppose this plan, despite the proponents' use of free-market rhetoric. (One free-market publication praised the Ecu as "an extension of Hayek's work on competitive currency.")

None of this is to say that I approve of the status quo. The world monetary system *is* shaky. The system of floating exchange rates between fiat currencies only adds to the volatility. And we do need more international cooperation. But we want *economic* integration without *political* integration.

We all know the troubles we have dealing with city hall, let alone the state house or Washington, D.C. A world system would be unimaginably worse. Internationally as well as domestically, the answers to economic problems are free markets, free trade, free labor, and a gold standard. All would build the only kind of world economic order consistent with sound economics and individual freedom.

8

REAGANOMICS

A Walk on the Supply Side

Murray N. Rothbard

Establishment historians of economic thought—they of the Smith-Marx-Marshall variety—have a compelling need to end their saga with a chapter on the latest Great Man, the latest savior and final culmination of economic science. The last consensus choice was, of course, John Maynard Keynes, but his *General Theory* is now a half-century old, and economists have for some time been looking around for a new candidate for that final chapter. For a while, Joseph Schumpeter had a brief run, but his problem was that his work was largely written *before* the *General Theory*. Milton Friedman and monetarism lasted a bit longer, but suffered from two grave defects: (1) the lack of anything resembling a great, integrative work; and (2) the fact that monetarism and Chicago School Economics is really only a gloss on theories that had been hammered out before the Keynesian Era by Irving Fisher and by Frank Knight and his colleagues at the University of Chicago. Was there nothing new to write about since Keynes?

Since the mid 1970s, a school of thought has made its mark that at least gives the impression of something brand new. And since economists, like the Supreme Court, follow the election returns, "supply-side economics" has become noteworthy.

Supply-side economics has been hampered among students of contemporary economics in lacking anything like a grand treatise, or even a single major leader, and there is scarcely unanimity among its practitioners. But it has been able to take shrewd advantage of highly placed converts in the media and easy access to politicians and think tanks. Already it has begun to make its way into last chapters of works on economic thought.

A central theme of the supply-side is that a sharp cut in marginal income-tax rates will increase incentives to work and save, and therefore investment and production. That way, few people could take exception. But there are other problems involved. For, at least in the lands of the famous Laffer Curve, income tax cuts were treated as the panacea for deficits; drastic cuts would so increase revenue as allegedly to yield a balanced budget. Yet there was no evidence whatever for this claim, and indeed, the likelihood is quite the other way. It is true that if income-tax rates were 98% and were cut to 90%, there would probably be an increase in revenue; but at the far lower tax levels we have been at, there is no warrant for this easy assumption. In fact, historically, increases in tax rates have been followed by increases in revenue and vice versa.

But there is a deeper problem with supply-side than the inflated claims of the Laffer Curve. Common to all supply-siders is nonchalance about total government spending and therefore deficits. The supply-siders do not care that tight government spending takes resources that would have gone into the private sector and diverts it to the public sector. They care only about taxes. Indeed, their attitude toward deficits approaches the old Keynesian "we only owe it to ourselves." Worse than that: the supply-siders want to maintain the current swollen levels of federal spending. As professed "populists," their basic argument is that the people want the current level of spending and the people should not be denied.

Even more curious than the supply-sider attitude toward spending is their viewpoint on money. On the one hand, they say they are for hard money and an end to inflation by going back to the "gold standard." On the other hand, they have consistently attacked the Paul Volcker Federal Reserve, not for being too inflationist, but for imposing "too tight" money and thereby "crippling economic growth."

In short, these self-styled "conservative populists" begin to sound like old-fashioned populists in their devotion to inflation and cheap money. But how to square that with their championing of the gold standard?

In the answer to this question lies the key to the heart of the seeming contradictions of the new supply-side economics. The "gold standard" they want provides only the illusion of a gold standard without the substance. The banks would not have to redeem in gold coin, and the Fed would have the right to change the definition of the gold dollar at will, as a device to fine-tune the economy. In short, what the supply-siders want is not the old hard-money gold standard, but the phony "gold standard" of the Bretton Woods era, which collapsed under the bows of inflation and money management by the Fed.

The heart of supply-side doctrine is revealed in its best-selling philosophic manifesto, *The Way the World Works* by Jude Wanniski. Wanniski's view is that the people, the masses, are always right, and have always been right through history.

In economics, he claims, the masses want a massive welfare state, drastic income-tax cuts, and a balanced budget. How can these contradictory aims be achieved? By the legerdemain of the Laffer Curve. And in the monetary sphere, we might add, what the masses seem to want is inflation and cheap money along with a return to the gold standard. Hence, fueled by the axiom that the public is always right, the supply-siders propose to give the public what they want by giving them an inflationary, cheap-money Fed *plus* the illusion of stability through a phony gold standard.

The supply-side aim is therefore "democratically" to give the public what they want, and in this case the best definition of "democracy" is that of H. L. Mencken: "Democracy is the view that the people know what they want, and deserve to get it good and hard."

The Case Against the Flat Tax

Murray N. Rothbard

1. "Special Interests": Good or Bad?

The flat tax draws virtually unanimous support from the right-thinking intellectuals in our society, including academics, writers, and media pundits. By "right-thinking" I mean all people who have managed successfully to identify their own views, whatever they may be, with the general welfare. By this time, however, the cautious should be on the alert: any policy that draws unanimous support from these people can't be all good. There must be a catch somewhere.

The flat tax has been cleverly labeled a tax "reform," the very word "reform" being heavy with the implication that no man or woman of good will, be they liberal or conservative, Democrat or Republican, can possibly stand opposed to such a plan. My favorite writer, H. L. Mencken, once wrote that he had learned at his father's knee in Baltimore what "reform" in politics really meant: "mainly a conspiracy of prehensile charlatans to mulct the taxpayer."

So convinced are the flat-taxers that only they have a pipeline to interpret the general welfare, that they invariably charge that any and all critics of their scheme are simply spokesmen for a sinister and shadowy group they commonly refer to as "the special interests." "Special interests" seems to be an effective way to write off substantial opposition to the flat-tax, especially since the convenient tendency of intellectuals is to dismiss all other interests but their own as "special" and hence somehow narrow and sinister.

But are special interests all bad? Some undoubtedly are. Take, for example, the sugar program to which all of us have been subjected for a half-century. In order to maintain and expand the inefficient U.S. sugar industry, the sugar interests have for decades propped up sugar prices by use of government, and lobbied for severe quotas on the import of sugar. As a result, American consumers (to say nothing of foreign sugar producers) have been hurt severely, the supply of sugar sharply restricted, and the price artificially raised—so that the support price of sugar in the U.S. is now no less than seven times higher than the world market price. Here is a clear-cut example of aggression by special interests.

But there are also cases of special interests acting defensively, rather than aggressively. Several years ago, for example, the movie theaters circulated petitions urging that a new tax on movie admissions be repealed. I was happy to sign that petition both because I believed that the cause of the theaters was just and also that my own and other movie consumers' rights and interests were being invaded by the government.

But wasn't this special pleading on the part of the movie theaters? Yes, and so what? There is no reason to expect that movie theaters will be in the forefront of actions to protect the rights and incomes of, say, restaurants. In all cases where special interests are acting defensively, the front fighters for the rights of consumers will naturally be the particular firms or industries that happen to be under attack. Who else would we expect to sound the alarm?

To return now to the flat tax: the seductive rhetoric invoking the "special interests" has lead most people to believe that everyone will benefit from the flat tax except a few wicked corporations or multi-millionaires. Nothing could be further from the truth. If the flat tax is enacted, millions of us will find out, too late and to our chagrin, that, to paraphrase Pogo: "We have met the special interests and they are us." Or as Senator Robert Dole (R-KS) put it recently on the issue of the flat tax as an allegedly fair tax: "Everybody believes in fairness unless they're involved."

Before we go down the list of "special interests" who would be hurt by the enactment of a flat tax, I want to stress that I'm talking about the *pure* flat tax concept, rather than the current approach to it submitted last fall by then-Secretary of the Treasury Donald Regan or this spring by Treasury Secretary James Baker. These present as much of the flat tax as the Treasury thought it could get away with politically. But the argument for these plans are that they approach the ideal of the flat tax, and so it is that ideal that should be examined.

The flat tax, quite simply, proposes that every individual and every organization be subjected to the same, uniform proportional income tax. To achieve that uniformity, the flat-taxers propose the ruthless suppression of all credits, deductions, exemptions, and shelters, all of which are sneered at as "loopholes" in the tax system. In the flat-taxers' pure theory, the proportional income tax would apply to everyone regardless of income. But early in the development of the flat-tax movement they decided that, politically, the poor would have to be exempt from the tax. As a result, all flat tax schemes are now "degressive": proportional above an arbitrary minimum income floor, below which line income receivers pay no taxes. The "degressivity" leaves an important element of progressivity in what has been touted as a strictly proportional plan.

2. What Is a "Loophole"?

It is instructive to pause for a moment to examine the pejorative term "loophole." What *is* a "loophole," anyway? It is never defined, but the flat-taxers seem to make the implicit assumption that the government *really* owns, or should be owning, all of what everyone makes, at least up to some arbitrary percentage decided by the government. Hence, any failure of government to confiscate everyone's property up to that amount is somehow a moral blot that needs to be rectified. But to me it is far from self-evident that the government, rather than we ourselves, should have the primary right to our own earnings.

The "closing of loopholes" under a flat tax will mean a merciless and continuing search-and-destroy mission by which the government will root out and obliterate every little hidey-hole in which many of us have been able to squirrel away a bit of our own earnings and our own property, and keep them safe from the ever-expanding maw of the federal government.

Wrapped up in the confusion over the role of "special interests" is a muddle over the concept of "subsidy." Flat-taxers call these exemptions, deductions, and loopholes "subsidies," and being staunchly opposed to subsidies, flat-taxers propose to eliminate them. But is it *really* a "subsidy" to be allowed to keep more of your own money? *Only* if we agree with the curious implicit assumption of the flat-taxers that the government, not us, really owns our earnings and our property, and that therefore being allowed keep some of them is an arbitrary indulgence on its part.

I submit, to the contrary, that there is a big and crucial difference between the government's taxing Peter to pay Paul, which is a "subsidy" to Paul, and the government's allowing Paul to keep more of his own funds. *That* can only be called a "subsidy" on the grotesque assumption that the government really owns all of our property to begin with.

Before examining the "special interests" who will lose, and often lose heavily, from the imposition of a flat tax, let me say that, strictly for the sake of argument, I will begin by granting, for the time being, the flat-taxers their insistent point that the shift to their tax will be strictly "revenue-neutral," that is, that total tax revenue will remain exactly the same from the shift, and will not increase.

Let us now go down the list of heavy losers from the imposition of the flat tax:

a. Receivers of "Imputed" Income

The flat taxers are nothing if not sophisticated economic theorists, and they realize that we receive our incomes, not only in money but also in other ways, by goods or services "in kind," or in various psychic ways. They also realize that much of the flowering of non-money incomes, to which they "impute" monetary value, has come about precisely in order to avoid some of the confiscations of the taxing system. Since income taxes are levied on money income, people tend to shift as much income as possible from monetary to non-monetary forms.

And so, people pay and receive income in non-monetary ways: if a carpenter goes to a physician for treatment, he may meet his bill by fixing the doctor's house rather than by money payment. Employees receive much of their income in non-monetary "fringe benefits," which may accrue in money only in the future. Salesmen and executives take some of their salary, not in money income, but in blissfully tax-free "perks" such as expense accounts, and the much-cherished business lunch.

But the flat-taxers, in their puritanical frenzy at seeing anyone escape their allotted payment of taxes, are out to get rid of all that. It is good-bye to the tax-free fringe benefit, the expense account, the business lunch. And what will happen to the restaurant business, the hotel business? The flat-taxers, like all puritans, like all fanatics, care not; they are ready to wreak unlimited havoc in the name of attaining their ideal.

For one thing, there is the American homeowner. Every homeowner is going to get it, but good, under the flat-tax regime. The flat-taxers, for example, have figured out that homeowners benefit, in a real though non-monetary way, by *not* having to pay rent. And so the flat-taxers propose to tax every homeowner on the "imputed rent" they are earning by not having to pay rent to a landlord. If, for example, you own your own home, and some officials figure out that you would have been paying $1,200 a month if you had been renting the home, then you will have to pay a proportional tax on this imputed total.

Unfortunately, no one has yet figured out a way to pay "imputed" taxes. The IRS insists on cold hard cash. And so it is going to be very painful for many people to have to pay taxes in money on income which is only psychic. As we will see shortly, the flat-taxers are out to tax capital gains fully as much as if they were earned income, as indeed they are. But if they had their druthers, they would tax these gains, not when we realize them in money form, but every year, as they accrue.

It is going to be very difficult for many people to pay through the nose on capital gains from increases in the value of their stocks or their homes, gains which they can only reap when they come to sell their asset. In the regime of the flat-taxers, there will be a great deal of painful forced-selling of homes and other assets. And to think, all this in the sacred name of the twin watchwords of the flat-taxers: "Simplicity" and "Fairness!"

It's a good thing that the flat-taxers haven't yet figured out how to tax us on our leisure, although as good puritans I'm sure they're working on it.

b. Payers of Interest

Interest payments are expenses that the government allows us to deduct from taxable income. They will be brought under the heel by the flat-taxers. But if interest payments are no longer deductible, this means that one of the great economic advantages of owning a home, being able to deduct mortgage interest payments from taxes, will disappear. Notice that all of America's homeowners will be clobbered four ways by the ruthless ideologues of the flat-tax movement. One, as we have seen, homeowners will lose by being forced to pay taxes on their "imputed rent"; two, they will no longer be able to deduct interest payments on mortgages; and three and four, the value of their homes, on which they count when they wish to move, will be forced down because the after-tax return on the house will decline from the two increased tax levies.

I fail to follow the logic on this one: I can see why those who *earn* interest have to pay taxes on this income; but I fail to see why those who *pay* interest have to shell out more as well. In fact, this looks to me like double taxation on the same income, and if the flat-taxers were not self-proclaimed experts on "fairness," I would even go so far as to say that double taxes on the same income are unfair.

c. Receivers of Capital Gains

The flat-taxers are also astute enough to realize that capital gains constitute income. But on the other hand, profits add to capital gains, and since they propose to tax profits too, they are, once again, double-taxing the same income. At the very least then, profits should no longer be taxed if capital gains are as well. Relentless in pursuing any bit of untaxed income, the flat-taxers note that capital gains have been taxed much less in recent years than other income, and so they propose to pile on higher taxes so as to bring about the desired uniformity.

But higher capital gains taxation will strike hardest and foremost at the new, young, venture capitalists going into high-risk, progressive industries. Heavy capital gains taxation will strike a deadly blow precisely at new, high-risk venture capital. Do we really want to cripple these firms and ventures?

We have already pointed to the extra difficulties if flat-taxers pursue their prey to the last ounce and insist on taxation of accrued, and not just realized, capital gains.

It is common knowledge that Great Britain's economy since World War II has suffered grievously from very high levels of income tax. One of the reasons that Britain has not gone completely down the drain is that, fortunately, its government has levied no tax on capital gains, thus allowing many capital ventures to flourish. Our implacable flat-tax Jacobins would make sure to close *that* loophole.

d. Accelerated Depreciators and Investors

But let it not be thought that our flat-taxers are *only* out to make life difficult for new venture capitalists. The old-line smokestack industries, already in decline, will get theirs too. One of the great problems of the older, heavily capitalized industries is that their profits have not been high enough to permit them to maintain and modernize their capital to allow them to compete with newer firms at home and abroad.

Two highly beneficial tax reforms of the first year of the Reagan Administration were (1) allowing investment credit on corporate and personal income tax for investing in capital; and (2) permitting business firms to accelerate the depreciation of their capital at virtually any speed. The investment credit has allowed heavily capitalized firms to keep more of their profits, and invest them in maintaining and expanding their capital.

Now, under the thrall of the flat-tax ideologues, the Administration proposes to get rid of its own salutary reforms. Both of them are now derided as "subsidies." But, once again, the investment credit allows people to keep more of their money if used for investment. Neither can one call accelerated depreciation a subsidy. There is no reason why a business should not be able to depreciate its capital at any pace it wants. Its total, long-run tax bill does not even decline; what a business is permitted to do is, instead of extending a depreciation allowance over, say, the ten-year life of a machine, to choose instead to take the entire allowance off now, so as to be able to buy a new machine and pay the same total tax bill out of the returns of the new machine over the next nine years. Accelerated depreciation simply allows firms to arrange the time-schedule of their payments in the most convenient and efficient ways.

e. Owners of Natural Resources

Let it not be thought that owners of natural resources, such as oil, natural gas, and metallic mines, will get off scot free. On the contrary, they will be among the worst losers from the tyranny of the flat-taxers. Economists in general, let alone flat-taxers, have long denounced depletion allowances of natural resource owners as an outrageous subsidy. Since oil and natural gas companies, in the public's folk mythology, are considered especially wicked, this part of the flat-tax creed enjoys wide popularity. Yet, in actuality, apart from the fact that the right to keep one's own money can hardly be called a subsidy, there is another important fallacy in calling depletion allowances a subsidy.

An income tax, by its very name, is designed as a tax on annual income, not on accumulated wealth. A tax on wealth directly confiscates property and brings about a decline in the structure of capital and hence of everyone's standard of living. But then we must realize that if we make the grave mistake of treating a using-up of capital as a firm's income, and tax it accordingly, we will precipitate a decline in its capital structure and impose severe losses upon the firm.

Suppose, for example, that a crude oil company produces and sells oil, and makes a net income from the sale of $100 million. But the oil in its reserves has now been diminished; if we can determine, say, that the value of its underground oil has gone down by $70 million, then the net income of the company has only been $30 million. To tax it as if its income has been $100 million will unwittingly impose crippling losses upon the company. And yet, our flat-taxers, true to form, propose to do precisely that. And the value of stock investments in oil and mineral resource companies will, of course, decline as well.

f. Corporations

Lest we think that only the new venture firms and the older smokestack industries will get the axe from our flat-taxers, we should know that *all* corporations will suffer, for the corporate income tax will increase substantially, to make the tax on a par and uniform with the tax on the income of individuals. Everything, again, looks neat and "fair," with all individuals *and* organizations paying a uniform rate.

But if, in the famous Milton Friedman formula, TANSTAAFL (there ain't no such thing as a free lunch), then we can also add the term TANSTAAC (there ain't no such thing as a "corporation"). There is no existing entity called a "corporation" that feels, works, thinks, earns income, and then enjoys that income. A "corporation" is only a label for individuals who organize themselves, and hope to earn income, in certain ways. There is no income-earning *thing* called a "corporation" that exists and earns income above and beyond the people, that is, the stockholder-owners, who constitute that corporation. Therefore, a tax on corporate income is an unjust and "unfair" (if I may use that term) double tax on the same income, as well as a tax hitting at savings and investment. Instead of raising income tax rates on corporations, as the Treasury plan and the flat-taxers would do, we should move in the other direction, end double taxation, and cut the corporate tax to zero. Stockholders should be taxed just once, on the income they individually earn from the corporate form. Even President Reagan himself had been known to voice such sentiments.

g. State and Local Taxpayers

And now we come to a category of losers from the flat tax that I find particularly outrageous, since I live in New York City, where I and millions of other hapless citizens are mulcted into paying the highest state income tax in the nation, the highest city income tax in the country, and the highest sales tax.

After having been chastised for so many years with whips, the flat-taxers now arrive on the scene to chastise us with scorpions. It seems that being able to deduct our massive state and local taxes from our federal taxable income has only been a wicked "subsidy," and so now even that small consolation will be snatched from us.

It goes without saying that flat-taxers are zealots in favor of taxing the interest from municipal bonds—a long-standing goal of liberals in order to aggrandize the power of the federal government as against the states. If municipal bonds are taxed, their value will of course plummet, as will the credit and the power of state and local government to float bonds. More and more spending will then be centralized in the hands of a super-powerful federal government.

Is that all we really want? I suppose there is no reason to raise the point that federal taxing of municipal bonds is clearly unconstitutional, as would be state taxation of Treasury bonds, for since when has anyone worried about the provisions of the Constitution of the United States?

h. The Charitable and the Non-Profitable

One important tax deduction to be swept away would be gifts to charities or other non-profit organizations. Since much charity is now done under the gun of the IRS, the result of the flat-tax would be a drastic crippling of private charitable and educational organizations. Why should giving to charities, the arts, and educational institutions be hobbled and penalized, in the name of "simplicity" and "fairness?" The severe losses of many of these organizations, would lead them to turn to the federal government to bail them out, in effect nationalizing private charity and expanding and aggrandizing the federal welfare state. All universities and non-profit institutions that depend on voluntary giving would be victims of the zeal of our single-minded flat-taxers.

i. Victims of Fire, Sickness, and Accident

There are even more helpless victims who will fall under the heel of the flat-taxers. Every man or woman who falls sick and whose medical payments are not insured, will, in flat-taxland, be unable to deduct these payments from his taxable income. No victim of fire, uncovered by insurance, will any longer be able to deduct his losses. And so life's unfortunates, run over by accident or disease, will be run over a second time, this time in the name of "equality" and "fairness."

j. Entrepreneurial Losers

Some entrepreneurs make profits; others suffer losses. That is the essence of entrepreneurship. While I don't believe that losers should be bailed out or subsidized by the government, it seems like excessive punishment for government to kick them while they're down. But this is precisely what our flat-taxers are planning to do. For while it is difficult to claim that losses, like profits, somehow constitute net income, this is precisely how flat-taxers regard them: as hidden income to be ferreted out and taxed. We have heard for years about those evil "tax shelters" which "they," the wicked rich, like to indulge in. But mainly these "shelters" are losing propositions, the losses of which partially offset net income in other areas. How can we call such shelters "income"?

I, for example, in addition to being a salaried professor, am a self-employed author and lecturer. Some years, I make a net income from this business, other years I suffer losses. Who are the flat-taxers to come swooping down, and they or the IRS to try to pry into my soul, and announce either that I am a genuine but sometimes losing entrepreneur, *or* that in my secret heart of hearts I rejoice in my losses because it lowers my taxable income? Are the flat-taxers or the IRS truly qualified to examine everyone's heart and soul and decide on everyone's inner motives? And, in the last analysis, how dare they anyhow?

Let everyone, then, realize that the "they," the "special interests" who will be hurt, and perhaps hurt badly, from the flat tax, are not just a few shadowy and malevolent millionaires.

While it is not really possible to average out pain or loss among individuals and make it disappear, there is every reason to believe that, on the average, upper-income groups will probably benefit on net from the fall in tax rates under the flat tax, whereas the middle class, as usual, will be hit and hit hard. So what else is new?

3. The Argument From Fairness

The major argument for the flat tax is not economic but moral, namely that this is the only fair way to distribute taxation. The assumption is that, *given* an arbitrarily determined total revenue to the government, that revenue should be distributed in a uniform, flat-tax manner.

But the flat-taxers do not really *argue* their point; they simply assume it as self-evident to all people of good will. Well, sorry, but I don't see it. I don't see why it is particularly "fair" to clobber the sick, the sufferers from accidents, or the homeowners, or why it is fair to impose monetary taxes on earners of non-monetary income.

More specifically, I don't see why proportional taxation is any "fairer" than many other possible patterns of distribution. Take, for example, Mr. A and Mr. B, each of whom earns a net income of, say, $50,000 a year. But Mr. A is a young man, just starting in life, with virtually zero assets. He depends on personal savings to finance a future business.

Mr. B, on the other hand, is an older man who has already built up or inherited millions of dollars in assets. Why is it manifestly fair for him to pay the same tax as Mr. A? Neither is it obvious to me that a sick person with heavy medical bills should pay the same tax as a healthy man with the same income. Note that I am not saying the opposite: I am not advocating a tax on health or on wealth. I'm simply saying that there seems to be no convincing argument for the fairness of one pattern of taxation over another.

In fact, I will go even further, and say that fairness has little or nothing to do with the matter, that, in fact, TANSTAAFT ("there ain't no such thing as a fair tax"). Conservative flat-taxers like to analogize to the free market, and maintain that they are trying to achieve neutrality to the market. But consider: what in the world is a "fair" price on the market?

Many medieval economists came to grief on this issue. What is the "fair price," for example, of Wonder Bread? Who knows? For my part, as a Wonder Bread consumer, I'd love to see the price down to about a penny a loaf, and the Wonder Bread Company would undoubtedly love to be able to charge $100 a loaf. As it is, after the higgling and haggling of the market, we all settle for about one dollar a loaf. There seems to be no sense to the concept of fairness in price *except* what is arrived at, from day to day, as the result of voluntary transactions on the market.

But what of taxation? Unfortunately, we can't even apply the voluntary transaction criterion here, because by its very nature, taxation is coercive, and is not arrived at by the voluntary bargaining of individuals on the market. So what then is a "fair" tax? I submit that the concept simply doesn't apply.

All I know is that, as a taxpayer, I would like my taxes to be as low as possible. I suggest, then, that we cease the impossible quest for fairness in taxation, and try to arrive at taxes as low as possible. For whom? For everyone.

One of my favorite economists, the 19th-century Frenchman, J. B. Say, after pointing out that taxation is a coercive transfer from individuals and groups to the government, crippling their ability to produce and consume, concluded: "The best scheme of finance is to spend as little as possible; and the best tax is always the lightest." In short, to paraphrase Jefferson, "That government is best which spends and taxes least."

Instead of worrying about distributing taxes "fairly," or what is supposed to amount to the same thing, allocating tax suffering equally, we should set about trying to *minimize* tax suffering as much as we can down the line. And if we approach the problem *that* way, we should find it easier to gain broad agreement. Rather than trying to figure out whether a proportional, degressive, regressive, or progressive income tax structure is "fairest," we may find we can agree on reducing the tax burden of everyone.

Thus, let us compare two hypothetical tax systems. In system A, there is a progressive income tax, ranging from one to ten percent. In system B, everyone pays a flat, strictly proportional income tax, of 20%. I have a hunch that, in choosing between these systems, even the upper-income groups would opt for the far more progressive, but much lower tax burden. The central point is the lowness of each tax, rather than the distribution of the burden.

People are, or should be, interested in lowering their own tax burden rather than enviously trying to aggravate the burdens of other people. And here is a genuine basis for solidarity among taxpayers of all groups and sizes. The point, then, is not that "they"—whoever "they" are—are paying too little taxes and should be brought to heel. The point is that all of us are paying too much. The flat-tax movement is part of a process by which the government and its allies have been able to split and deflect the tax protest movement from trying to lower the taxes of everyone, into trying to force everyone into paying some arbitrarily defined "fair share."

4. The Argument From Neutrality to the Market

An important argument of the flat-taxers, especially those who claim devotion to the free market, is that their plan is needed to restore the allocation of resources to what would have been the pattern on the market: in short, that the flat tax is uniquely neutral to the market.

The argument runs as follows: credits, deductions, loopholes distort resources relative to the free market because more resources go into the loopholes than would otherwise. Thus, an investment tax credit means that more resources will go into investment than would a free market.

Suppose that there are only two industries in the economy, machine tools and wheat. If machine tools receive an investment tax credit, more resources will be poured into machine tools relative to wheat than on the purely free market. Therefore, the tax credit distorts resources, and a flat tax, by eliminating that credit, will correct the distortion and restore genuine market conditions.

But this argument overlooks a crucial point: namely, that even in our simple model, much less in the real world, there is still *another* channel for the allocation of resources, namely *government*. In our example, if resources did not go into machine tools because of the special credit, they would have gone not into wheat but into government, and *government* is far less neutral to the market than any other allocation.

In other words, from the point of view of the free market, *any* allocation of economic resources in the private sector, whether machine tools, wheat, or whatever, is better, that is, closer to the free market, than those resources going into the maw of government. If neutrality to the free market is really the consideration, then free-marketeers would rejoice with the creation of one more loophole, one more nook and cranny safe from the tax-man. The key point to focus on is private resources vis-à-vis government.

It has been completely overlooked that the Reagan Administration, while submitting the Treasury flat-tax plan, has at the same time called for further tax credits: for private school tuition and for enterprise zones. Both are laudable, but both are completely opposed to the flat-tax concept.

There is another important point about neutrality to the market, one which also speaks to the fairness issue. The flat-taxers have strongly implied that, in contrast to the progressive tax, the uniform proportionate tax is neutral to the market—for the market would pay in this way for the services of government. But would it really? Where *on the market* is the price of *anything* proportionate to the income of the customer? I pay approximately one dollar a loaf for Wonder Bread; if and when David Rockefeller goes to the market to buy a loaf of Wonder Bread, is he forced to pay one million dollars a loaf—or whatever the proportion would be for our respective annual incomes? One of the great things about the market is that every good or service tends to be at one price: regardless of the race, creed, personality, or income of the customer.

5. The Argument From Simplicity

Perhaps the most seductive argument of the flat-taxers is the argument from simplicity: that, in contrast to the maddening complexity of today's tax code, a code that even the IRS itself cannot fully understand, the flat tax would be simplicity itself. Everyone, they promise, would be able to make out their income tax "on a postcard."

But in the first place, it wouldn't be that simple. We would still need a complex process to determine what our net, taxable income might be. Those of us who are self-employed would still have to figure out our expenses and net incomes. But let us set that aside. What the flat-taxers don't seem to realize is that there are worse things in the world than complexity. And one of them is paying higher taxes. In short, they don't seem to understand some of the reasons for all the tax complexity.

The reason is that many people are willing to wade through a great deal of complexity in order to lower their tax burden. So that, in a sense, given the tax system, much of the complexity that everyone denounces is voluntary. In fact, if we desire simplicity, we can achieve it right now, and without the flat tax. Two-thirds of Americans do so now by filling out the simple short form for their taxes. The one-third of us who choose the wearying long-form route do it for one reason alone: to lower our tax bills. Why in the name of simplicity, are the flat-taxers trying to take this choice away from us? Let them keep their gift of simplicity to themselves, thank you.

One variant of the simplicity argument proved so alluring to a friend of mine that he was almost persuaded by the flat-taxers: the promise that the flat tax would get rid of what are apparently one of the most disliked groups in our society: tax lawyers and accountants.

Apart from the fact that the flat tax would still require a lot of cogitating over net income, let me be one of the few Americans to put in a good word for this much vilified and beleaguered group. Denouncing tax lawyers and accountants is like blaming doctors for the existence of disease, or attacking expenditures on guards, locks, and fences for protecting oneself against crime. Our complaint should not be with tax lawyers and accountants, but with the system that makes them necessary. So long as that system exists, we must realize that they are our shield and our buckler, our defense against the depredations of the tax system.

6. Revenue-Neutral?

It is now time for us to relax the original assumption that I granted the flat-taxers: that their plan would be and remain revenue-neutral. Even if the flat tax would not raise total revenue immediately, who here is naive enough to believe that the government will sit still for long for revenue-neutrality?

The government may be willing to lull us into a false sense of security by promising no increase in total revenue. It doesn't mind cutting tax rates a bit temporarily, for the sake of bringing more revenue sources into its clutches. It is worth a lot to bring previously sheltered hiding places into the grasp of the federal government. I can make that point most dramatically by pointing to the fact that eminent left-liberal economists like Walter Heller champion the flat-tax plan. We might almost point to a picture of Professor Heller, and ask: why is this man smiling? He is smiling because, as he has frankly written, the cut in present tax rates is worth the broadening of the tax base, that is, the bringing of previously exempt income under the grip of federal taxing power.

7. The Terrible Simplifiers and the "General Interest"

If the flat tax is neither evidently fair not genuinely simple nor neutral to the market, if it is merely a snare and a delusion for more confiscatory taxation, it is easy to understand why politicians and bureaucrats may love the idea. But why the enthusiasm of the intellectuals—the alleged spokesmen for the "public" interest? The answer is that the intellectuals may well have a "special interest" of their own.

Jacob Burckhardt, the great 19th-century Swiss historian, referred to many of the intellectuals of his day as "terrible simplifiers." What he meant is that many intellectuals, right, left, or center, are opposed to the messy individuality, the untidy diversity of real life. It is an occupational disease of intellectuals to simplify the reality of people, of *other* people that is, in order to try to understand them. And so intellectuals like to pigeonhole their subjects—other people—into neat, orderly, and simple categories, and to classify and then deal with them in neat and orderly ways. From that way of thinking is an easy step to classify and then treat people as mere pawns to be pushed around.

To do so, the intellectual turns to the secular arm—that is the enforcement power of government—to do the pushing. Intellectuals, in short, are all too often terrible simplifiers, willing and eager to impose massive and painful losses upon other people for the sake of symmetry, uniformity, flatness, or some other simple and abstract ideal. The nature of the creed, the specific content of the ideal, is not nearly as important as the eagerness to override and bulldoze out of existence the diverse and rumpled reality of individual life. We have, alas, come to know in the twentieth century that totalitarianism can have many faces.

When the Regan plan toward a flat tax was announced last fall, an anonymous White House aide attacked the proposal as one "that looks like a tax system designed by a lot of academics." And a leading New York broker charged that "those guys at Treasury are tax lawyers, assistant professors, or statisticians. They have no understanding of what makes an entrepreneur tick."

Indeed, the main designer of the Regan plan, a former academic, proudly proclaimed his lack of realism. Admitting that the plan was written "in an ivory tower," he declared that "one nice thing you get from the ivory tower, is that you get opinions that tend to be unbiased, that are not affected by special interests, that have the public interest in mind." I hope that we will now begin to treat such arrogant claims with the skepticism they so richly deserve.

Is There Life After Reaganomics?

Murray N. Rothbard

I come to bury Reaganomics, not to praise it—and there can be no more fitting epitaph for Reaganomics than the October massacre, especially Black Monday of October 19. The stock market crash brought an end to the so-called Reagan "miracle" not with a whimper but a bang. The crash showed dramatically once again that every time—as in the late 1920s—the financial and political establishment begins to talk about a new era of permanent prosperity and perpetual boom in the stock market, the time has come to head for the hills. Before Monday, the largest stock collapse had occurred in October 1929, when stock prices fell 12.8% in one day; this Monday, stock prices fell almost twice as hard, by 22.6%. That is a *crash*, not a "correction."

As usual, the crisis was met by deception and soft soap. Day after day, as the crash continued, our political, economic, and financial leaders continued to assure us that nothing was wrong, that stock prices are bargains and we should all buy right now, that stocks could not drop further, that 1929 could never happen again. At first, we were told that the market crash was unimportant because trading volume was small, only to be greeted a few days later by unprecedented and enormous trading volume, setting records at over 600 million daily shares.

Leading the parade was President Reagan. Delivering a bromide eerily reminiscent of Herbert Hoover, the president assured us that the "economy is fundamentally sound." A dubious consolation for those who lost one-half trillion dollars in wealth on Black Monday, and one trillion dollars since the stock market began its steep decline this August.

In his now traditional "press conferences" shouted over the roar of helicopter motors, President Reagan followed up his assurance by yelling that "there is nothing wrong with the economy," and, besides, that "Congress is responsible for the deficit." However, it was hardly reassuring for him to shout that if a recession *does* come, the fault will be the media's for alarming us, a classic case of the king reacting to bad news on the front by shooting the messenger.

The crash came because several years of monetary expansion finally resulted this year in the return of price inflation, which accelerated from about one percent last year to about five percent in 1987. But during the years of the Reagan "miracle"—heavy monetary expansion, prosperity, but low price inflation—real interest rates still remained high, a sign that the public remembered the bad not-so-old days of double-digit inflation. As inflation accelerated in 1987, interest rates rose inexorably in response to the return of inflation, and in anticipation of more to come. High interest rates put a chronic damper on the stock market during the inflationary boom of the 1970s, and only the fall in nominal interest rates caused by the whopping recession of 1981-82 could generate the boom of the last few years in the stock market. Now that inflation and higher interest rates reappeared, the stage was set for the stock market crash.

The timing of the crash was insured by the Federal Reserve. After pumping in more money into the economy at the rate of over 10% a year for several years, the Fed became worried at the rising inflation and interest rates this April and stopped its policy of monetary inflation. From April on, the money supply has been flat, an admirable policy, but one that almost always triggers a recession. A recession is inevitable once a credit boom has been launched. The stock market is often an indicator of the near future of the economy, so it is very likely that this crash presages an imminent recession, one that is long overdue.

It is the view of the Austrian School of Economics that a boom in bank credit will lead inevitably to a corrective recession, and that the sooner the boom is stopped, and the recession is allowed to liquidate the unsound investments of the boom, the better. Having expanded credit and brought about a return of inflation, the Reagan administration quickly reacted to the crash by promising to protect us by virtually unlimited doses of inflation in the future. Thus, our monetary czar, Federal Reserve Chairman Alan Greenspan, assured the banks and the financial markets of enough liquidity (that is, new money) to bail everyone out. On Tuesday Greenspan declared that "the Federal Reserve . . . affirmed today its readiness to serve as a source of liquidity to support the economic and financial system." Hence, the "cure" for what ails us—monetary inflation—is to be a lot more of the same. Consistent with this program, the Fed has already pressured the banks to lower their prime interest rates, and has already driven down the federal funds rate by pumping in more bank reserves. On the international front, Secretary of the Treasury Baker, who had been having trouble with the West Germans trying to induce them to inflate and lower their interest rates, announced success in the wake of U.S. pressure after the crash.

Unfortunately, the Fed and the administration are caught in a trap of their own making—in what the British call a "cleft stick." As the Fed expands credit and pushes interest rates down, price inflation will accelerate, and this will inexorably raise interest rates via an inflation premium—precisely what happened in the double-digit inflation of the late 1970s. By frantically trying to stave off an inevitable recession, the administration can only make it worse—and also make it inflationary, as in the 1970s. The administration is busily working to bring about its own worst fears: the so-called "nightmare scenario" of a simultaneous inflation and recession, accompanied by a falling dollar and a collapsed stock market—all neatly in time for the presidential election year of 1988.

Let us now turn from the crash, for the moment, and assess how well Reaganomics has done over the seven years of its reign.

The first question to ask is: how well has Reaganomics achieved its own goals? Perhaps the best way of discovering those goals is to recall the heady days of Ronald Reagan's first campaign for the presidency, especially before his triumph at the Republican National Convention in 1980. In general terms, Reagan pledged to return, or advance, to a free market and to "get government off our backs." Specifically, Reagan called for a massive cut in government spending, an even more drastic cut in taxation (particularly the income tax), a balanced budget by 1984 (that wild-spender, Jimmy Carter, you see, had raised the budget deficit to $74 billion a year, and this had to be eliminated), and a return to the gold standard, where money is supplied by the market rather than by government. In addition to a call for free markets domestically, Reagan affirmed his deep commitment to freedom of international trade. Not only did the upper echelons of the administration sport Adam Smith ties, in honor of that moderate free-trader, but Reagan himself affirmed the depth of the influence upon him of the mid-19th century laissez-faire economist, Frederic Bastiat, whose devastating and satiric attacks on protectionism have been anthologized in economics readings ever since.

The gold standard was the easiest pledge to dispose of. President Reagan appointed an allegedly impartial gold commission to study the problem—a commission overwhelmingly packed with lifelong opponents of gold. The commission presented its predictable report, and gold was quickly interred. Let's run down the other important areas:

Government Spending. How well did Reagan succeed in cutting government spending, surely a critical ingredient in any plan to reduce the role of government in everyone's life? In 1980, the last year of free-spending Jimmy Carter, the federal government spent $591 billion. In 1986, the last recorded year of the Reagan administration, the federal government spent $990 billion, an increase of 68%. Whatever this is, it is emphatically *not* reducing government expenditures.

Sophisticated economists say that these absolute numbers are an unfair comparison, that we should compare federal spending in these two years as percentage of gross national product. But this strikes me as unfair in the opposite direction, because the greater the amount of inflation generated by the federal government, the higher will be the GNP. We might then be complimenting the government on a lower percentage of spending achieved by the government's generating inflation by creating more money. But even taking these percentages of GNP figures, we get federal spending as percent of GNP in 1980 as 21.6%, and after six years of Reagan, 24.3%. A better comparison would be percentage of federal spending to net private product, that is, production of the private sector. That percentage was 31.1% in 1980, and a shocking 34.3% in 1986. So even using percentages, the Reagan administration has brought us a substantial increase in government spending.

Also, the excuse cannot be used that Congress massively increased Reagan's budget proposals. On the contrary, there was never much difference between Reagan's and Congress's budgets, and despite propaganda to the contrary, Reagan never proposed a cut in the total budget.

Deficits. The next, and admittedly the most embarrassing, failure of Reaganomic goals is the deficit. Jimmy Carter habitually ran deficits of $40-50 billion and, by the end, up to $74 billion; but by 1984, when Reagan had promised to achieve a balanced budget, the deficit had settled down comfortably to about $200 billion, a level that seems to be permanent, despite desperate attempts to cook the figures in one-shot reductions.

This is by far the largest budget deficit in American history. It is true that the $50 billion deficits in World War II were a much higher percentage of the GNP; but the point is that that was a temporary, one-shot situation, the product of war finance. But the war was over in a few years; and the current federal deficits now seem to be a recent, but still permanent part of the American heritage.

One of the most curious, and least edifying, sights in the Reagan era was to see the Reaganites completely change their tune of a lifetime. At the very beginning of the Reagan administration, the conservative Republicans in the House of Representatives, convinced that deficits would disappear immediately, received a terrific shock when they were asked by the Reagan administration to vote for the usual annual increase in the statutory debt limit. These Republicans, some literally with tears in their eyes, protested that never in their lives had they voted for an increase in the national debt limit, but they were doing it just this one time because they "trusted Ronald Reagan" to balance the budget from then on. The rest, alas, is history, and the conservative Republicans never saw fit to cry again. Instead, they found themselves adjusting rather easily to the new era of huge permanent deficits. The Gramm-Rudman law, allegedly designed to eradicate deficits in a few years, has now unsurprisingly bogged down in enduring confusion.

Even less edifying is the spectre of Reaganomists who had inveighed against deficits—that legacy of Keynesianism—for decades. Soon Reaganite economists, especially those staffing economic posts in the executive and legislative branches, found that deficits really weren't so bad after all. Ingenious models were devised claiming to prove that there really *isn't* any deficit. Bill Niskanen, of the Reagan Council of Economic Advisors, came up with perhaps the most ingenious discovery: that there is no reason to worry about government deficits, since they are balanced by the growth in value of government assets. Well, hooray, but it is rather strange to see economists whose alleged goal is a drastic reduction in the role of government cheering for ever greater growth in government assets. Moreover, the size of government assets is really beside the point. It would only be of interest if the federal government were just another private business firm, about to go into liquidation, and whose debtors could then be satisfied by a parceling out of its hefty assets. The federal government is not about to be liquidated; there is no chance, for example, of an institution ever going into bankruptcy or liquidation that has the legal right to print whatever money it needs to get itself—and anyone else it favors—out of any financial hole.

There has also been a fervent revival of the old left-Keynesian idea that "deficits don't matter, anyway." Deficits are stimulating, we can "grow ourselves out of deficits," etc. The most interesting, though predictable, twist was that of the supply-siders, who, led by Professor Arthur Laffer and his famous "curve," had promised that if income tax rates were cut, investment and production would be so stimulated that a fall in tax rates would increase tax *revenue* and balance the budget. When the budget was most emphatically *not* balanced, and deficits instead got worse, the supply-siders threw Laffer overboard as the scapegoat, claiming that Laffer was an extremist, and the only propounder of his famous curve. The supply-siders then retreated to their current, fall-back position, which is quite frankly Keynesian; namely deficits don't matter anyway, so let's have cheap money and deficits; relax and enjoy them. About the only Keynesian phrase we have *not* heard yet from Reaganomists is that the national debt "doesn't matter because we owe it to ourselves," and I am waiting for some supply-sider to adopt this famous 1930s phrase of Abba Lerner without, of course, bothering about attribution.

One way in which Ronald Reagan has tried to seize the moral high road on the deficit question is to divorce his rhetoric from reality even more sharply than usual. Thus, the proposer of the biggest deficits in American history has been calling vehemently for a Constitutional amendment to require a balanced budget. In that way, Reagan can lead the way toward permanent $200 billion deficits, while basking in the virtue of proposing a balanced budget amendment, and trying to make Congress the fall guy for our deficit economy.

Even in the unlikely event that the balanced budget amendment should ever pass, it would be ludicrous in its lack of effect. In the first place, Congress can override the amendment at any time by three-fifths vote. Secondly, Congress is not required to actually *balance* any budget; that is, its actual expenditures in any given year are not limited to the revenues taken in. Instead, Congress is only required to prepare an *estimate* of a balanced budget for a *future* year; and of course, government estimates, even of its own income or spending, are notoriously unreliable. And third, there is no *enforcement* clause; suppose Congress *did* violate even the requirement for an estimated balanced budget: What is going to happen to the legislators? Is the Supreme Court going to summon marshals and put the entire U.S. Congress in jail? And yet, not only has Reagan been pushing for such an absurd amendment, but so too have many helpful Reaganomists.

Tax Cuts. One of the few areas where Reaganomists claim success without embarrassment is taxation. Didn't the Reagan administration, after all, slash income taxes in 1981, and provide both tax cuts and "fairness" in its highly touted tax reform law of 1986? Hasn't Ronald Reagan, in the teeth of opposition, heroically held the line against all tax increases?

The answer, unfortunately, is no. In the first place, the famous "tax cut" of 1981 did not cut taxes at all. It's true that tax rates for higher-income brackets were cut; but for the average person, taxes rose, rather than declined. The reason is that, on the whole, the cut in income tax rates was more than offset by two forms of tax increase. One was "bracket creep," a term for inflation quietly but effectively raising one into higher tax brackets, so that you pay more and proportionately higher taxes *even though* the tax rate schedule has officially remained the same. The second source of higher taxes was Social Security taxation, which kept increasing, and which helped taxes go up overall. Not only that, but soon thereafter, when the Social Security System was generally perceived as on the brink of bankruptcy, President Reagan brought in Alan Greenspan, a leading Reaganomist and now Chairman of the Federal Reserve, to save Social Security as head of a bipartisan commission. The "saving," of course, meant still higher Social Security taxes then and forevermore.

Since the tax cut of 1981 that was not really a cut, furthermore, taxes have gone up every single year since, with the approval of the Reagan administration. But to save the president's rhetorical sensibilities, they weren't *called* tax increases. Instead, ingenious labels were attached to them; raising of "fees," "plugging loopholes" (and surely everyone wants loopholes plugged), "tightening IRS enforcement," and even revenue enhancements." I am sure that all good Reaganomists slept soundly at night knowing that even though government revenue was being "enhanced," the president had held the line against tax increases.

The highly ballyhooed Tax "Reform" Act of 1986 was supposed to be economically healthy as well as "fair"; supposedly "revenue neutral," it was to bring us (a) simplicity, helping the public while making the lives of tax accountants and lawyers miserable; and (b) income tax cuts, especially in the higher income brackets and in everyone's marginal tax rates (that is, income tax rates on additional money you may earn); and offset only by plugging those infamous loopholes. The reality, of course, was very different. In the first place, the administration has succeeded in making the tax laws so complicated that even the IRS admittedly doesn't understand it, and tax accountants and lawyers will be kept puzzled and happy for years to come.

Secondly, while indeed income tax rates were cut in the higher brackets, many of the loophole plugs meant huge tax increases for people in the upper as well as middle income brackets. The point of the income tax, and particularly the marginal rate cuts, was the supply-sider objective of lowering taxes to stimulate savings and investment. But a National Bureau study by Hausman and Poterba on the Tax Reform Act shows that over 40% of the nation's taxpayers suffered a marginal tax *increase* (or, at best, the same rate as before) and, of the majority that *did* enjoy marginal tax cuts, only 11% got reductions of 10% or more. In short, most of the tax reductions were negligible. Not only that; the Tax Reform Act, these authors reckoned, would lower savings and investment overall because of the huge increases in taxes on business and on capital gains. Moreover, savings were also hurt by the tax law's removal of tax deductibility on contributions to IRAs.

Not only were taxes increased, but business costs were greatly raised by making business expense meals only 80% deductible, which means a great expenditure of business time and energy keeping and shuffling records. And not only were taxes raised by eliminating tax shelters in real estate, but the law's claims to "fairness" were made grotesque by the retroactive nature of many of the tax increases. Thus, the abolition of tax shelter deductibility was made retroactive, imposing huge penalties after the fact. This is ex post facto legislation outlawed by the Constitution, which prohibits making actions retroactively criminal for a time period when they were perfectly legal. A friend of mine, for example, sold his business about eight years ago; to avoid capital gains taxes, he incorporated his business in the American Virgin Islands, which the federal government had made exempt from capital gains taxes in order to stimulate Virgin Islands development. Now, eight years later, this tax exemption for the Virgin Islands has been removed (a "loophole" plugged!) but the IRS now expects my friend to pay full retroactive capital gains taxes plus interest on this eight-year old sale. Let's hear it for the "fairness" of the tax reform law!

But the bottom line on the tax question: is what happened in the Reagan era to government tax revenues overall? Did the amount of taxes extracted from the American people by the federal government go up or down during the Reagan years? The facts are that federal tax receipts were $517 billion in the last Carter year of 1980. In 1986, revenues totaled $769 billion, an increase of 49%. Whatever that is, that doesn't look like a tax *cut*. But how about taxes as a percentage of the national product? There, we can concede that on a percentage criterion, overall taxes fell very slightly, remaining about even with the last year of Carter. Taxes fell from 18.9% of the GNP to 18.3%, or for a better gauge, taxes as percentage of net private product fell from 27.2% to 26.6%. A large absolute increase in taxes, coupled with keeping taxes as a percentage of national product about even, is scarcely cause for tossing one's hat in the air about a whopping reduction in taxes during the Reagan years.

In recent months, moreover, the Reagan administration has been more receptive to loophole plugging, fees, and revenues than ever before. To quote from the Tax Watch column in the *New York Times* (October 13, 1987): "President Reagan has repeatedly warned Congress of his opposition to any new taxes, but some White House aides have been trying to figure out a way of endorsing a tax bill that could be called something else."

In addition to closing loopholes, the White House is nudging Congress to expand the usual definition of a "user fee," not a tax because it is supposed to be a fee for those who use a government service, say national parks or waterways. But apparently the Reagan administration is now expanding the definition of "user fee" to include excise taxes, on the assumption, apparently, that every time we purchase a product or service we must pay government for its permission. Thus, the Reagan administration has proposed not, of course, as a tax *increase*, but as an alleged "user fee," a higher excise tax on every international airline or ship ticket, a tax on all coal producers, and a tax on gasoline and on highway charges for buses. The administration is also willing to support, as an alleged user fee rather than a tax, a requirement that employers, such as restaurants, start paying the Social Security tax on tips received by waiters and other service personnel.

In the wake of the stock market crash, President Reagan is now willing to give us a post-crash present of: higher taxes that will openly be *called* higher taxes. On Tuesday morning, the White House declared: "We're going to hold to our guns. The president has given us marching orders: no tax increase." By Tuesday afternoon, however, the marching orders had apparently evaporated, and the president said that he was "willing to look at" tax-increase proposals. To greet a looming recession with a tax increase is a wonderful way to bring that recession into reality. Once again, President Reagan is following the path blazed by Herbert Hoover in the Great Depression of raising taxes to try to combat a deficit.

Deregulation. Another crucial aspect of freeing the market and getting government off our backs is deregulation, and the administration and its Reaganomists have been very proud of its deregulation record. However, a look at the record reveals a very different picture. In the first place, the most conspicuous examples of deregulation; the ending of oil and gasoline price controls and rationing, the deregulation of trucks and airlines, were all launched by the Carter administration, and completed just in time for the Reagan administration to claim the credit. Meanwhile, there were other, promised deregulations that never took place; for example, abolition of natural gas controls and of the Department of Energy.

Overall, in fact, there has probably been not deregulation, but an increase in regulation. Thus, Christopher De Muth, head of the American Enterprise Institute and a former top official of Reagan's Office of Management and the Budget, concludes that "the President has not mounted a broad offensive against regulation. There hasn't been much total change since 1981. There has been more balanced administration of regulatory agencies than we had become used to in the 1970s, but many regulatory rules have been strengthened."

In particular, there has been a fervent drive, especially in the past year, to intensify regulation of Wall Street. A savage and almost hysterical attack was launched late last year by the Securities and Exchange Commission and by the Department of Justice on the high crime of "insider trading." Distinguished investment bankers were literally hauled out of their offices in manacles, and the most conspicuous inside trader received as a punishment (1) a fine of $100 million; (2) a lifetime ban on any further security trading, and (3) a jail term of one year, suspended for community service. And this is the *light* sentence, in return for allowing himself to be wired and turn informer on his insider trading colleagues. [Editor's note: Ivan Boesky has since been sentenced to three years in prison.]

All this was part of a drive by the administration to protect inefficient corporate managers from the dread threat of takeover bids, by which means stockholders are able to dispose easily of ineffective management and turn to new managers. Can we really say that this frenzied assault on Wall Street by the Reagan administration had no impact on the stock market crash?

And yet the Reagan administration has reacted to the crash not by letting up, but by *intensifying*, regulation of the stock market. The head of the SEC strongly considered closing down the market on October 19, and some markets were temporarily shut down—a case, once again, of solving problems by shooting the market—the messenger of bad news. October 20, the Reagan administration collaborated in announcing early closing of the market for the next several days. The SEC has already moved, in conjunction with the New York Stock Exchange, to close down computer program trading on the market, a trade related to stock index futures. But blaming computer program trading for the crash is a Luddite reaction; trying to solve problems by taking a crowbar and wrecking machines. There were no computers, after all, in 1929. Once again, the instincts of the administration, particularly in relation to Wall Street, is to regulate. Regulate, and inflate, seem to be the Reaganite answers to our economic ills.

Agricultural policy, for its part, has been a total disaster. Instead of ending farm price supports and controls and returning to a free market in agriculture, the administration has greatly increased price supports, controls and subsidies. Furthermore, it has brought a calamitous innovation to the farm program; the PIK program ["Payments In Kind"] in which the government gets the farmers to agree to drastic cuts in acreage, in return for which the government pays back the wheat or cotton surpluses previously held off the market. The result of all this has been to push farm prices far higher than the world market, depress farm exports, and throw many farmers into bankruptcy. All the administration can offer, however, is more of the same disastrous policy.

Foreign Economic Policy. If the Reagan administration has botched the domestic economy, even in terms of its own goals, how has it done in foreign economic affairs? As we might expect, its foreign economic policy has been the exact opposite of its proclaimed devotion to free trade and free markets. In the first place, Adam Smith ties and Bastiat to the contrary notwithstanding, the Reagan administration has been the most belligerent and nationalistic since Herbert Hoover. Tariffs and import quotas have been repeatedly raised, and Japan has been treated as a leper and repeatedly denounced for the crime of selling high quality products at low prices to the delighted American consumer.

In all matters of complex and tangled international economics, the only way out of the thicket is to keep our eye on one overriding question: Is it good, or bad, for the American consumer? What the American consumer wants is good quality products at low prices, and so the Japanese should be welcomed and admired instead of condemned. As for the alleged crime of "dumping," if the Japanese are really foolish enough to waste money and resources by dumping—that is selling goods to us below costs—then we should welcome such a policy with open arms; anytime the Japanese are willing to sell me Sony TV sets for a dollar, I am more than happy to take the sets off their hands.

Not only foreign producers are hurt by protectionism, but even more so are American consumers. Every time the administration slaps a tariff or quota on motorcycles or on textiles or semiconductors or clothespins—as it did to bail out one inefficient clothespin plant in Maine—every time it does that, it injures the American consumer.

It is no wonder then, that even the Reaganomist Bill Niskanen recently admitted that "international trade is more regulated than it was 10 years ago." Or, as Secretary of Treasury James Baker declared proudly last month: "President Reagan has granted more import relief to U.S. industry than any of his predecessors in more than half a century." Pretty good for a Bastiat follower.

Another original aim of the Reagan administration, under the influence of the monetarists, or Friedmanites, was to keep the government's hand completely off exchange rates, and to allow these rates to fluctuate freely on the market, without interference by the Federal Reserve or the Treasury. A leading monetarist, Dr. Beryl W. Sprinkel, was made Undersecretary of the Treasury for Monetary Policy in 1981 to carry out that policy. But this non-intervention is long gone, and Secretary Baker, aided by the Fed, has been busily engaged in trying to persuade other countries to intervene to help coordinate and fix exchange rates. After being removed from the Treasury after several years, Sprinkel was sent to Siberia and ordered to keep quiet, as head of the Council of Economic Advisors; and Sprinkel has recently announced that he will leave the government altogether. [Editor's note: Sprinkel has recently been rehabilitated, and given Cabinet status, in return for his agreement to take part in the disastrous Baker dollar policy.]

Moreover, the policy of foreign aid and foreign lending conducted or encouraged by the government has proceeded more intensely than even under previous administrations. Reagan has bailed out the despotic government of Poland with massive loans, so that Poland could repay its Western creditors. A similar policy has been conducted in relation to many shaky or bankrupt third world governments. The spectre of bank collapse from foreign loans has been averted by bailouts and promises of bailout from the Federal Reserve, the nation's only manufacturer of dollars, which it can produce at will.

Wherever we look, then, on the budget, in the domestic economy, or in foreign trade or international monetary relations, we see government even more on our backs than ever. The burden and the scope of government intervention under

Reagan has *in*creased, not decreased. Reagan's *rhetoric* has been calling for reductions of government; his *actions* have been precisely the reverse. Yet both sides of the political fence have bought the rhetoric and claim that it has been put into effect.

Reaganites and Reaganomists, for obvious reasons, are trying desperately to maintain that Reagan has indeed fulfilled his glorious promises; while his opponents, intent on attacking the bogey of Reaganomics, are also, and for opposite reasons, anxious to claim that Reagan has really put his free-market program into operation. So we have the curious, and surely not healthy, situation where a mass of politically interested people are totally misinterpreting and even misrepresenting the Reagan record; focusing, like Reagan himself, on his rhetoric instead of on the reality.

What of the Future? Is there life after Reaganomics? To assess coming events, we first have to realize that Reaganomics has never been a monolith. It has had several faces; Reaganomics has been an uneasy and shifting coalition of several clashing schools of economic thought. In particular, the leading schools have been the conservative Keynesians, the Milton Friedman monetarists, and the supply-siders. The monetarists, devoted to a money rule of a fixed percentage increase of money growth engineered by the Federal Reserve, have come a cropper. Fervently believing that science is nothing else but prediction, the monetarists have self-destructed by making a string of self-confident but disastrous predictions in the last several years. Their fate illustrates the fact that he who lives by prediction shall die by it. Apart from their views on money, the monetarists generally believe in free markets, and so their demise has left Reaganomics in the hands of the other two schools, neither of whom are particularly interested in free markets or cutting government.

The conservative Keynesians—the folks who brought us the economics of the Nixon and Ford administrations—saw Keynesianism lose its dominance among economists with the inflationary recession of 1973-74, an event which Keynesians stoutly believed could never possibly happen. But while Keynesians have lost their old eclat, they remain with two preoccupations: (1) a devotion to the New Deal-Fair Deal-Great Society-Nixon-Ford-Carter-status quo, and (2) a zeal for tax increases to moderate the current deficit. As for government spending, never has the thought of actually cutting expenditures crossed their minds. The supply-siders, who are weak in academia but strong in the press and in exerting enormous political leverage per capita, have also no interest in cutting government spending. To the contrary, both conservative Keynesians and supply-siders are prepared to call for an increasing stream of goodies from government.

Both groups have also long been keen on monetary inflation. The supply-siders have pretty much given up the idea of tax cuts; their stance is now to accept the deficit and oppose any tax increase. On foreign monetary matters, the conservative Keynesians and the supply-siders have formed a coalition; both groups embrace Secretary of Treasury Baker's Keynesian program of fixed exchange rates and an internationally coordinated policy of cheap money.

Politically, the Republican presidential candidates can be assessed on their various preferred visions of Reaganomics. Vice-President Bush is, of course, a conservative Keynesian and a veteran arch-enemy of supply-side doctrine, which he famously denounced in 1980 as "voodoo economics." Secretary of Treasury James Baker is a former Bush campaign aide. White House Chief of Staff Howard Baker is also in the conservative Keynesian camp, as was Paul Volcker, and is Alan Greenspan. Since former White House Chief of Staff Donald Regan was a fellow-traveller of the supply-siders, his replacement by Howard Baker as a result of Iranscam was a triumph of conservative Keynesians over the supply-siders. This year, in fact, our troika of Economic Rulers, Greenspan and the two Bakers, has all been squarely in the conservative Keynesian camp.

Senator Robert Dole, the other Republican front-runner for president, is also a conservative Keynesian. In fact, Bob Dole carried on the fight for higher taxes even when it was relatively unfashionable inside the administration. So devoted to higher taxes is Bob Dole, in fact, that he is reputed to be the favorite presidential candidate of the Internal Revenue Service. So if you like the IRS, you'll love Bob Dole.

Congressman Jack Kemp, on the other hand, has been the political champion of the supply-siders ever since supply-side was invented in the late 1970s. Kemp's call for higher government spending, and approval of deficits, monetary inflation, and fixed exchange rates, all attest to his supply-side devotion.

Jack Kemp, however, has for some reason not struck fire among the public, so Mrs. Jeanne Kirkpatrick stands ready in the wings to take up the cause if Kemp should fail to rally. I confess I have not been able to figure out the economic views of the Reverend Pat Robertson, although I have a hunch they do not loom very large in his world outlook.

Although there are a lot of Democratic candidates out there, it is hard at this point to distinguish one from another, on economic policy or indeed on anything else. As Joe Klein recently wrote in a perceptive article in *New York* magazine, the Republicans are engaged in an interesting clash of different ideas, while the Democrats are all muddily groping toward the center. To make the confusion still greater, Klein points out that Republicans are busily talking about "compassion," while the Democrats are all stressing "efficiency." One thing is fairly clear; Congressman Gephardt is an all-out protectionist, thoroughly jettisoning the old Democratic commitment to free trade, and is the most ardent statist in agricultural policy.

On monetary and fiscal policy, the Democrats are the classic party of *liberal* Keynesianism, in contrast to the Republican policy of *conservative* Keynesianism. The problem is that, in the last decade or two, it has become increasingly difficult to tell the difference. Apart from supply-sider Kemp, we can expect the president of either party to be a middle-of-the-road liberal/conservative Keynesian. And so we can expect the next administration's economic policies to be roughly the same as they are now. Except that the *rhetoric* will be different. So we can, therefore, expect diverse perceptions and responses to a similar reality by the public and by the market. Thus, if Jack Kemp becomes president, the public will wrongly consider him a champion of hard money, budget cutting, and the free market. The public will therefore underestimate the wildly inflationist reality of a Kemp administration. On the other hand, the public probably perceives the Democrats to be wilder spenders relative to the Republicans than they really are. So should the Democrats win in 1988, we can expect the market to *over*estimate the inflationary measure of a Democratic administration.

All of this, along with the universal misperception of Reaganomics, illustrates once more the wisdom of those incisive political philosophers, Gilbert and Sullivan: "Things are not always what they seem; skim milk masquerades as cream."

Ronald Reagan: Protectionist

Sheldon L. Richman

Mark Shields, a columnist for the *Washington Post*, recently wrote of President Reagan's "blind devotion to the doctrine of free trade." If President Reagan has a devotion to free trade, it must be blind because he has been way off the mark. In fact, he has been the most protectionist president since Herbert Hoover.

Admittedly, his rhetoric has been confusing. In 1986 Reagan said, "Our trade policy rests firmly on the foundation of free and open markets. I recognize . . . the inescapable conclusion that all of history has taught: the freer the flow of world trade, the stronger the tides of human progress and peace among nations."

But he advocated protectionism early in his 1980 campaign, saying to the U.S. auto industry: "Japan is part of the problem. This is where government can be legitimately involved. That is, to convince the Japanese in one way or another that, in their own interests, that deluge of cars must be slowed while our industry gets back on its feet. . . ."

When he imposed a 100% tariff on selected Japanese electronic products for allegedly "dumping" computer memory chips, he said he did it "to enforce the principles of free and fair trade." And Treasury Secretary James A. Baker has boasted about the protectionist record: Reagan "has granted more import relief to U.S. industry than any of his predecessors in more than half a century."

It's true that the administration has fought with protectionists in Congress, but only over who should have the power to restrict trade. As Reagan put it, "It's better policy to allow for presidents—me or my successors—to have options for dealing with trade problems."

Defenders of the Reagan policies will say that he has engaged in protectionism to open foreign markets. But they cannot deny that one-quarter of all imports are today restricted, a 100% increase over 1980.

Nor are foreign markets more open. The Reagan administration talks about exporting free enterprise, but in fact it has exported economic intervention to Japan, South Korea, and other nations. When the United States imposes import quotas or pressures a foreign government to do so, a compulsory cartel must arise in the exporting country, since its government will assign the quotas among private firms and administer the system. Ronald Reagan has forced nations that export textiles, apparel, sugar, steel, and other products to cartelize these industries.

Can trade restrictions open foreign markets? The use of government power to regulate trade is more likely to produce conflict of which American consumers and exporters become the victims. It is also naive, because it ignores the political pressure to maintain existing restrictions. The United States, for example, could impose new limits on Japanese autos to force Japan to accept beef exports from Iowa. But, as syndicated columnist Stephen Chapman asks, "Does anyone believe that when Japan starts buying Iowa beef, Ford and Chrysler will stop trying to keep out Japanese cars?"

Considering our own intricate web of trade restrictions, it is sanctimonious for the U.S. government to lecture others about opening their markets. It might be in a better position to make demands if it first stripped our economy of those restrictions. But wouldn't we be giving up bargaining chips? Yes. But the objective is not to negotiate; it is to enjoy the benefits of productivity and the international division of labor. The bonanza of unconditional free trade would be so great for the United States that it would set a good example for the rest of the world.

The value of free trade does not depend on open markets abroad. It is good for the nation that practices it, regardless of what others do. The purpose of an economic system is not to produce jobs or sell products abroad. Those are means. The end is satisfaction of our material wants. Free trade is good because our standard of living depends on how easily we can get the products and services we want.

One is led to ask: with free-traders like this, who needs protectionists? The administration has thus far:

- Forced Japan to accept restraints on auto exports;
- Tightened considerably the quotas on imported sugar;
- Negotiated to increase the restrictiveness of the Multifiber Arrangement governing trade in textiles and apparel;

- Required 18 countries, including Brazil, Spain, South Korea, Japan, Mexico, South Africa, Finland, Australia, and the European Community, to accept "voluntary restraint agreements" that reduce their steel imports to the United States;
- Imposed a 45% duty on Japanese motorcycles for the benefit of Harley Davidson, which admitted that superior Japanese management was the cause of its problems;
- Raised tariffs on Canadian lumber and cedar shingles;
- Forced the Japanese into an agreement to control the price of computer memory chips;
- Removed third-world countries on several occasions from the duty-free import program for developing nations;
- Pressed Japan to force its automakers to buy more American-made parts;
- Demanded that Taiwan, West Germany, Japan, and Switzerland restrain their exports of machine tools;
- Accused the Japanese of dumping roller bearings on grounds that the price did not rise to cover a fall in the value of the yen;
- Accused the Japanese of dumping forklift trucks and color picture tubes;
- Extended quotas on imported clothes pins;
- Failed to ask Congress to end the ban on the export of Alaskan oil and timber cut from federal lands;
- Redefined dumping so domestic firms can more easily charge foreign competitors with unfair trade practices;
- Beefed-up the Export-Import Bank, an institution dedicated to distorting the American economy at the expense of the American people in order to artificially promote exports of eight large corporations.

The World Bank estimates that import restrictions in 1984 had the same effect as a 66% income tax surcharge on America's poorest citizens. Less obvious is the harm to American producers, who lose exports and pay more for capital goods because of protectionism. For example, everyone, including the beleaguered American auto industry, has to pay more for steel because of the Reagan administration's restrictions on imports. Even the steel industry is hurt because artificially high prices stimulate the search for alternative materials.

President Reagan missed a unique opportunity to begin freeing the American economy from the shackles of trade restrictions. He need not have given the American people a technical lesson in economics. He could have said that free trade requires no more justification than domestic economic freedom; indeed, it requires no more justification than the traditional American values of a humane and open society.

The Sad Legacy of Ronald Reagan

Sheldon L. Richman

On August 2, 1988, President Ronald Reagan announced that he had changed his mind about the pro-union plant-closing bill. He had vetoed it three months earlier, but now let it become law without his signature after intense pressure from presidential nominee George Bush and former Treasury Secretary James Baker, now Bush's campaign chairman. Reagan claimed that only this action would enable him to sign a Congressional trade bill almost unequaled in its anti-consumer protectionism.

Ronald Reagan's faithful followers claim he has used his skills as the Great Communicator to reverse the growth of Leviathan and inaugurate a new era of liberty and free markets. Reagan himself said, "It is time to check and reverse the growth of government."

Yet after nearly eight years of Reaganism, the clamor for more government intervention in the economy was so formidable that Reagan abandoned the free-market position and acquiesced in further crippling of the economy and our liberties. In fact, the number of free-market achievements by the administration are so few that they can be counted on one hand—with fingers left over.

Let's look at the record:

Spending

In 1980, Jimmy Carter's last year as president, the federal government spent a whopping 27.9% of "national income" (an obnoxious term for the private wealth produced by the American people). Reagan assaulted the free-spending Carter administration throughout his campaign in 1980. So how did the Reagan administration do? At the end of the first quarter of 1988, federal spending accounted for 28.7% of "national income."

Even Ford and Carter did a better job at cutting government. Their combined presidential terms account for an increase of 1.4%—compared with Reagan's 3%—in the government's take of "national income." And in nominal terms, there has been a 60% increase in government spending, thanks mainly to Reagan's requested budgets, which were only marginally smaller than the spending Congress voted.

The budget for the Department of Education, which candidate Reagan promised to abolish along with the Department of Energy, has more than doubled to $22.7 billion. Social Security spending has risen from $179 billion in 1981 to $269 billion in 1986. The price of farm programs went from $21.4 billion in 1981 to $51.4 billion in 1987, a 140% increase. And this doesn't count the recently signed $4 billion "drought-relief" measure. Medicare spending in 1981 was $43.5 billion; in 1987 it hit $80 billion. Federal entitlements cost $197.1 billion in 1981—and $477 billion in 1987.

Foreign aid has also risen, from $10 billion to $22 billion. Every year, Reagan asked for more foreign-aid money than the Congress was willing to spend. He also pushed through Congress an $8.4 billion increase in the U.S. "contribution" to the International Monetary Fund.

His budget cuts were actually cuts in *projected* spending, not absolute cuts in current spending levels. As Reagan put it, "We're not attempting to cut either spending or taxing levels below that which we presently have."

The result has been unprecedented government debt. Reagan has tripled the Gross Federal Debt, from $900 billion to $2.7 trillion. Ford and Carter in their combined terms could only double it. It took 31 years to accomplish the first postwar debt tripling, yet Reagan did it in eight.

Taxes

Before looking at taxation under Reagan, we must note that spending is the better indicator of the size of the government. If government cuts taxes, but not spending, it still gets the money from somewhere—either by borrowing or inflating. Either method robs the productive sector. Although spending is the better indicator, it is not complete, because it ignores other ways in which the government deprives producers of wealth. For instance, it conceals regulation and trade restrictions, which may require little government outlay.

If we look at government revenues as a percentage of "national income," we find little change from the Carter days, despite heralded "tax cuts." In 1980, revenues were 25.1% of "national income." In the first quarter of 1988 they were 24.7%.

Reagan came into office proposing to cut personal income and business taxes. The Economic Recovery Act was supposed to reduce revenues by $749 billion over five years. But this was quickly reversed with the Tax Equity and Fiscal Responsibility Act of 1982. TEFRA—the largest tax increase in

American history—was designed to raise $214.1 billion over five years, and took back many of the business tax savings enacted the year before. It also imposed withholding on interest and dividends, a provision later repealed over the president's objection.

But this was just the beginning. In 1982 Reagan supported a five-cent-per-gallon gasoline tax and higher taxes on the trucking industry. Total increase: $5.5 billion a year. In 1983, on the recommendation of his Social Security Commission—chaired by the man he later made Fed chairman, Alan Greenspan—Reagan called for, and received, Social Security tax increases of $165 billion over seven years. A year later came Reagan's Deficit Reduction Act to raise $50 billion.

Even the heralded Tax Reform Act of 1986 is more deception than substance. It shifted $120 billion over five years from visible personal income taxes to hidden business taxes. It lowered the rates, but it also repealed or reduced many deductions.

According to the Treasury Department, the 1981 tax cut will have reduced revenues by $1.48 trillion by the end of fiscal 1989. But tax increases since 1982 will equal $1.5 trillion by 1989. The increases include not only the formal legislation mentioned above but also bracket creep (which ended in 1985 when tax indexing took effect—a provision of the 1981 act despite Reagan's objection), $30 billion in various tax changes, and other increases. Taxes by the end of the Reagan era will be as large a chunk of GNP as when he took office, if not larger: 19.4%, by ultra-conservative estimate of the Reagan Office of Management and Budget. The so-called historic average is 18.3%.

Regulation

For all the administration's talk about deregulation (for example, from the know-nothing commission which George Bush headed), it has done little. Much of what has been done began under Carter, such as abolition of the Civil Aeronautics Board and deregulation of oil prices. Carter created the momentum and Reagan halted it. In fact, the economic costs of regulation have grown under Reagan.

Some deregulation has occurred for banks, intercity buses, ocean shipping, and energy. But nothing good has happened in health, safety, and environmental regulations, which cost Americans billions of dollars, ignore property rights, and are based on the spurious notion of "freedom from risk." But the Reagan administration has supported state seat-belt and federal air-bag requirements. This concern for safety, however, was never extended to the Corporate Average Fuel Economy (CAFE) rules, which, by imposing fuel-efficiency standards, promote the production of small cars. The shift to small cars will cause an estimated 10,000 to 20,000 highway deaths over the next ten years.

Bureaucracy

By now it should not be surprising that the size of the bureaucracy has also grown. Today, there are 230,000 more civilian government workers than in 1980, bringing the total to almost three million. Reagan even promoted the creation of a new federal Department of Veterans' Affairs to join the Departments of Education and Energy, which his administration was supposed to eliminate.

Trade

The Reagan administration has been the most protectionist since Herbert Hoover's. The portion of imports under restriction has *doubled* since 1980. Quotas and so-called voluntary restraints have been imposed on a host of products, from computer chips to automobiles. Ominously, Reagan has adopted the bogus fair-trade/free-trade dichotomy, and he was eager to sign the big trade bill, which tilts the trade laws even further toward protectionism.

Results

Reagan's fans argue that he has changed the terms of public-policy debate, that no one today dares propose big spending programs. I contend that the alleged spending-shyness of politicians is not the result of an ideological sea-change, but rather of their constituents' fiscal fright brought about by $250 billion Reagan budget deficits. If the deficit ever shrinks, the demand for spending will resume.

This is the Reagan legacy. He was to be the man who would turn things around. But he didn't even try. As he so dramatically illustrated when he accepted the plant-closing bill, there has been no sea-change in thinking about the role of government.

About the Contributors

Tucker Alford is a student and Mises Institute fellow at Washington and Lee College.

Tom Bethell is a media fellow at the Hoover Institute at Stanford University.

Walter Block is chief economist at the Fraser Institute and senior fellow at the Mises Institute.

Richard Ebeling is Ludwig von Mises assistant professor of economics at Hillsdale College.

David Gordon is senior fellow at the Mises Institute.

Robert Higgs is William E. Simon professor of political economy at Lafayette College.

Hans-Hermann Hoppe is associate professor of economics at the University of Nevada, Las Vegas, and senior fellow at the Mises Institute.

Mark D. Hughes is a graduate student and Mises Institute fellow at George Mason University.

Graeme B. Littler is an economic consultant.

Bradley Miller is director of publications for the Heritage Foundation.

Ludwig von Mises (1881-1973) was the greatest economist of the twentieth century.

Margit von Mises, widow of Ludwig von Mises, is an author and chairman of the Mises Institute.

Ron Paul is a former U.S. Congressman, 1988 presidential candidate of the Libertarian Party, and distinguished counsellor to the Mises Institute.

William H. Peterson is a resident scholar at the Heritage Foundation.

Lawrence W. Reed is president of the Mackinac Institute.

Sheldon Richman is director of public affairs at the Institute for Humane Studies at George Mason University.

Llewellyn H. Rockwell, Jr., is founder and president of the Mises Institute.

Murray N. Rothbard is S. J. Hall distinguished professor of economics at the University of Nevada, Las Vegas, and vice president for academic affairs at the Mises Institute.

Mark D. Skousen is editor of *Forecasts and Strategies* and adjunct professor of economics at Rollins College.

Kathleen M. Spotts is a social worker.

Jeffrey A. Tucker is managing editor of the *Free Market* and a graduate student and Mises Institute fellow at George Mason University.

Charlotte Twight, a member of the Washington State Bar, teaches economics at Boise State University.

Patrick W. Watson is a Ph.D. student in political science at Rice University in Houston, Texas.

Sam Wells is a free-lance writer.

Index

Compiled by Nancy Oliver

Act for Better Child Care Services (ABC bill), 287, 288
Action Committee for Europe, 336
Acton, Lord, 208
Adams, Ted, 132
Africa, East, 224
  South, 97, 131-33, 146, 148, 189
Aquired Immune Deficiency Syndrome (AIDS), 325
Airport congestion, 257
Airports, 259
Aldrich, Nelson W., 116
Alford, J. Tucker, 105
Algeria, 321
Amalgamated Clothing Workers, 251
American Association of Retired Persons, 284
American Bar Association, 251, 319
American Eagle coin, 98
American Enterprise Institute, 374
American Mercury, 210
American Spectator, 282
America's Great Depression, 192
Andreas, Dwayne, 317
Andrew, Piatt A., 116
Andropov, Yuri, 229
Anti-trust laws, 16
Anti-Capitalistic Mentality, 181
Apartheid, 131, 190
Aquaculture, 265
Archer-Daniels-Midland, 317
Arnold, Roger, 202
Arrow, Kenneth J., 331
Articles of Confederation, 128, 129, 295
Atlas Economic Research Foundation, 167
Auburn University, 168, 201, 202, 204
Auchincloss, Kenneth, 209
Austrian, 73, 90, 95
  Chamber of Commerce, 174
  School of Economics, 93, 100, 165, 171, 172, 184, 201, 333, 364
  Institute for Business Cycle Research, 174
Baker, Howard, 379
Baker, James, 112, 344, 364, 376, 377, 379, 382, 385
Balance of Payments, 112, 159
Balance of Trade, 126, 127, 138, 142, 143
Balanced Budget Amendment, 296ff.
Balladur, Edouard, 338
Bank, Banking
  of Boston, 252
  Central, 28, 52, 53, 86-88, 93, 100, 102, 110, 116, 118, 122, 160, 173, 186, 192, 195, 220, 304, 333, 337
  credit, 52, 63, 85
  commercial, 78
  of England, 84
  free, 100
  for International Settlements (BIS), 338
  of Japan, 335
  runs, 77, 79
  Second Bank of United States, 300, 301
  thrifts, 78
Bargaining chips, 383
Barnum, P. T., 299
Baruch, Bernard M., 94
Baruch College, 205
Bastiat, Frederic, 127, 153, 366, 376, 377
Batemarco, Robert, 40
Bauer, Peter T., 320
Becker, Horace, 36
Bell, Alexander Graham, 215
Bennett, William, 284, 285
Berkeley, University of California at, 325
Bethell, Tom, 226
Billings, Josh, 209
Bimetallism, 300
Black, Angus, 133
Black Monday, 62, 64, 275, 308ff., 362
Bland-Allison Act, 302
Block, Walter, 41, 65, 195, 201, 266, 270
Blue Eagle, 251
Blumert, Burton S., 213
Böhm-Bawerk, Eugen von, 45, 89, 100, 171, 187, 195, 217

Boesky, Ivan, 374
Body Parts, 270ff.
Bogart, Ernest Ludlow, 303
Bolingbroke, Lord, 286
Boskin, Michael, 323-27, 332, 334
Bradley, Bill, 88
Brady Commission, 316
Brady, Nicholas, 314ff.
Brezhnev, Leonid, 184
Brokerage Industry, 274
Brookings Institution, 333
Brooklyn Polytechnic, 192
Buchanan, James, 179
Buckley, William F., Jr., 210
Budget
  balanced, 296ff.
  Balanced Budget Amendment, 396
  cut, 32, 34
  deficit, 310
Burckhardt, Jacob, 361
Bureaucracy, 187, 293
Bureaucracy, 291ff.
Bureaucrats, 66, 261, 292ff.
Burns, Arthur F., 73, 120, 191, 326
Bush, George, 211, 323, 329, 379, 388
Business
  big, 57, 289
  cycles, 63, 69, 70, 88-91, 93ff., 115, 119, 177, 220, 299ff., 324
Butcher, Willard C., 55

Calculation, economic 48, 49, 236, 239, 246, 252, 253
Calhoun, John C., 14
California, 82
Cambodian genocide, 256
Canada, 107, 111
Cantillon, Richard, 142
Cape Town, University of, 189
Capital, 95, 125, 172, 247
  budget, 324, 325
  gains, 347-49
Capitalism, 40, 48, 56, 57, 240, 244, 246, 248, 249
Carlson, Chester, 35, 36
Carter, Jimmy, 16, 37, 38, 82, 146, 286, 292, 322, 365-367, 372, 379, 386, 387, 389
Caste analysis, 17
Caste conflict, 39
Catallactic, 70
Central planning, 240, 250, 252, 255
Chapman, Stephen, 383
Chase Manhattan Bank, 38, 55, 101, 121
Chicago School, 340
Child care, 286ff.
China, 230, 255
Chrysler, 130, 253
Civil Aeronautics Board (CAB), 258, 260
Civil War, 264
Clear Springs Trout Company, 265
"Cluster box" system, 277
Cochran, Bourke, 303
Colbert, Jean-Baptiste, 131
Columbia University, 191
Commerce Department, 39, 70, 127, 251, 319
Commodity Credit Corporation, 319, 322
Communist, communism, 60, 168, 224, 232, 256
Communist Manifesto, 45
Comparable worth, 67
Conceived in Liberty, 194, 197
Conservative Digest, 185
Constitution, 125, 126, 129, 295-97, 306ff., 353, 372
Consumer Price Index, 93
Consumer Product Safety Commission, 15, 319
Consumer sovereignty, 57-59
Continental, 107, 114
Confederacy, 302
Corporate Average Fuel Economy (CAFE), 389
Corporations, 351, 352
Costs
  of production, 141, 247
  subjective, 141, 144, 157
Council for a Competitive Economy, 128
Council of Economic Advisors, 104, 368, 377
Credit Lyonnais, 335
Crime, victimless, 274
Cronkite, Walter, 170
Crowding-out effect, 21
Cuomo, Mario, 136
Czechoslovakia, 183

Dairy, 317
Dallas, University of, 188, 201
Dames & Moore v. Regan, 147
Davison, Henry P., 116
Debt, 121
  Mexican, 120
  Third World, 121
Deficit Reduction Act, 388
Deficits, 19ff., 34, 96, 296, 305, 367
Deflation, 27, 28
DeGaulle, 176
Degressive, 345
Democrat, Democratic 104, 332
Democracy, 342
Denationalized, 100
Denson, John V., 203
Department of Education, 285ff., 386, 389
Department of Energy, 37, 286, 374, 386, 389

Department of Justice, 266, 374
Department of Veterans' Affairs, 389
Depreciators, accelerators, 349
Depression, 90
Depression, the Great, 94, 110, 119, 129, 175, 195, 373
Deregulation, 373, 389
DeMuth, Christopher, 374
D'Estaing, Valery Giscard, 336
Digital Equipment Corporation, 252
Discrimination, 41-43, 44
Disinvestment, 132
Dodd, Christopher, 287
Dole, Robert, 344, 380
Drought-relief, 386
Drucker, Peter, 208
Dukakis, Michael, 251, 252, 323, 329, 330
Dumping, 141, 144, 155ff.

Eastern Airlines, 259
Ebeling, Richard, 201, 239
Ebsen, Alf, 213
Economic calculation, 48, 49, 236, 239, 246, 252, 253
  warfare, 146
Economic Recovery Act, 387
Economist, 337
Economy, mixed, 240
Ecu Banking Association, 335
Egypt, 321
Einaudi, Luigi, 176
Eisenhower, Dwight, 32, 38
Ellis, Abraham, 281
Emergency Economic Powers Act, 147
Employment, 66
  protection, 68
Entitlements, 386
Entrepreneur, 241, 268, 269, 278, 354
Environmental Protection Agency (EPA), 15, 286, 319
Envy, 181ff.
Epistemological Problems of Economics, 175, 219
Erhard, Ludwig, 176
Erickson, Nellie, 165, 203
Establishment, 83, 103, 298, 314
Ethics of Liberty, 194, 199
Ethiopia, 321-24
Europe, Western, 88, 110, 307
European
  Central Bank, 335ff.
  Currency Unit (Ecu), 335ff.
  Investment Bank, 335
  Monetary System, 336
Evolution, 47
Exchange
  rate, 54, 62, 83ff., 86, 87, 110
  fixed, 53, 83, 109, 111
Export-Import Bank, 123, 127, 322, 384

Fair Deal, 379
Fairness, 355 ff.
Famine, 223, 224, 225
Farmland Dairies, 135
Farm programs, 386
Fascist, fascism, 60, 250, 253.
Federal Aviation Agency (FAA), 258-60
Federal Deposit Insurance Corporation (FDIC), 75, 77, 79
Federal Express, 278, 279
Federal Insurance Contributions Act (FICA), 282
Federal Register, 123
Federal Reserve, 20, 21, 62, 64, 65, 69, 70, 76, 79, 88, 90, 91, 101, 105-08, 114-19, 121, 160, 173, 191, 209, 277, 299, 304, 305, 311-17, 319, 325, 326, 328, 335, 336, 341, 364, 365, 377, 378
  Act, 38, 94
Federal Savings and Loan Insurance Corporation (FSLIC), 75-77, 79
Federal Trade Commission, 16, 116, 286, 319
Feldstein, Martin, 327ff., 331, 334
Fertig, Lawrence, 176, 178, 179, 187, 212
Ferrara, Peter, 284
Feudalism, 254
Fisher, Anthony, 167
Fisher, Irving, 208, 340
Flew, Antony, 231
Food and Drug Administration, 319
For a New Liberty, 192, 198
Forbes, 337
Forecasting, economic, 25
Foreign Aid, 320ff., 387
Foreign Economic Policy, 376ff.
Ford, Gerald, 104, 322, 378, 379, 386, 387
Ford Motor Company, 125
Fort Knox, 99
Foundations of Morality, The, 228
Founding Fathers, 122, 134, 147
Fractional reserves, 78, 107, 160
France, 111
The Freeman, 210
Free Market, 200
Friedman, Milton, 22, 120, 207, 339, 351, 355, 378
Friedmanite, 53, 54, 86, 87, 113
Fuller, Ida, 282
Fund, John, 209

Galbraith, J. K., 112, 237
Garrison, Roger, 201
General Accounting Office (GAO), 278
General Electric, 251, 252
General Motors, 125
General Theory, 175, 188, 189, 329
George Mason University, 40, 43

Gephardt, Richard, 380
Germany, West, 111, 112, 364, 384
Girard College, 214
Glasnost, 255
Glass-Steagall Act, 275
Gold, 84, 86, 88, 91, 97, 99, 100, 102, 160, 337
Gold coin standard, 53, 54, 64, 83, 89, 93, 104, 109, 114, 118, 159, 168, 191, 296, 299, 300, 301, 304, 338, 341
Gorbachev, Mikhail, 226, 227, 229, 230
Gordon, David, 45, 201
Gramm-Rudman, 368
Great Britain, 109, 111, 349
Great Society, 379
Greed, 183
Greenspan, Alan, 103-05, 312, 314, 326, 364, 379, 388
Greider, William, 117, 119, 120, 121
Gresham's Law, 54, 110, 113, 302
Gross Federal Debt, 387
Gross National Product, 32, 39, 40, 71, 91, 193, 297, 366, 367, 372, 388
Group of Seven, 111, 112
Gyoten, Toyo, 55

Haberler, Gottfried, 167
Haloid Company, 36
Hamilton, W. P., 215
Hammer, Armand, 317
Harley Davidson, 384
Harper, Baldy, 167
Harper's, 292
Hatch, Orrin, 288
Hawley, E. W., 319
Hayek, F. A., 88, 89, 165, 167, 174, 175, 177, 199, 211, 221, 228, 234, 338
Hayes, President, 302
Hazlitt, Henry, 43, 136, 176, 178, 179, 184, 185ff., 187, 189, 194, 200, 202, 203, 204-06, 208, 209, 212, 213, 214, 228, 325
Heller, Walter, 360
Henry Hazlitt Fund, 201
Hefner, Hugh, 183
Hegel's Geist, 47
Higgs, Robert, 146, 306
Hiroshima, 149
Hoff, Trygve, 227
Homoeconomicus, 178
Hong Kong, 139, 315
Hoover, Herbert, 14, 120, 251, 273, 305, 311, 373, 376, 381, 389
Hoppe, Hans-Hermann, 201, 244
Hospitals, 272
Howe, Neil, 282
Hughes, Mark D., 40, 134
Human Action, 48, 50, 164, 187, 216, 240, 242
Hungary, 255
Hutt, William H., 52, 179, 184, 185, 188ff., 194

Iacocca, Lee, 128, 130, 145
Idle Capacity, 50-56
Idleness, 52
Ignatius, David, 230
Import, 123, 124
Income, "imputed," 346
India, 321
Industrial Revolution, 27, 152
"Infant industries," 158
Inflate, 375
Inflation, 19, 22, 24, 26, 27, 51, 53, 69, 79, 84, 88, 89, 91, 94, 96, 97, 100, 117, 119, 173, 192, 261, 313, 326, 363, 375
  "bracket creep," 370
  double-digit, 62
  expectation, 24
  hyper, 84, 302
  premium, 64
  recession, 50
Insider trading, 274
Institute for Humane Studies, 167
Institute of Sociology, 231
Institutionalism, 175
Interest group, 13, 38
  special, 333, 342, 343
Interest rates, 21, 22, 24, 62-65, 89, 96, 120, 173, 311, 333, 363
International Business Machines (IBM), 36, 76
Internal Revenue Service, 330, 347, 353, 354, 370, 371, 372, 380
International Monetary Fund, 102, 112, 187, 207, 337, 338, 387
Interstate Commerce Act, 318
Interstate Commerce Commission (ICC), 116, 318, 319
Intervention, government 86, 170, 193, 242-44, 299
Investment, 22, 245, 311
Iran, 146
Iran-United States Claims Tribunal, 146
Israel, 321
Italy, 111

Jackson, Andrew, 101, 117, 122, 301
Jagger, Mick, 294
Jagiellonian University, 234
Japan, 111, 112, 123, 125, 139, 141, 145, 148, 157, 382, 384
Japanese, 127
Jefferson, Thomas, 295, 296, 356
Jobs, 65ff.
John Hancock Mutual Life, 252
Johnson, Lyndon, 178

Johnson, Samuel, 216, 220
Jordan, Jerry, 113
Joseph, Sir Keith, 262

Kahn, Alfred E., 258
Kaiser, Robert, 226, 230
Kemp, Jack, 88, 112, 380, 381
Kennedy School of Government, 329
Kennedy, Ted, 38
Keynes, 101, 175, 188, 323-25, 328, 329, 339
Keynesian, 26, 34, 50, 52, 51, 53-56, 83, 84, 86, 90, 104, 112, 175, 184, 190, 197, 204, 205, 283, 311-13, 323, 324, 327, 330, 332-34, 340, 368, 369, 378-80
Kildee, Dale, 287
Kirkpatrick, Jeanne, 380
Kirzner, Israel, 165, 177, 178, 202
Klein, Joe, 380
Knight, Frank, 340
Koch, Edward, 82, 136
Kodak, 35, 36
Koether, George, 166
Kolko, Gabriel, 318
Korea, South, 139, 382
Kourouma, Michelle, 133
Kristol, Irving, 285
Krugerrands, 132
Kuhn Loeb & Company, 116

Labor, 125
  child, 69
  division of, 124
Laffer, Arthur, 368, 369
Laffer Curve, 29, 340, 342
LaGendre, Thomas, 131
Laissez-faire, 17, 89, 131, 153
Lange, Oskar, 50, 228
Las Vegas, Nevada, 202
Law of the Sea Treaty, 266
Legal-tender laws, 101, 301
Lenin, Vladimir, 181, 229, 330
Leningrad, 238
Less Developed Countries (LDCs), 320
Liberalism, 46
Libertarian, 232
Libya, 146, 148
License, licensing, 68, 69, 137, 287, 290
Liggio, Leonard, 178
Littler, Graeme B., 273
London School of Economics, 189
Loophole, 345ff.
Loot seekers, 134
Luddite fallacy, 375
Louvre Accord, 64

Machlup, Fritz, 165, 167
Malthus, Thomas, 56
Man, Economy and State, 192, 193, 197, 199, 221
Marketing, 57
Marx, Karl, 14, 46, 49, 171, 172, 183, 237
Marxism/Marxist, 45, 47, 49, 62, 90, 171, 187, 190, 224, 232, 248
  Christian, 183
Massachusetts, 107, 250, 251
Massachusetts Capital Resources Corporation, 252
Massachussetts Industrial Finance Agency, 252
Mathematics, 49
McCaffrey, Neil, 166
McClure, Jessica, 288
Medicaid, 119, 386
Meese, Ed, 285, 286
Mencken, H.L., 186, 200, 205, 342, 343
Menger, Carl, 100, 171, 187, 217
Mercantilism, 161
Mercantilist, neo, 140
Methodology, 70, 73, 175, 219
Mill, John Stuart, 221
Miller, Bradley, 180, 291
Minorities, 67
Mises, Ludwig von, 13, 14, 34, 39, 41, 45-48, 56, 70, 88, 100, 101, 115, 119, 122, 128, 135, 139, 144, 145, 163, 166-69, 170ff., 177ff., 184, 187, 190, 191, 197, 200, 216ff., 227, 234, 239, 242, 252, 255, 293, 300, 305, 333, 336
Mises, Ludwig von Institute, 168
Mises, Margit von, 163, 176, 202, 213
Misesian, 95
Mitchell, Wesley C., 73
Mitin, M. B., 47
Mitterrand, Francois, 336
Mondale, Walter, 116, 117, 292
Monetarists, 86, 90
Monetary policy, 97ff.
Monetary Control Act of 1980, 121
Money
  fiat money standards, 53, 84, 105, 160
  M-1, 121
  prices, 236, 246
  supply, 23, 93, 108, 109
  True Money Supply, 121, 193
Monopolist, 262
Monopoly, 317ff.
  natural, 280
  prices, 196, 276
Montesquieu, 221
Mont Pelerin Society, 179
Morgan, J. P., 105, 116, 118
Morgan Guaranty, 102, 105, 335
Morgenstern, Oskar, 167

Morocco, 321
Mozambique, 224
Mundell, Robert, 112
Municipal bonds, 352
Mussolini, Benito, 250, 251
Mystery of Banking, The, 192, 234

Nagasaki, 149
National Association of Blacks, 132
National Association of Manufacturers, 251
National Bureau of Economic Research (NBER) 70ff., 331, 371
National City Bank, 116
National Conference of Black Mayors, 133
National curriculum, 284
National Health Federation, 279
National income, 297, 387
National Industrial Recovery Act, 319
Nationalism, Nationalist 148, 152
Nationalokönomie, 175
National parks, 373
National Recovery Administration (NRA), 251
National Review, 198, 210
National Tax Association, 325, 331
National Urban League, 132
Nation, State, and Economy, 218
Natural resources, 263ff., 350
Nazi, 60, 220
Netherlands, 146
Nevada, University of, 192, 201
New Deal, 15, 198, 273, 324, 329, 379
New Order, 112, 113
Newsweek, 187, 205, 209, 210
New York, 69, 80, 81, 82, 135, 138, 352
New York, College of the City of, 215
New York Evening Post, 215
New York Federal Reserve Bank, 314
New York Magazine, 380
New York Stock Exchange, 375
New York Times, 104, 170, 187, 188, 215, 323, 326, 373
New York Times Magazine, 250
New York University, 176, 178, 180, 187, 191, 200, 202, 212
New Zealand, 237
Nicaragua, 146, 148
Nietzsche, 181, 294
Nihilism, 226
Niskanen, William, 368, 376
Nixon, Richard, 85, 110, 115, 121, 209, 322, 324, 378, 379
North, Oliver, 291
Nozick, Robert, 199
Nutter, Warren, 179
Nyerere, Julius, 321

Occidental Petroleum, 317
Occupational Safety and Health Administration (OSHA), 15, 286
Office of Foreign Assets Control, 147
Office of Management and the Budget, 374, 388
Omnipotent Government, 187
OPEC, 96, 312
Opel, John, 314
Orwell, George, 294
Overseas Private Investment Corporation, 127, 322

Pace University, 202
Pakistan, 321
Panic of 1819, 151, 191, 195, 300
Parkinson's "Law," 23
Pascal, 294
PATCO, 258
Paul, Ron, 37, 97, 115, 122, 123, 206, 213, 295, 314
Payments in Kind (PIK), 375
Pechman, Joseph A., 333
Peddling, 69
Perestroika, 255, 256
Peterson, William, 177
Phillips, A. W., 26
Phillips Curve, 26, 27, 313, 314, 331
Poland, 231-34
Politicians, 66, 261
Ponzi, Charles, 283
Poor, 119
Post Office, 192, 261, 276ff., 317
Power and Market, 192, 193
Praxeology, 175, 180, 219
Pressure groups, 81
Price
  controls, 243, 275, 326
  market, 246
  monopoly, 196
  predatory price-cutting, 156
  system, 41, 42, 51
Privacy, 275, 279
Private enterprise, 78, 80
Private Product Remaining, 40, 193
Privatization, 260ff., 266, 326
Production, mass, 57
Profit, 268
Progressive Era, 198, 318
Property, 56
  private, 57, 61, 236
  rights, 264, 266, 389
Protectionism, 87, 124, 127, 145, 148, 152, 153, 158, 160, 381, 382ff.
PTL, 294

Quotas, 125, 150ff., 383ff.
  import, 31, 32, 159

Raico, Ralph, 178

Racism, 40, 42, 44, 149
Rahn, Richard W., 70
Raiders, 274
Rand, Ayn, 104
Randianism, 105
Reagan, Ronald, 93, 116, 123, 211, 229, 284, 285, 352, 363, 366, 367, 369, 373, 381ff., 390
 Administration, 14, 38, 87, 96, 113, 138, 144, 266, 277, 373, 375
 "Reagan miracle," 312
 Reaganomics, 362, 365, 370, 376, 378ff., 381ff.
Raytheon, 252
Read, Dillon, 314, 315
Read, Leonard, 167, 179
Recessions, 90, 95, 119, 313
Redistribution, 95
Red Square, 238
Reed, Lawrence W., 233, 235, 299
Reed, Leonard, 292
Regan, Donald, 344, 361, 362, 379
Regulation, 32, 288, 290, 328, 375, 388ff.
Regulatory-Industrial Complex, 316ff.
Reich, Robert, 329ff., 334
Rent, imputed, 347
Republican, 285, 332
Republican National Convention, 365
Reserve requirements, 100
Revenue neutral, 360, 371
Revisionism, 198
Revolutionary War, 107
Ricardo, David, 173, 216
Richman, Sheldon L., 381, 385
Roads, 266ff.
Roberts, Oral, 181
Robertson, Pat, 380
Roche, George, 167
Rockefeller, David, 358
Rockefeller, John, 55, 105, 118, 121
Rockwell, Llewellyn H., Jr., 37, 39, 75, 100, 114, 116, 128, 144, 163, 164, 168, 170, 184, 195, 202, 203, 206, 212, 250, 276, 284, 295, 304, 323
Rollins College, 202
Roman Empire, 225
Romania, 123
Roosevelt, Franklin D., 97, 115, 120, 251, 273, 280, 293, 318, 324, 324, 333
Rothbard, Murray N., 19, 32, 35, 39, 40, 48, 50, 62, 70, 77, 83, 93, 97, 101, 108, 109, 115, 121, 122, 126, 127, 131, 148, 167, 170, 176-78, 185, 191ff., 201, 205, 213, 220, 223, 231, 234, 254, 257, 260, 263, 296, 300, 308, 332, 339, 362
Ruder, David, 275
Rueff, Jacques, 176, 179
Salerno, Joseph, 121, 202
Samuelson, Paul A., 208, 331
Savings, 63, 245, 311
 private, 22
 rate, 90
Savings and Loan Industry, 76
Say, J. B., 356
Scarcity, 66, 244, 249
Schultz, George, 326
Schumpeter, Joseph, 339
The Secrets of the Temple, 122
Securities and Exchange Commission (SEC), 273ff., 315, 319, 374, 375
Sherman Silver Purchase Act, 302, 303
Shields, Mark, 381
Shortages, water, 77
Skousen, Mark, 88, 194, 202, 209
Smith, Adam, 124-26, 161, 171, 172, 216, 365, 376
 "value paradox," 171
Smith, Hedrick, 237
Smith, Lee, 284
Smith, Winston, 294
Smithsonian Agreement, 85, 88
Smoot-Hawley tariffs, 124
Socialism, 48, 59, 223, 244ff., 254-56, 317
Socialism, 174, 234, 235
Socialists, 59, 260, 280
 Utopian, 49
Social Security, 280ff., 386
 Commission, 105, 388
 program, 104, 118
 system, 370
 tax, 33, 38, 282, 370, 373
Society for Worldwide Interbank Financial Telecommunications (SWIFT), 335
Somalia, 321
Soviet Russia, 48, 226, 235, 237, 238, 255, 330
Special Drawing Rights (SDRs), 55, 337
Spending, 386ff.
"Spoils system," 296
Spotts, Kathleen M., 286
Sprinkel, Beryl W., 87, 113, 377
Stalinist, 47
Stanley, Scott, 185
Stanford University, 284, 323
Steel Industry, 385
Stigler, George, 179
Stock index futures, 309
Stock market crash of 1987, 62, 64, 275, 308ff., 362
Subsidy, 345, 350
Sugar Industry, 343
Summers, Lawrence, 326, 330ff.
Supply-side economics, 112, 113, 187, 298, 339, 340ff., 379

Supreme Court, 298, 307, 340, 369
Switzerland, Basle, 338
Swope, Gerard, 251, 319
Syria, 146, 148

Taiwan, 139, 384
Tanzania, 321
Tariffs, 31, 32, 124, 129, 150ff., 157, 158
Tax, 29, 95, 307, 341, 387-88
  business, 38
  credit, 290
  cut, 33, 34, 370ff.
  flat, 28, 342ff.
  hidden, 118
  income, 29, 30
  increases, 22, 33, 297, 310-11, 327, 373
  payroll, 68
  simple, 359ff.
  Social Security, 33, 38, 282, 370, 373
  tariff as a, 124
  watch, 372
  "windfall profits," 37
Tax Equity and Fiscal Responsibility Act of 1982 (TEFRA), 387
Taxi, 317
Tax Reform Act of 1986, 371ff.
Tehran, 146
Thatcher, Margaret, 262, 336
Theory and History, 47, 175, 187, 219
The Theory of Money and Credit, 172, 174, 217, 234
Third World, 224, 320, 330
Tocqueville, Alexis 221
Tories, 114
Trade, 389ff.
Trade deficit, 138ff., 193, 310
  fair, 153ff.
  surplus, 142
Transportation, 267
Treasury, 352, 358
  bonds, 20, 281, 353
Treasury Department, 84, 97, 99, 388
Trust fund, 281
Trilateral Commission, 105, 327
Triumph of Conservatism, 318
Tucker, Jeffrey, 17, 216
Tullock, Gordon, 179
Turgot, A. R. J., 128, 129, 131
Twight, Charlotte, 146

Ultimate Foundation of Economic Science, The, 175, 219
Underground economy, 237, 247, 289
Unemployment, 26, 27, 30, 51, 52, 67, 69, 89
  insurance, 68
Unfairness, 240
Unions, 38, 52, 68, 385
United Auto Workers, 127
United Mine Workers, 251
United Nations, 266
United Parcel Service (UPS), 278, 279
United States, 111, 123, 154
United Way, 282
USA Today, 140
"User fee," 373

Value paradox, 171
Vanderlip, Frank A., 116
Vieira, Edwin, 337
Vienna, University of, 174, 180, 217
Virgin Islands, 372
Volcker, Paul, 38, 51, 104, 121, 191, 341, 379
Voltaire, 221

Wage, 43
  controls, 326
  minimum, 38, 43, 44, 52, 67, 89, 151, 290, 327
  rates, 26, 30, 31, 154, 155
Wall Street, 88, 374, 375
Wall Street Journal, 187, 209, 215, 323, 326
Wanniski, Jude, 341
Warburg, Paul, 116
Warsaw, University of, 231, 234
Washington, Harold, 133
Washington, D.C., 42, 69, 76, 119, 279
Washington Post, 117, 251, 381
Water, 80, 81
Watson, Patrick W., 280
Weaver, Richard, 167
Webster, Pelatia, 114
Welfare economics, 196
Wells, Sam, 138, 316, 320
Wexler, Leonard D., 137, 138
Whip Inflation Now (WIN), 104
White, Harry Dexter, 55, 84
Wicksteed, Phillip, 187
Williams Act, 274
Williams, Walter E., 43, 191
Woods, Bretton, 53, 54, 84, 85, 88, 110, 111, 113, 187, 188, 207, 341
  From Bretton Woods to World Inflation, 187, 207
Working conditions, 68
World Bank, 112, 187, 338, 384
World Central (Reserve) Bank, 55, 84, 113, 335ff.
World War I, 109, 174, 198, 310
World War II, 86, 349, 367

Xerox, 35-37

Yeager, Leland, 202
Yugoslavia, 255

Made in the USA
Monee, IL
04 June 2026

51526054R00223